"I am encouraged and challenged these passionate pages. She has been a sl... ... y serious Christian who desires to make it to Heaven, and to tak... as many others, as possible, with her."

Rev. Charles Pahlman, D.Min, Pastor of Central Assembly, Mentor, Ohio; Author of Several Books, including *The Decorated Disciple Book Series, A Plea for Preachers*; Has led many missions teams, and ministered in 18 Nations.

"I feel honored to endorse this second book by Claire Goodwin, who has lived the life of her stories. My wife and I always admired her life of enthusiastic dedication to the Lord. Get ready for adventuresome excitement as you read this book."

William F. Hill, TH.D, Pastor of Calvary Evangelistic Center, Independence, Iowa; Author of 31 books, including *What Is Holiness?* ; Ministered in many countries during 36 overseas trips.

"This tremendous volume has been placed before us like a fine meal on the menu of life. I suggest that you peel back the cover, taste the text, and enjoy what Sister Claire Goodwin has set before all of us."

Rev. Joey D. Hight, Pastor of Calvary Pentecostal Tabernacle, West Plains, Missouri; Campmeeting Speaker.

"Claire Goodwin is an expert teacher of evangelism. I know, because she was my instructor at Free Gospel Bible Institute. Sister Goodwin lives what she teaches. I do not know of anyone who takes personal evangelism of the lost more seriously than this wonderful lady. She has my respect for her life; my thanks for her sacrificial service; and my hearty endorsement of this book."

Pastor Lloyd Shuecraft, Fairland Holiness Church, Fouke, Arkansas; Campmeeting Speaker.

"It is an honor to endorse and recommend Compelled To Tell. As you read it you will feel the passion flowing from the heart of Sister Goodwin. Through her teaching at Free Gospel Bible Institute hundreds were challenged to rise and seek for the lost. She has heard and responded to the clarion call, and continues to lead by example. With joy, I highly recommend this book."

Pastor Mike Shaffer, Lighthouse Full Gospel Church, Roanoke, Virginia.

Claire Goodwin is devoted to the work of God. We have known her since 1976, and witnessed her faithful labor in ministry. Her book will encourage your heart. Here is a woman who is not afraid to stop and talk to anyone about the Lord. Her life is proof that whoever you are, God will use you, if you will just step out!"

Shirley A. Savage, Pastor's Wife, Bible Holiness Church, Elkton, Virginia; 58 years of ministry including evangelizing and missions; Author of 9 books and speaker at women's conferences.

Claire Goodwin has been a tremendous blessing to the Pentecostal/ Holiness people. We have seen the fruitfulness of her life, but most of us have not seen the details of how her life came to be. These twenty-three chapters of the journey of her life, set forth in Compelled to Tell, will lead us to more fully appreciate that she is our acquaintance and fellow laborer in Christ. Her story is captivating as you see the sovereignty of God overruling her life and placing her at the crossroads of His divine purpose. I hope this book will find its way into many hands, for without a doubt, from there it will find its way into the heart."

William F. Parks, Editor, *The Holiness Messenger*, Pastor of House of Prayer, Tulsa, Oklahoma.

It was great to meet you Amber. I pray that you will let the Lord have His way in your life. There is no greater life than one lived in the center of Gods will!

COMPELLED TO TELL

A Fascinating Journey from a New York Dead-End Street to a Lifetime of Ministry and Soul-Winning

Claire H. Goodwin

Claire H. Goodwin

Prov. 11:30

WestBow
PRESS
A DIVISION OF THOMAS NELSON

WestBow Press books may be ordered through booksellers or by contacting:

WestBow Press
A Division of Thomas Nelson
1663 Liberty Drive
Bloomington, IN 47403
www.westbowpress.com
1-(866) 928-1240

Scripture taken from the King James Version of the Bible.

Some names and other identifying details have been changed to protect the privacy of individuals.

ISBN: 978-1-4908-0537-5 (sc)
ISBN: 978-1-4908-0538-2 (e)

Library of Congress Control Number: 2013914751

Printed in the United States of America.

WestBow Press rev. date: 8/16/2013

Dedicated to my daughter, Rebecca C. Hawk, her husband Jim, and their children, Jessica, Briana, Andrew, David, and Wesley—my precious grandchildren.

—

Special appreciation to my husband Bob for his love, patience encouragement, and many guiding words, during all the hours and days it has taken to complete this book.

—

I owe many thanks to my sister, Barbara C. Haas, for her diligent editing of this manuscript and for her dedicated, personal interest in the story of *Compelled To Tell*.

—

Above all, my thanks goes to my Lord and Savior, Jesus Christ, for without Him, there would be no story to tell.

TABLE OF CONTENTS

FOREWORD

"We think you are all heretics! Even the Catholics!" That is the angry response that came right before the door went SLAM! The lady informed us that they were Russian Orthodox, just before she blurted out that rude goodbye. We met all kinds and, as you can see, not everyone wanted to talk. But we still had to tell them. We were *"Compelled to Tell"* them! The Great Commission compelled us, and we were also compelled by an energetic teacher. That teacher is the author of this book and I know from personal experience that her heart beats for personal evangelism. I was a Bible school student in Sister Claire Goodwin's class when I had that experience. She divided us into teams and sectioned off communities around the Bible school into our "personal mission fields." Out we went into the harvest field that Jesus spoke of. Sister Goodwin constantly reminded us that the harvest field was all around us.

She still has a heart to win souls. I have no doubt that her story will inspire you to win souls too. I was captivated by her first book, *"Reach Them One By One,"* and I couldn't go to sleep till I finished it. This story is the biography of a burden. It was born in the heart of a young girl. This burden grew and lived through transition and temptation. This burden can transfer from one heart to another. It's a burden that began in the heart of Jesus. It lives in the heart of this woman. It wants to live in your heart too.

So often we know what should be done but we can't imagine ourselves doing it. We don't know where to start. We want to see an example. Even a minister's vision can be blurred by the swift transition of life. As I read this story that starts on a "dead-end street," I have chuckled, rejoiced and cried as I traced the hand of providence in a life. In the pages of this story, that providential hand has touched my heart again. Because of that hand, ordinary lives can experience extraordinary living.

The early church spread the gospel in troublesome times. They faced persecution from many directions. The government turned on them. False religions resisted them. Secular society laughed at them. But they went forward. They were armed with a personal experience and a personal testimony. God used those powerful tools to break through satanic strongholds. The times are still troublesome today. The tools are still available. Will you pick them up? Do you have a personal experience with Jesus? Then you also have a testimony. Tell it to someone! You will be amazed at how God can use your willing heart. God is still looking for someone to stand in the gap. There is a gap near you, and that gap is just your size.

J. Kevin Lloyd, Pastor of First Pentecostal Church of Murlin Heights, Dayton, Ohio; Assistant Editor at Hope that Purifieth Ministries; Campmeeting Speaker.

1

THE GIRL ON THE FRONT STOOP

Fighting Back Tears

Defenseless! That's how I felt as the walls of the room seemed to close in on me. What was my boss trying to do? His words dripped with sarcasm: "Can you believe what Claire is going to do?" Like those led by the Pied Piper of Hamlin, these men followed along with mocking words, rising louder and louder. I stood there staggered by this senseless scene. They were taunting me. I had done nothing wrong. So why this?

I forced a weak smile through my intimidation, while fighting back tears. Then in a moment that seemed to stretch into many minutes, my thoughts leaped beyond the looks on their faces to the secure place of my continual unfailing Help. I needed Him now and my silent, urgent prayer flew heavenward, "Lord, help me! What should I say?"

No sense of forewarning predicted what would happen next. I could feel it beginning deep inside. Then suddenly the Spirit of God rose up from the depths of my being, and out of my mouth came a strong voice of authority that boldly declared to these men, "This day you will see what God will do!" My raised hand pointed straight at them, as amazement swept over me. What had I said? Such strength had poured through me. Where did that come from? It must have shocked the whole mocking bunch, because for a long moment, they just stared at me...and then slowly walked away. What followed is nothing short of a miracle of divine intervention that is woven into the pages of the adventurous story ahead.

Such memories of the past reach down like lively hands out of decades of experience and touch the trigger to an inner spring. Slowly, quietly a trickle begins. The gate opens wider and I am weeping. Words leap spontaneously from my heart, pouring forth like unhindered flowing water, tumbling from a mountain stream. My bended knees sink into soft carpet as the first rays of morning sun shimmer through partially open patio blinds. "Dallas, Texas. Here I am, Lord." A slightly worn but favorite blue wing chair poses before me as a willing altar, and my warm tears gently pattern themselves into the fabric. The words are intense. Though unadorned, they are bursting with condensed emotion. I feel these words. They are like containers filled with countless years of memory. They tip and reveal their passionate contents. Don't underestimate their significance. Hear them as they pour forth, "Oh, Lord, what a life You have given me!" Slowly, intently they flow from my quivering lips once more, "Oh, Lord, what a life You have given me!" Such words! Nine words of profound utterance.

It hardly seems possible that in such a short time on my knees so many flashes of memory flew by. Like quickly turning pages from the illustrated book of my life came vivid recollections of the time the Lord saved me and baptized me with the Holy Ghost at ten, of his voice calling me at eleven, of his mercy preserving me through my teen years and setting me in Bible school at seventeen, where he molded and prepared me for his purposes. The years that followed dynamically affirmed to me that the Lord would "perfect that which concerneth me...." (Psalm 138:8 King James Version).

I couldn't help but tell Him, "Lord, I'm just *that girl on the front stoop of that dead-end street?* How could all of this be happening to me?" Countless times these words ascended from my lips, as I observed with great wonder the Lord's plans and direction for my life. If anyone had told me in advance that I would do the things I have done, go to the places I have gone, and experience the things I have experienced, my mind would have struggled to believe it. I don't think there can be anything more awesome than walking into the amazing story of your life as planned by God.

A kind lady once suggested to another that God had his hand on my life for something special. That woman responded, "On Claire? She's no different than any other girl." My ordinary life was showing, but beneath it stretched an underlying flow of desire for God's will. When God works in unexpected ways with ordinary people, the outcome always boggles the human mind.

With this book, I am attempting to step back through the doors of my life to catch a faint glimpse of his wonders. Although it has been no dream of mine to write a book—especially a book about my life—God interrupted my busy life at about the time my years rose to the late sixties. I felt compelled to tell of the great works of God, of his supernatural shaping of events and providential intervention. I only know of one way to do this—by painting the story of my life—some of which I planned and, thankfully, most of which God planned. I invite you now to come with me to the place where it all began.

On a Dead-End Street in Corona

When my mother and father eloped in January 1931, their uncertain path eventually took them to a late 19th century residential development in Queens. As one of the five boroughs that make up New York City, Queens is the most ethnically diverse urban area in the world with a population of over 2.2 million. The area where my parents settled became known as Corona, meaning "Crown" in Italian or Spanish.

In this unique place, God's foreordained plan for my life burst into reality on the seventh day of March 1941. My parents, Bill and Helen Wilmerton, welcomed me as the second of their four children. As they carried me home from the hospital that day, not even they could have imagined the future that God had planned for this screaming bundle of energy.

My earliest memories were of living in one of the many duplex houses on 97th Street, a dead-end street with the Long Island Railroad at the upper end. The constant clatter of buses, taxies, fire engines, ambulances, police cars, and trains, all created a plethora of unmatched sound. This was Corona.

Forever branded on my brain are the sounds of blaring horns from locomotives, as they thundered and screeched toward multiple destinations, pulling scores of freight trains. Their turbine powered

3

wheels rolled down the tracks with a rhythmic chug-a-chug-a-chug-a that could be heard blocks away.

It must be necessity that persuaded thousands of people to squeeze into commuter trains like a bunch of sardines in a can. But they depended on that transportation to get to city jobs. Jammed into crowded seats and hanging onto swinging overhead handgrips, their dazed looks seem oblivious to the possibility of trouble around the next curve of the tracks.

Death on the Tracks

At the upper end of our street, train tracks towered above street level on top of a graffiti-marked, concrete abutment. We were never allowed to go up on those tracks. However, one day word reached us that a train hit a boy, several blocks down from our street. My brother and I were alarmed. Could it be someone we knew? We had to find out.

Without further thought, we climbed quickly up the concrete abutment, hurrying to the top and onto the heavy gravel and rock alongside the tracks. A sudden flash of guilt hit us. We weren't supposed to be up here. Determined, we simply bent down as low as possible so my father would not see us.

Full of foolish curiosity, our cautious first steps rapidly turned to careless jogging along the edge of the tracks. Then as we approached the spot where people stood in a huddle near the tracks, we hesitated. Two steps further and we saw him. Squinting at the scene before us revealed more than we wanted to see. We saw blood. Such a terrible sight made us cringe and decide that we shouldn't go any closer. To us, he seemed to be dead. Emergency workers were standing around him when we turned back with hearts racing from the horror of it all. Very slowly, very deliberately, we retraced our steps over that rough, rocky path toward home. Dreadful thoughts persisted, penetrating our consciousness, and distracting us as we came closer to the place where we would climb back down to our street.

Our eyes looked down each house-filled street as we passed it. They were neatly arranged, perpendicular to the tracks—100th Street, 99th Street, 98th Street. We had to be careful! If we were not bent low when we came to our street, our father would see us on the tracks—if he happened to be outside the house. Maybe our concentration was effected by our anxiety, or perhaps a little guilt, but we somehow lost count of the street numbers. There was no time to make a correction, and much to our dismay, we were still standing tall and obviously visible when we reached 97th Street. Disaster! There stood my father! Seeing his face turned directly up toward the tracks, we knew it would be hard for him to miss us. Were we caught? At lightning speed, we leaped to escape his view, dropping down to the ground and scurrying across the tracks to the opposite side. We descended past old factories and buildings toward Junction Boulevard, but dread struck us the moment we caught sight of Dad coming around that corner. His rapid, purposeful, intentional walking never slowed down, nor did the methodical swinging of that object in his hand. I saw it coming—that old, double-edge razor strap. I could almost hear those two leather straps slapping against each other.

Strong words flew out of his mouth like arrows, "I told you to never go up on those tracks! You could be killed!" Simultaneously, I could now feel those leather straps applied to the back of my legs as my father took one hand and led me down the hill. My brother's turn came next and, by the time we concluded our long march homeward, each of us bore more than a memory of that well-deserved restraining action. No, we didn't want to wind up dead like that poor boy. Yes, we would do a better job of obeying our father. I still remember that event almost sixty years later, and shake my head at what God had to work with as He prepared me for his divine plan.

It's a Wonder You're Still Alive

Only one tree rose from the concrete sidewalks on our dead-end street. It stood right in front of our house and when my mother would come out the door to call for me, she said she would just look straight up, and often that live-wire daughter sat right there, on a branch of that tree. As if that wasn't enough to make a mother grow old fast, some of our other activities surely led her down that path.

A large double billboard, two stories high, displayed its advertisements to traffic on Junction Boulevard. Standing exactly on our corner, it became our delight to play tag on the back of it. With toes on one of the support beams that stretched horizontally across the back of the sign and fingers holding tightly to an upper parallel beam, we would inch our way along to keep from getting caught by the one chasing us. My father declared that I climbed to the top of that sign at just three years of age, and he had to climb up it to get me down. My mother used to say it was a wonder I was still alive.

We grew up playing in the street with dozens of other kids, all finding our own space. There were no computer games or iPods, so we spent free hours playing outside. Street games prevailed with stoop-ball and stick-ball taking precedence. All the kids on the block played their own style of football. You couldn't be from Corona without playing kick-the-can, "I-declare-war," or ringolevio. Skully took us to the ground, where we used chalk to draw a giant square with corner boxes, and shot soda-pop caps from one corner to another with the snap of our fingers. Imagine, also, the ingenuity of playing hide and seek with only cars and alleys as places to hide! Intrigue filled the street as cops and robbers roamed, and cowboys and Indians reined in their "horses" with their own created adventures. I always had to be Hopalong Cassidy. We also played "king of the mountain" in the vacant lot and hopscotch on the sidewalk, plus jump rope and high-water low-water in the street.

I don't remember having many toys. We invented our own fun. One time we charged kids on the block one penny to come through our alley to the back where they would get to see a live anteater! Wow! They went running home to get their pennies and we were more than happy to lead them back to see my father in a lawn chair. The living anteater—that's who he was! They stared with a mixture of awe and disappointment as they watched us place live, crawling ants on my father's tongue. Gulp! Down they went—but only the red ones! He helped make the fun!

Sometimes in the hot summer, my dad would be the hero of the block as he pulled out the long garden hose and sprayed a whole gang of yelling kids in the street. What relief that cool water brought! Yet even more excitement and joy came when we sold Kool-Aid on Junction Boulevard, under the shade of the Long Island Railroad bridge. Cars would stop, people walking past would buy, and one time a bus actually stopped and many passengers bought our precious, cool drink. One day we made eight dollars! Besides buying more sugar, Kool-Aid and cups, we splurged by going into Bellaccico's Italian Deli and buying big, luscious green olives and large, cool and juicy dill pickles to devour slowly while sitting under that same railroad bridge.

There were times my mother did not display much pleasure at our youthful entrepreneurial skill. It seemed like a great idea to Bill and me when we devised a plan to dress up our little sister Barbara and created an original sign for her to wear around her neck. Additionally we gave her a lovely can she could hold in her hand. She so obediently followed our instructions to simply walk down Junction Boulevard. When Barbara returned, our brilliant success was quickly dimmed by my very embarrassed mother. Looking into the can, she saw money. Then came that fierce look as she glared at the sign that read, "I need shoes." Our fun came to an end! Evidently, we had much to learn.

Caught by a Policeman

I shamefully admit that at such an early age I walked right into guilt from both stealing and lying. The first occurred on a day that my mother stood outside talking to our landlord, Mrs. Stewart. They were busily chatting, but I needed to ask her an important question. Mrs. Stewart held the chain that leashed her playful boxer. Why didn't she take him for a walk? I would just have to find a lull in their conversation and blurt out what I wanted. Finally I had my chance. It was now or never. "Mom, can I have some money to buy candy?"

She stopped talking just long enough to look down at me, irritated, and tell me, "No!" I did not want to hear that answer. Her "No!" did not settle well in my yet unconverted mind. I wandered back into the house sulking. Roaming through the hall and past my parents' bedroom, the thought crept furtively into my mind that I knew where my mother kept her purse. I remembered her opening the dresser drawer and placing it on the left side. Why did this idea even form in my head? I stood there hesitating for just a moment, until that dark thought edged its way through the wavering boundaries of my conscience.

Recklessly ignoring all inhibitions, I inched toward the dresser and gently pulled at the rickety, aging drawer. Why did it have to be so tight? I tugged harder and flinched as the drawer abruptly flew open with a loud, unwelcome screech which, at that moment, seemed loud enough to break the sound barrier. Oh, no! Did anyone hear that? What reasonable answer could I give for having my hand in my mother's dresser drawer? An awful, gnawing feeling edged its way through my being, but I had no time to ponder such dreadful considerations. There lay Mom's purse.

"It's not yours!"

Did I hear a voice? Looking around and seeing no one, I decisively opened the purse, took one little dime, closed it, and carefully slid the drawer back in place. I hastily hurried out the back door, through the hedges of our little backyard, over our brown picket fence, and around a weed-and-debris-filled vacant lot. Moving quickly, I finally placed my feet on the street that would take me to my destination---the candy store! Phew! I made it!

Out of breath from my hasty escape, I slowed down, but just for a moment...a moment that ended in serious alarm as soon as I saw what came around the corner in my direction—a police car! I stood frozen with unbelief as it pulled right up to the curb where I stood. Immediate recognition occurred as I saw the face of my policeman father and heard his voice calling to me, "Claire, where are you going?"

I could hardly talk. "To the candy store," I mumbled weakly. No true policeman can miss the obvious sound and clear look of plain old guilt.

Next I heard, "Come over here." I did and when he asked, "Where did you get the money?" everything fell to pieces and I burst into tears. Into the police car he called me and there uncovered my secret sin. I thought I could sneak away and no one would know but, early on, the Lord let me see that sin will be found out.

Although not a Christian at this time, my father counseled me lovingly and commended me for admitting the truth.

He told me, *"Always tell the truth, no matter how hard it is."*

He took my stolen little dime and, flashing a forgiving smile, replaced it with a quarter. It felt so good to be forgiven. That awful, gnawing feeling was gone too, and I determined never to do such a thing again. Perhaps I later tried to make up for my behavior when someone stole Barbara's tricycle. I became the self-appointed detective searching for it and successfully found the thief—a boy on the next block—who was busily disguising it with fresh paint!

Your Tongue Is Green

It happened during a third grade lineup in the school yard of Public School 19 that I became a liar. I can't justify my sin, but it will help for you to understand why I lied. If you knew this girl in my class named Deborah, you would understand. She always had the most outrageous tales for "show and tell." First it was a grandmother who fell down the stairs and broke both legs. Then her dog ate two of the live chickens she was raising, and every day we heard one more wildly, dramatic story. Sometimes I thought she just made them up, but everyone loved her stories. I never had stories like that. Who could like such a person? I certainly didn't envy her—or did I?

Well, one afternoon everything culminated. As we waited to return to class after lunch, I watched her. There stood Deborah, again the center of attention. She boasted about seeing the new building that was going up a few blocks away from the school. "She knows everything," I whispered under my breath.

My yet unsaved flesh could not stand it, so I jumped into the conversation and declared, "Oh, yeah. I saw it too!" (I did not!)

Like a flash, Deborah howled, "No, you didn't! If you did, what color is the door?"

I guessed, "It's blue."

"It is not!" she jubilantly shouted. "It's yellow!" She stood there absolutely in charge and talking so fast that when she ordered me to stick out my tongue, I obeyed and did. She yelled, "Your tongue is green. You're a liar. You're a liar. Your tongue is green."

As we marched into the school room, I felt worse and worse. "My tongue is green," I thought to myself. The pit of my stomach squirmed with an awful creeping nauseous feeling. The queasiness made me sink into my seat and feel sicker every minute. Fighting back tears, I went to the teacher and told her I felt sick and had to go home. Can you guess what I did when I arrived there? I rushed to the bathroom, grabbed a chair, stood on it and looked at my tongue in the mirror. It WAS NOT green! That really made me think twice about ever lying again. What if every liar's tongue did turn green?

God surely had an interesting project on his hands, as He relentlessly observed me, even in elementary school, and worked to shape my life. Perhaps He had a part in my surprise, one day, as I sat down in the school cafeteria and opened my brown-bag lunch, finding inside only a bag of carrot and potato peels. What a predicament! What happened to my lunch?

A teacher happened to pass by just as the carrot and potato peels made their humorous appearance on my table. I wonder what thoughts must have gone through her head....

"Poor deprived child! Her family must be very poor. I never saw such an awful lunch!"

Perhaps it was out of pity, but she invited me to get a free hot lunch at the cafeteria. Her sympathy must have increased, because she then offered me, a sixth grader, a job! In exchange for free hot meals, each day I stood guard at the plate collection location where I checked the plates of students who had "finished" eating. If they left food, I sent them back to the table to finish it. I wonder what the ACLU would say about that. Hmmm! I still remember all those uneaten, big, healthy red kidney beans looking so lonely spread out on beds of unwanted lettuce.

The redeeming benefit of this unusual experience is that I learned how God could take a bad situation and turn it around for good. He must have watched when my mother handed me those two bags as I left for school and clearly instructed me, "Now, Claire, be sure to throw this bag in the garbage and take this other bag to school with you." Sometimes we all make mistakes.

An Uncle Who Cared

No one in my family had become Christians yet; however, my brother and I, and my sisters, Jean and Barbara, were regularly picked up for Sunday school by my uncle, Burtis Becker. He served faithfully as the Sunday School Superintendent at the Free Gospel Church of Corona. Surely stars await him in Heaven for the impact that he had on our lives. We could always tell when the time arrived to run outside for our ride, because he would begin repeatedly honking his horn as he came under the Long Island Rail Road (LIRR) bridge. We could hear the resounding echo at our house, just one block away, and he warned us to be out there and ready if we wanted a ride.

Uncle Burtis had a unique car with little fold-down seats behind the front seats, facing backward, making room for extra passengers. It became our flying chariot to the house of God. What great reward awaits such unseen and unnoticed people who care enough to go out of their way to take others to church and Sunday school!

It was a Heavenly ordained pathway—my introduction to anything spiritual. The fingerprints of God pressed their imprints upon my young life. If only Uncle Burtis could see the future results of those faithful trips! He was married to my mother's twin sister, Anna Becker. I vividly remember attending Uncle Burtis' funeral where Aunt Anna's hands were raised in worship to the Lord, in the midst of her sorrow. Beautiful, comforting words flowed through the sanctuary as the caring congregation sang out the old hymn, "Satisfied:" "Hallelujah! I have found Him, Whom my soul so long has craved!" Yes, Uncle Burtis is now satisfied in the presence of Jesus.

I'll Never See Her Again!

One day our phone rang and I jumped up to answer it. My mother's twin sister Anna was on the line and wanted to talk to her. "It's for you, Mom," I said, handing her the phone.

I had not walked three feet away when I heard my mother scream, "No! I'll never see her again!" We quickly learned that my mother's elderly mother had been found dead in her bedroom at Aunt Anna's house. She was a Christian and my mother was not. The sudden thought of eternal separation from her mother became an unbearable reality that pierced her unsaved soul. It drove her to lingering despair. Something had to change.

The next Sunday was Mother's Day, and my mother headed back to the Free Gospel Church that had now moved to Flushing and that day met God at an altar of repentance and forgiveness. She came home a new person with a determination that kept her true to God in the face of resistance from my unsaved father. She started immediately to find ways to get all four of her children to Sunday school and church with her. Stepping out of our door to that dead-end street, she led the way for Billy, Jean, and me, while carrying one-year-old Barbara in her arms, for those challenging trips. God put strength in my mother that enabled her to press through some very difficult obstacles in order to finally arrive at that sacred destination.

2

A POWERFUL TURNING POINT

A strange thing happened one Sunday morning as I sat next to my mother in church. I looked up at her and noticed something unusual about her. Her hand was raised and tears were coming down her shining face, but what especially caught my attention were the strange sounds coming out of her mouth. I couldn't understand what she said. My mind could not recall my mother ever acting like that before. After a moment of observing her, this ten-year-old girl tapped her on the arm and asked, "Mom, what is that?"

I suppose that could compare to the astonished crowd in the book of Acts, chapter two, asking "What meaneth this?" And my mother might have answered, "This is that which was spoken of by the prophet Joel....," but as a new convert, she hardly knew how to even explain to me that the Lord had baptized her with the Holy Ghost and that she was speaking in tongues. Her simple explanation intrigued me—"It's the Holy Ghost!"—so in a minute, I tapped her again and asked, "How old do you have to be to get that?"

With a look of amazement at my question, she responded, "You can have it! Do you want it?"

Why wouldn't I want what made my mother look so happy? "Yes!" I quickly said.

"Well, we will start to ask the Lord for it when everyone goes up to the altar to pray."

I will never forget that day, kneeling between those first pews and for the first time feeling the power of God surging through me. I hardly knew how to pray, so when my mother said, "Praise the Lord!" I said, "Praise the Lord!" and when she said, "Hallelujah!" I said, "Hallelujah!" Soon tears began to roll down my face, and a new kind of joy engulfed my rejoicing heart. It is the first time I remember ever praying with such faith and vocal intensity.

On that day in 1950, Heaven was accomplishing a deeper work in my heart than I even understood at that moment. In my own way, I gave my whole life to the Lord, and He responded to my surrendering heart according to his promise: "For whosoever shall call upon the name of the Lord shall be saved" (Romans 10:13).

Together, mother and I continued to pray. Simultaneously, the Lord drew my tender ten-year-old life into a relationship with Him that would take me down a lifelong path I could not have imagined.

From that day on, my mother attempted to get me to some church somewhere, almost every night of the week. She didn't drive and Dad didn't go, so our transportation came from friends, or by bus or train, but everywhere we went I headed to the altar to pray to receive the Holy Ghost. I thank God that my mother so intensely desired that I receive that holy baptism. Every time I prayed I came closer. Then came that victorious day about one month later when the Lord filled me with his Spirit at the altar of the Community Gospel Tabernacle in Astoria, New York.

As Pastor Williams and others gathered around me encouraging me on, I soon felt that anointing of stammering lips that the Bible foreordained in Isaiah 28:11 "For with stammering lips and another tongue will he speak to this people." Moments later those stammering lips started to clearly speak in tongues as the Spirit gave the words. No one told me what to say. I didn't think up the words before I spoke them. They simply flowed out of my mouth as I yielded myself to the Lord. The Third Person of the Trinity had come to dwell within this child. The preacher rejoiced! The church people shouted, and my mother was thrilled beyond words.

I went home so happy that I marched up and down our hallway, jubilantly playing all sorts of imaginary instruments in an expression of my inward joy. I was baptized with the Holy Ghost!! It was the beginning of a walk with God that would take me on journeys and adventures that I could never have imagined at the age of ten. My jubilant hallway march and playing of invisible musical instruments was actually a prophetic display of what would take place in the future. At the time of this writing, I have now played piano for over fifty-five years and organ for over forty-five years, in ministry for the Lord.

God had begun a work in me at that early age that would keep me praying and wanting to be in his presence. At the age of eleven, I didn't fully understand what was happening, but God began to call me to work for Him. I can remember so clearly those nights in bed when I lay awake and talked to the Lord. For several nights, the same sort of thing happened. God put in my mind a dangerous or difficult situation—like a jungle scene—and asked me, "If I wanted you to go there, would you go?"

I cried and prayed after each scene, considering the things that an eleven-year-old girl regarded as difficulties and dangers, and finally told the Lord, "Yes, even if you wanted me to go there, I would go." It was a call from beyond the universe to the heart of a little girl. A hand reached out from Heaven to prepare a life of full surrender to the will of God. What a privilege! I was only *that little girl sitting on that stoop, on that dead-end street in Corona*, New York. Who was I? What abilities did I have? I stand amazed at the workings of God in the life of a child. He saw me, as insignificant as I was. Divinity knew me and already had a plan for my life. Can anything be more astounding?

It took me a long time to fully understand that God had called me. One significant memory is the growing desire in my heart for spiritual things. However, that evidently interspersed with some of the immature occurrences of my growing up years, because sometimes I was just plain carnal. People usually think I was pretty tough when I tell them my box story, but I'll risk telling it again.

My Embarrassing Box Story

My cousin Andy and I spotted it at the same time. "Look down there. Let's go and get it before anyone else sees it!" We ran down the street and grabbed the big, empty refrigerator box and started dragging it around the corner, to the empty lot filled with weeds and old bedsprings. It was a perfect place to hide our newfound treasure.

No one else that we knew had a refrigerator box. We were so excited as we placed it in the weeds and crawled inside. It would be our club house. It would be our hiding place. We thought of all sorts of things we could do, even to charging kids to come in and be part of our club. With a sharp rock, we cut a little hole in the side to be a window and just sat there dreaming. Then suddenly, BOOM! Something hit our box. Again it happened. BOOM! And several more times, until I looked out the hole and saw them.

"Andy, there are three kids out there walking along the railroad and they're throwing rocks at our box. Tell them to get away, that they can't have this box. It's ours!" Something had to be done, but Andy didn't move. So I announced, "Okay, I'll go out," and I did. Two of them were as big as I was and one was just a little guy. I stood tall with my hands on my hips and declared ownership. "Hey! You guys quit throwing rocks! This is our box and you can't have it."

"Oh, yeah?" they defiantly hissed, as they stepped closer. I took another step toward them. Our eyes met and I could see that one was about to jump at me, but I beat him to it and pushed him down. Arms were flying. The second one went down next, but I didn't see the little guy coming at me with that short, stumpy log raised high. Thud! It hit me right on the head and I saw stars.

Down I went and lay there dizzy with my eyes closed. I was not unconscious, but as I squinted and saw these culprits coming closer and looking very worried, I pretended I was dead. I didn't move. And they came closer. I could see them through my mostly closed eyes. And they came closer. Then I saw my moment and I suddenly leaped up and grabbed the arm of the closest one, yelling, "I have you now. You're not getting away." The other two took off running up Junction Boulevard, but I was not about to lose my prisoner. "I'm taking you to my father! He's a policeman and is right up the street at the police station, and he'll put you in jail." I dragged him up the boulevard, ignoring curious looks from passing traffic, while also trying to keep my focus on the other two criminals as they fled backwards to escape. What a strange spectacle! My prisoner struggled, but I tightened my grip, even though I was still feeling lightheaded.

"It's not fair. They did it too. Let me go and I'll go get them, and you can take all of us to the police station," he pleaded.

In that moment, my dizzy head thought that sounded quite reasonable and I let him go. The last thing I remember seeing is the three of them running backwards up the boulevard, waving and laughing at me. What a dreadful dilemma! And that is my well-loved box story...and a clear picture of what God had to work with to try to make me his profitable servant. Most of us didn't start out well. Most of us needed the hard clay to be heated and molded into the image that the Lord desired. Such was the evident need of this twelve-year-old girl.

A Flying Knife, Makeup, and an Evil Man

Surely the mercies of God and the ever-watching angels of the Lord kept me through my young years. Living in the city did require caution and sometimes defense and escape. More than once I had to flee from people, even when minding my own business. Sometimes I had to scream for help which I am thankful came to my rescue. Can you imagine that over fifty years ago I had to jump out of the way of a knife thrown toward me?

I had returned to my junior high school a few minutes late after lunch and had taken the back stairway to avoid being seen. It was a bad choice. Suddenly I heard someone at the top of the stairs yell, "I'll get you now!" as he threw a knife in my direction. It flew past me to a boy at the bottom of the stairs—its intended victim. It didn't take long for me to race to my classroom. There I found out what all those police cars and ambulances were doing outside the school. There had been a gang war between black, white, Puerto Rican, and Italian students and one boy had been stabbed beneath the heart.

My father warned me about the girls in my ninth grade class. He directed the JAB, the Juvenile Aid Bureau at the police department, and told me, "Claire, stay away from those girls! They belong to gangs that rob local stores."

Nice! Well, he didn't have to worry about me. As a loner with only one or two friends in the school, I kept to myself and usually went straight home after school.

When those girls were flirting and boasting about boys, I still had more interest in climbing on the monkey bars at the park across the street. Yet one day some of them decided to exert their group "authority" over me and my friend Rachel, the only other Christian I knew in the school. As class ended, I saw them whispering and looking our way, then purposely walking toward us. Five or six of these tough girls moved in and surrounded us as we sat trapped at our desks. They looked down at us, exuding arrogance by their glaring looks and posturing.

"What was this all about?" I wondered. Neither Rachel nor I had any personal association with these girls. We were simply students in the same class. I wonder if they practiced making those mean looking faces.

Then, it came—the unbelievable, bold threat: "You are the only girls in this class who don't wear makeup, and tomorrow our class picture will be taken. We won't let you ruin it! You had better come to school with makeup on, or we will beat you up!"

I was either too carefree or naive to worry about what I considered a ridiculous threat. That's life in Corona—with just one more little "bump" in the road. I doubt if I even mentioned it to my parents, but I had no intention of giving in to their demands.

Lo and behold, when I got to school the next morning, without makeup, I couldn't believe my eyes. There stood Rachel with makeup on! Talk about making it hard on another Christian! What a disappointment! My good friend! What was she trying to do? The fact is that no one tried to beat me up. The threatening big bullies were silent, but sadly, Rachel's choice became a first step downward for her testimony. It may have seemed like just a little thing, but her compromise of a believed standard led her down a path further away from the Lord. An inch of compromise grew into a yard of spiritually damaging choices, as one bad decision led to another. God's will calls to us clearly, "And be not conformed to this world: but be ye transformed by the renewing of your mind, that ye may prove what is that good, and acceptable, and perfect, will of God" (Romans 12:2).

There is no doubt that I could have been dead numbers of times in my loosely supervised younger life. Once during an excursion with my dad to Flushing Meadow Park, my brother Bill and I wandered off from the Police Athletic League ball game my father coached. We played by the tall metal structures that still remained from the 1939 World's Fair. A stranger came along and began talking friendly to us, giving us candy. He asked if we wanted to play hide and seek and, of course, that sounded exciting. I was ten and my brother was twelve, and we were both very naive. He wanted my brother to be "it" and to count to 100 while he and I would hide. What took place next will not be described, except for saying that only the Lord's mercies kept me from something worse, or even fatal that could have happened to me. In a moment of panic I yelled loudly for my brother who arrived just in time for me to escape, as the vile man disappeared in the dust of his fleeing footsteps. It is not hard to look back and see how many times Satan attempted to distract or destroy me before I could ever do anything for the Lord in ministry. To this day, I praise Him for his mighty power and protection. The angel of the Lord does encamp around about them that fear Him and delivers them. Through many diverse experiences of life, God faithfully taught me.

Our Neighbor in the Alley

My brother Bill and I took turns bringing our garbage can in from the front of the house to the back. My turn came and, as I carried it through the narrow alley, our neighbor Bob also carried his to the back. Although Bob worked as a baker, addiction to alcohol ensnared his life. Step by step we ambled on, passing the open windows of our separate duplex houses. Occasionally a waft of supper smells breezed past, stirring hungry visions of a plate full of home cooked food. Bob was now just a couple of feet ahead of me and, as I walked, the thought occurred to me, "Tell Bob about the Lord." I wavered, afraid, not knowing what to say. "Tell him about the Lord!" There it is again! I faltered as my heart pounded harder at the thought—then I almost did it—but it was too late. He turned the corner to walk up the steps to his house and was gone.

That evening as our family sat together in the screened porch eating supper, our other neighbor Phil came running through our door, yelling to my father, "Bill, come quick! Bob is on the floor!" Bob lived with Phil and his wife. My dad rushed out the door, and I jumped up and ran to my room and fell on my knees crying out to God, "Please don't let him be dead, and I'll tell him." This difficult moment pained me as a young teenager when I realized that I might have been the last chance of hope for my lost neighbor and failed. Yes, Bob was dead. My young heart grieved. This experience stuck with me for a long time. I didn't want that to ever happen again. The value of a soul and the uncertainty of time became a strong motivator in later soul winning efforts in my life.

A Paralyzing Fear

God had already dealt with me, drawing me closer and filling me with a desire to do something for Him. I sometimes hesitate to reveal the terrible fear that Satan tried to use on me to destroy me before I ever had a chance to do anything for God. It has shown me how cruel he is and how he hates those who have a future as a servant of the Lord.

My earliest memory of this terror stems from the night when I opened sleepy eyes and called for my mother to please bring me a drink of water. When she did, I saw something that frightened and horrified me. Pushing the glass away, I yelled, "There are webs all over that glass!" Her face twisted with a concerned frown as she went through the hall to the kitchen to get another glass. It was a frightening moment for both of us when I again saw the webs—as clearly as I saw her standing by my bed. She saw none. If this was childish imagination, it became a long-term nightmare. Who could have guessed that several years of dreadful fear would follow?

As kids on my block discovered my fear, they chased me up and down the street with webs and even roots that looked like webs—and I ran. The fear increased to the point that I literally felt webs on me when there were none there. Frantically, I called for my mother to please come and take the webs off me. One evening I went down to our dimly lit basement to get something and suddenly they were there again—webs! I felt them as they swept across my face. I froze in terror and screamed for my mother to come and rescue me again. She always came and pretended to wipe the invisible things away and, as she did, I actually felt them tear from my face, but she felt nothing.

A very significant episode occurred one dark night when my

mother sent me to get something from a store. As I rode my bicycle from the road up onto a sidewalk, I came between trees on both sides and panicked as I felt as if a thick web, like tennis net, caught me across my face. I immediately stopped in my tracks and froze, not daring to move an inch. I stood like a statue, fearing even to breathe too hard lest even a subtle movement would make those "webs" tear across my face again, with their sticky, clinging strands. One foot trembled on a bike pedal and one foot on the ground, as terror swept over me. Tears streamed down my face. There I stood, so hopeless, all alone with no one to help. Was there no way out of this unending terror? It was right at that darkest moment, that seemed like the edge of an abyss, that a crucial thought pierced through my darkness:

"Sometimes, in church, the preacher talked about the power of the name of Jesus."

I pondered the idea for just a moment before urgently pleading, "In the name of Jesus, webs go away from me!" As I urgently cried out the words, something amazing happened. The webs went away immediately!

It was a sudden moment of truth that became a turning point for me. "This fear must be from the devil," I realized, and that revelation flashed like a shaft of light piercing through what had become a dark tunnel for this fourteen-year-old girl.

Interestingly, my worst episodes occurred in church. Yet this is exactly where defeat turned into victory. Early on Sunday mornings, my father left me there all alone to set up Sunday School chairs while he picked up people for the service. As soon as I began walking through the building, I felt the webs. They were stretched across that church! Every place I moved I felt them. My only relief was to resort to the protective habit I had developed over time. With no one around to see me, I would walk holding my arm up in the air, shielding my face from any possible contact with webs.

On this particular morning, distress from this problem overwhelmed me. My footsteps came slow. Shielding my face, I carefully made my way to the back pew, sat down all alone and cried in agony. "Lord, how can I ever do anything for you with this problem?" My heart was breaking apart inside. "How can I possibly overcome what has tormented me for several years now?" At the moment, I did not know. With rare exceptions, I had kept this fear a secret. However, today things will change! This will be my day of victory! This will be my moment of fierce battle with the enemy, and I will win! As I sat there with hot tears dropping on my dress, my eyes diverted to the far wall of the sanctuary. A blue cardboard scripture sign hung from one nail. Silver glitter formed the border and shadowed the words. I had seen it many times, but this time was different. I could almost hear God's voice speaking the words to me, "Fear Not, Only Believe." A light lit in my spirit. Suddenly I understood the message. God was giving me a choice. Now it was up to me. I had to make a choice. Faith slowly built in my heart, as a new spiritual strength seemed to surge through me. God was here! He was with me right there in the back of that church. The Holy Spirit within urged me on—this was my time!

I stood up and proclaimed, "Lord, I will believe. I will not fear." Then I made a bold declaration, "With your help, I will walk down this aisle to the altar with my hands at my side, without holding up my arm to protect me from webs." You cannot imagine what a difficult challenge that was to someone who had been held in the grip of fear for so long. I walked and at each step cried, "In the name of Jesus!" My arms are still at my side. Just one more step—"In the name of Jesus!" The altar! I made it all the way to the front. I dropped to my knees at that altar and raised my hands, crying out to the Lord in faith, praising Him, and continuing to declare, "I believe You, Lord. I believe You, Lord."

A mighty miracle took place in my young life that morning! From that moment, complete deliverance was mine, and I was set free from the torment of the enemy of my soul. Jesus declared it: "He whom the Son sets free is free indeed."

I was so free that in the following days, I deliberately looked for webs and tore them down with my hands, declaring my victory! Hallelujah! It is hard to believe that such a small, insignificant thing like a spider web could hold such power over a life, but that is the way Satan works. He will use anything to stop a person from doing the will of God. I praise God today for the immeasurable lesson that I learned from this experience. He has filled me with courage and boldness and rarely do I ever have a fear. He makes us more than conquerors through Jesus who died for us. How I praise the Lord for his mighty power! "God hath not given us a spirit of fear but of power, and of love, and of a sound mind" (2 Timothy 1:7).

Before I turned seventeen, I wrote out this testimony and sent it in to the Pentecostal Evangel in Springfield, Missouri. They wanted to publish it but first wanted me to answer some questions, particularly about what initially caused this fear. I didn't know, so never replied to them. Then as I pondered the question, I remembered that during the only year we had a television, I had seen some movie about a giant web that enveloped a man, trapping him for the approaching giant spider.

Soon after this my fear began. Perhaps that frightening scene became a triggering mechanism that initiated all of those days of horror. Does this not serve as a warning regarding the susceptibility of children to negative influences of some types of media programming? It isn't worth it to provide a channel through which Satan can influence children or adults. We lived without television for all the remaining years, and would not have one in our home. Our commitment is: "I will set no wicked thing before my eyes" (Psalm 101:3).

Days of Dedication

I began to be conscious of the hand of God working in my life stronger than ever in the fourteenth year of my life. These became blessed days of serious dedication for me. I knelt at my bed and wept, praying and giving my life to the Lord in deeper consecration. He was there in that room with me. No wonder my heart swelled with joy and awe! The Spirit of God stirred me from deep inside and, like a gushing river of living water, He flowed forth in a torrent of Heavenly language. My hands were raised in surrender to my Lord, as I continued to pray in the Spirit. This became a frequent experience for me. Many times the Lord drew me to the words of a very old song that soon became my deep and earnest prayer to the Lord.

I'LL LIVE FOR HIM
By Ralph E. Hudson

My life, my love I give to Thee,
Thou Lamb of God Who died for me;
O may I ever faithful be,
My Savior and my God!

Chorus:
I'll live for Him Who died for me,
How happy then my life shall be!
I'll live for Him Who died for me,
My Savior and my God!

O Thou Who died on Calvary,
To save my soul and make me free,
I'll consecrate my life to Thee,
My Savior and my God![1]
Copyright: Public Domain

My bedside became a sacred altar absorbing the tears of my life offered to God. From the depths of my heart came intense words, "I consecrate my life to Thee." I sang it to Him. "I consecrate my life to Thee." I sang those words again. It seemed as if I could peer through the ceiling, past the first floor, the second, past the roof, and into the throne room of God. I knew I was talking to my precious Lord. "I consecrate my life to Thee, my Savior and my God." Tears streamed down my face as I sang the same few words over and over again. I wanted the Lord to know that I really meant it, and that I wanted to do whatever He wanted me to do in my life.

My red leather Bible lay open on my bed with my hand resting on the words to that song that I had written with ink on the front pages. That old Bible is still my precious possession, a valuable reminder of those days of consecration. As my tears flowed, they dropped onto the words of that song, leaving rings of blue stains. Those tear stains are mine! I treasure the sight of them! They are my testimony that I show to young people today, urging them to make that same dedication to the Lord too. What indescribable joy and privilege has been mine through these years, as I have continued to serve my Savior and to walk with Him!

"God, Save Daddy!"

I loved my father. When I saw him stand so tall and handsome in his police uniform, it made me feel important. He was my dad, and that made me proud. Yet, because I knew he was not saved, a troubling ache lodged in my young heart. The more I read my Bible, the greater my burden grew for him to become a Christian. For a long time, Mother and I had prayed at my bedside night after night, "God, save Daddy!" We wept, and prayed in tongues, and believed God for an answer. With spiritual desire for the future, my mother wept, envisioning our entire family sitting together in church.

One night when I was younger, we were praying quite late when Dad came home and angrily pounded on the door of the bedroom yelling, "Put that child to bed. It's almost midnight!" I cringe at the awful memory of seeing him push the door open and then proceed to shove my mother down onto the bed. He was angry. We knew that part of it was conviction. Another part of it was the fact that he was drinking.

Sometimes he made it nearly impossible for us to go to church. He stayed at the house until it was almost past time for us to leave for church, if we were going. He intended to stop us from going. Yet sometimes, after he left, we quickly got ready and headed out the door. We could see him walking up Junction Boulevard and would follow him at a distance, hiding behind parked cars, and then running to hide behind the next cars until we reached the train. With that kind of courageous determination, my mother faithfully designed ways to keep us under the influence of the gospel and the power of God. Even when it got complicated to go, we went. Sometimes we had to ride a train for about twenty minutes, get off and walk a block to a bus stop, wait for that bus and ride it until our stop, and then walk several more blocks to get to the church that had now relocated to Flushing, New York. It was that important to my mother!

I remember times when my mother and I returned from a Sunday night service to find a crowd on our stoop. They sat there—these men from our street—along with my father, and a keg of beer that all of them were consuming.

"Oh, look who's here! Have you finally come home from church?" slurred one inebriated man in a wavering, singsong voice.

He needed the support of the wall behind him, but still attempted to stretch out his unsteady hand to touch my face. Trying to reach closer, he lost his balance and fell forward, scratching the side of my nose and drawing blood. For a long time I carried a small scar from that incident, a subtle reminder of the misery of sin.

In spite of obstacles and difficulties along the way, I remember my mother keeping joy in her soul, even while her hands were in the sink doing dishes. I could hear the quiet melody of a song, a heartfelt "Hallelujah!" or a prayer for her family. The water in the sink didn't hinder the spiritual river in her soul. She was overjoyed to be filled with the Spirit. Many times she could be heard praying and speaking in tongues someplace in the house. One time she was so full of the Spirit that it just continued to flow when she opened the door in response to our landlord's knock, still speaking in tongues.

I don't want to give the impression that my father was a terrible man. While it is true that he was unsaved and resistant to the Lord, he, nevertheless, gave us many enjoyable memories. Sometimes we would just go for a drive "out to the country" to see trees and grass, and farms, and fresh vegetable stands. He took us to the Catskill Mountains across the Hudson River, where we saw live deer and other animals. It thrilled us. When we were little, we would go to the old remains of the 1939 World's Fair Grounds and play. Sometimes he would lie on his back in the grass, stretch out his arms for us to step onto his hands while grasping his upraised feet. We knew he was strong—because he then gave us a ride, lifting us high in the air. He gave us money to ride a bus and go swimming at a pool.

He began a photography club in our basement to teach local kids the trade and began to take unending pictures of us. He arranged for a policeman to let us in a side door to go skating at the local roller rink. He took us on P.A.L. (Police Athletic League) sponsored trips to Coney

Island and Rockaway Beach. I would have many things to learn about some of these activities as I grew in age and experience with the Lord, but they were Dad's way of providing us with things to keep us busy and out of trouble.

I Wanted to Play the Piano

I didn't know anything about music. But the time came when I had a strong desire to learn to play the piano. I believe the Lord shapes the desires of those who seek Him. He certainly had a plan for my life that was totally unknown to me at this time, and was beginning to lay the groundwork, preparing me for future ministry.

I approached my father with my request, "Dad, I would love to learn to play the piano! Can you get one for me?"

That was a big request, probably beyond my father's present financial ability. He had a wise answer for me. "Claire, we don't have a piano, but there is a cornet in the closet. Take that to school and learn to play it. If you show me you can do it, I'll get you a piano."

It was a challenge, and I took it! Off I went, heading down the street to Junior High School 16, several blocks from my house. That neat cornet case swung proudly from my hand, as I entered the band room and presented my petition to the music teacher. I was in! Accepted! I learned to read notes, to practice the fingering, to blow properly through the mouthpiece, and was playing in the horn section of the junior high school band, along with several boys. Since I was the only girl playing a cornet, after awhile I began to feel somewhat out of place and self-conscious. My friend, Rachel, was playing a French horn, so after persuading my teacher to give me permission, I switched and joined her, learning to play that too. I still remember sitting on the auditorium platform with the school band, playing "From the halls of Montezuma to the shores of Tripoli; we will fight our country's battles in the air, on land and sea." It was the official song of the Marines and sounded wonderful, even if I only played those rhythmic low bass notes—boom-boom, boom-boom. Well, I convinced my father of my interest in music and he somehow managed to get me an old, upright piano that I cherished. He also arranged for me to have weekly, piano lessons from a woman on the local city council. She taught me for a year and a half, and I am grateful for all I learned. Yet she didn't give me hymns or spiritual songs to practice. My heart longed to play Amazing Grace, and Leaning on the Everlasting Arms, and more of the songs I loved so much. Eventually, I stopped the lessons and became like a lion in battle, attacking my task—focusing hard on hymns from a regular hymnal and persisting in practice. I struggled and succeeded in joining the right and left-hand notes, making them sound like a song I could recognize!

"Did you hear that, Mom? I played it!"

It was exciting! I wanted to play the Lord's songs, and I practiced and practiced, slowly gaining ground. At the same time, I nearly drove my mother crazy with the constant pinging, often in perfect discord. Neither she nor I could have guessed that some day that piano playing for the Lord would be heard in places across America and in several other countries.

3

THE MIRACLE OF DAD'S SALVATION

A Divine Connection

Step by step, God supernaturally intervenes in the affairs of men to accomplish his divine purposes. One year I had the opportunity to go to a youth and adult campmeeting at Old Bridge, New Jersey. God was in it! Mom arranged for us to get a cabin but we had to clean out the spider webs to make it livable for that week. The big, long tabernacle filled with people, and the power of God moved mightily. Many young people starve for time together with others their age, who also love the Lord. I was blessed to be here! The greatest thrill came when the evangelist preached so powerfully and then invited all of us to come to the altar to pray.

Kneeling before those dusty old metal chairs I entered into the presence of God. It seemed that He reached out on all sides of my life to speak to me, trying to direct me. That's when my thoughts zeroed in on my father's need for the Lord. I wondered, "God, are You placing these ideas in my mind?" As I walked out of the tabernacle and started down the lane toward our cabin, I caught sight of the camp evangelist standing nearby. Instantly, I knew what I had to do. Working up enough courage to go to him, I addressed him politely and asked, "Brother, I know you don't live near us in Corona, but if you ever get the chance, could you please come to our house and talk to my father about the Lord? I really want him to get saved."

The next Saturday he showed up, knocking on our door.

"I came to talk to Mr. Wilmerton," he announced, and we

wondered if Mr. Wilmerton would even talk to him. It honestly surprised us when my dad invited this brother to a back room where they stayed for a long time. The next Saturday, he came back and they talked again. We were in awe and praying hard for God to save Dad.

This same evangelist began revival meetings that week in the church my mother and I started to attend in Astoria. We were dressing for the Sunday morning service as my father walked out all dressed and stated in a deliberately disinterested voice, "Well, maybe I'll go with you this morning."

Amazing! We were stunned! We were thrilled! We wanted to jump up and down and shout, "Hallelujah! Praise the Lord! Glory to God!" but thought it best to remain subdued, lest he change his mind. Mother restrained herself instead, sweetly voicing calm words, "That's nice! I'm sure you'll enjoy it."

My father had not been in church in years, with perhaps a very few exceptions. This was astounding! Then when Sunday night came, we were amazed beyond words when he said with a slight grin, "Well, I guess I'll go again tonight." But what really sent shimmering chills of excitement through us was his announcement on Monday night when he again said he would go.

Most Unusual Pentecostal Service

I wasn't there for that service, but at about one in the morning I woke up and found my mother sitting alone in the kitchen. "Mom, why are you up? What's going on?" Then I heard the words I had waited so long to hear: "Claire, Dad got saved tonight!!" Now I couldn't hold back the "Hallelujah! Praise the Lord! Glory to God!"

It had been a most unusual service for a Pentecostal church. When the evangelist stood to preach, someone suddenly spoke out loudly, by the Spirit, "Be still and know that I am God!" He sat down. Awhile later he tried again and the same thing happened. Sixty minutes of silence passed in a Pentecostal church! It was unheard of! But there was no silence in my father's heart and conscience. A war was raging, and God was winning.

Unknown to everyone else, Dad had bargained with God like a

negotiator sealing a deal. He poured out his intent to the God he had omitted from his life for so long,

"God, if you're really interested in me, I want you to make something very unusual happen in tomorrow night's service. Then I'll give my life to you and serve you as hard as I served the devil."

"Then the earth shook and trembled…the Lord thundered in the Heavens…he rode upon a cherub and did fly upon the wings of the wind" as he came down to respond to the psalmist David's cry (Psalm 18:7-17). This same God, who is not willing that any perish, came down into that little church in Astoria, to uniquely intervene and bring a lost sinner home.

When the pastor finally said, "Let's all get down to pray," my mother tapped my father's knee and pleaded, "Bill isn't it time for you to pray?" Like a bolt of lightning, he dropped to his knees weeping loudly—this hard-hearted New York City policeman who had seen it all, done it all, and resisted God so long. Tears freely flowed, but not only from Dad. These people grew up with Dad. They knew him. They knew how he had lived his life. This was an overwhelming miracle that caused a church full of people to cry and pray and rejoice with fervor. That night God not only saved my forty-six-year-old father and made him a new creature, but He also healed him of peptic ulcers, duodenal ulcers, and more.

The chief police surgeon of New York City had told him, "Mr. Wilmerton, you might as well retire, go out west, put your feet up, and do nothing." They had no cure for the painful condition that caused him to be eating nothing but baby food.

It didn't take long for him to react to the new peace and joy that now filled his heart. Sudden realization of God's mighty power stirred so much faith in his heart that after church he went out and ate a hot pastrami sandwich with no ill effects. He was, indeed, completely healed by the same power of God that cleansed and saved his soul. Praise the Lord!

Going back to the police station the next morning would present the first great test of his newfound faith, but he was determined to pass it with flying colors. Would he succeed? Dad had worked in this 110th precinct for eighteen years. These men knew him well. Some were his fishing and drinking buddies. My dad had once told me, "Claire, you'll never know all the things I was involved in." No doubt, these close knit police partners knew more than I did.

As he climbed the few narrow steps of his assigned command post and moved past the cold, grey stone exterior, patrolman William W. Wilmerton stepped through the heavy wood framed door a different man than he was yesterday. This day will be like an opening ceremony with everyone watching to see what comes next. There was a boldness in my father as he walked tall to his determined, first point of destination—the captain's office.

"Captain, I want you to be the first to know that last night I gave my life to the Lord and He saved me."

No doubt the Captain could have fallen off his chair in shock, but with visible amazement he slowly uttered, "That's good. That's good. I wish you well."

By the time my father made it through the precinct and around the corner to his office there was already a crowd of policemen gathered at the door. Word had spread that quickly. Jammed together in a little sea of blue, this usually-friendly gang of uniformed policemen stared at their fellow officer.

"Well, well, well! We hear that Bill got religion! We'll give you two weeks!" they chanted, adding a few more jibes.

But that two weeks turned into two months, and two years, and into the call of God to Bible school at about 47 years of age, and graduation, and pastoring for years, and then teaching in Ozark Bible Institute (O.B.I.), Neosho, Missouri for about fifteen years until the Lord took him home to Heaven.

A Great Change to Our Family

It was just before my fourteenth birthday when my father got saved. His salvation brought a great change to our family. New interests drove him to search for churches holding revivals, places where the Word of God was preached and where the power of God was manifest. Eventually, He got all of us involved in establishing a new church that began in our own house on our dead-end street. We set up chairs and invited people to the services and some came.

Our next-door neighbors in the duplex where we lived were Puerto Rican. They were very nice people, except for the fact that their one son Tony was a car thief and their mother was into some kind of witchcraft and spell casting. One day I had to jump out of the way of a speeding car that Tony had stolen. Police with flashing lights were in hot pursuit as Tony and his gang fled to a screeching halt at the end of our dead-end street where they threw open all four doors and jumped out from both sides, racing in every direction through narrow alleys and away.

One Sunday, his mother, Mrs. Cantini, agreed to come to our service. After the preaching, the pastor invited people to come up front for prayer if they wanted the Lord's help in their lives. Mrs. Cantini was one of the first to go forward. We prayed for her just a few minutes when all of a sudden she screamed very loudly and ran out of the house. Later she told us that while she stood there Jesus appeared to her and she was afraid of him. That's why she ran out. Too bad she didn't bow to Him and let Him set her free.

Later we moved our house church to a storefront and finally to a rented Lutheran church building. There Violet Witteman and I became the official usherettes to take up the offering. We wore neat white suits with pleated skirts made for us by a relative of Dr. C. I. Scofield. I was just learning to play piano and, since no one else was available, I played for church using just one hand, sometimes just one finger.

Once, a rather "starchy" visiting preacher came and wanted to sing a special. Ding, ding, ding went my one-finger playing for his song until right in the middle he stopped and barked, "Please stop playing! I can do much better without the music!" I left the piano and took a seat in the congregation, my face still hot red. Amazingly, such an embarrassing beginning didn't stop me. Neither did it take very long to discern the deplorable character of this man who called himself a "missionary." No doubt we were a little misinformed, and this led to several bewildering incidents.

When we picked him up at the airport late Saturday night, we had our first unexpected surprise. He was white! Since he was from Africa we mistakenly presumed he was a black man and had arranged for him to stay at the home of a very nice black family from our church. When we explained this to him we were very disturbed at his reproachful response. It was clear that he was agitated and perhaps offended at such a suggestion. He refused to stay at that home. That was just the beginning of our troubling revelation about this man.

Our little duplex barely held our family of six and was certainly not prepared for a guest at this hour. With no other option, we brought him to our house and gave him the best room. Before he retired to bed, he walked out into the kitchen carrying three suits and asked my worn out mother if she would be kind enough to press them for him before tomorrow. It was nearly midnight, but my mother did it.

Something about his presence in the house actually brought a fear in our hearts. I can remember my sisters and I creeping away to hide in our bedroom where we frantically prayed the Lord's Prayer, asking Him to protect us. There is even more to this story, but what a relief it was to finally get rid of him when he left the next day. We then learned from other missionaries that this man lived in luxury with many servants in Africa and showed little love for the people. How different it is when you are in the presence of a godly servant of the Lord!

Evangelists Allen, Osborn, Hicks, and Coe

When our little church didn't have services, Dad took us to meetings wherever he could find them. We drove almost every night to a theater in New Jersey where A. A. Allen had a month of meetings. It certainly kept our attention when the song leader led songs as he leaped across the platform. The preachers on the platform were also jumping until dust came up in a cloud. It was then announced that the cloud was the Shekinah glory. For some reason, I doubted it. Certainly there were some amazing miracles and many people who came for salvation. My dad was a new Christian and was just so hungry to be in church. Undoubtedly, because he was a policeman, he was appointed head usher in the meetings and guarded the money. He even caught one usher pocketing some of the offering for himself.

We also drove to an arena in New York City to hear a young T. L. Osborn and Tommy Hicks. It astounded us to hear of the great missionary work they were doing. Tears filled my eyes as I heard of the multitudes coming to Christ, and of blind eyes opening, the crippled walking, deaf ears hearing, and much more. So many people needed the Lord. My heart melted with desire to do something. Interest in ministry was blossoming in my soul. God was working.

Then Evangelist Jack Coe put up his huge gospel tent for one month in Jackson Heights, about two miles from our house, for one of his last crusades. We went every day and night except for our own church service times. My cousin and I walked a couple of miles to the afternoon service and stopped at big apartment buildings on the way, putting tracts under every door. We arrived at the tent early, ate the lunch that we brought with us, and then went to the afternoon service.

My parents arrived for the night service, and we all listened in awe and expectantly watched and rejoiced to see healings and miracles. Crutches and canes from healed persons were hanging across the tent. Just as he did for the Allen meetings, my Dad became an usher for these meetings. Huge crowds filling the tent were sometimes disorderly and had to be controlled. The singing, preaching and praying impacted my teenage life. My mother and I would sometimes stay late and pray with people in the prayer tent. I was just fourteen years old then, but I can remember one night that we both prayed until four o'clock in the morning with people seeking the Baptism of the Holy Ghost. My mother reported that as one woman received the infilling, a mighty rushing wind filled the tent. Such an eruption of God's power burst forth that Brother Coe came out of his trailer to see what was happening. This was an unforgettable experience that impacted my life. I became aware of increasingly frequent desires and thoughts of God's will. He was developing spiritual direction for my future, implanting in me a yearning to see his mighty power at work, and to touch the lives of others for Him.

Life started to become an adventure as God brought many changes into the Wilmerton household. By the time of my junior year in high school, my father already sensed that the Lord wanted him to preach. What an exciting difference this made in our lives! He retired from the police force, obeyed God's call and enrolled in Long Island Bible Institute in Oyster Bay, New York.

To be closer to the school we moved from Corona to Massapequa Park, Long Island, to a nicer house and a nicer neighborhood. Coming from a dead-end street to this place was awesome. By contrast though, these people did seem to be a lot richer than we were. It was just different being out of the city, and we were taking our time adjusting to our brand new life.

4

TEN FEET FROM MURDER

A Dark Shadow of Evil

My new high school had an impressive number of what seemed to be upper middle class students and, although I had a very small circle of friends, I was getting along well with them. However, much to my dismay, an alarming revelation dawned upon me one morning—that even in this kind of affluent atmosphere there could exist a creeping dark, shadow of evil.

It started out as a normal day. Students loaded with books were typically dragging through the halls for their early first period class. Yet even that accepted sense of usual normalcy was about to be cruelly squeezed from their grasp.

A dark, evil cloud of malevolence formed above that moving throng of humans and slowly slithered down to where we were. Suddenly on that dreadful morning, a terrifying explosive blast resonated from the men's restroom, bringing everyone to a startling standstill. Shock waves of uncertainty reverberated through each person's being. I had literally halted right outside that restroom door. In that brief instant of motionless silence, a teenager, in a tan trench coat, burst out of the door and pushed his way through the crowd, toward the school exit.

Mr. Mitchell, a tall strong science teacher, bounded through that bathroom door like a battle-bound warrior. Never was adrenaline energy so short-lived. Almost instantly, Mr. Mitchell struggled out of that door and nearly collapsed with his face against the wall. It was an emotional crisis to deal with the scene he had just observed. It was morally incomprehensible.

Inside that room was chaotic destruction. A fifteen-year-old boy lay dead. Only a day before, he sat across from me in study hall. He and a fifteen-year-old classmate had engaged in a series of escalating conflicts and fights. All of that came to a vengeful climax when a birthday gift of a shotgun became the concealed weapon of choice. With weapon ready, the angry and disturbed murderer hid behind a partition until his victim arrived and was standing before a mirror combing his hair. "You creep," he screamed, as he pressed the trigger, killing his rival instantly.

The devastation was complete and terrible. Needless to say, we all had to remain in our classrooms until authorities apprehended the murderer and restored order to the school. The awfulness of sin and the lost condition of this world gripped my heart. Even teenagers were vulnerable targets of Satan's evil designs. They needed a Savior. Only Jesus could change and transform their hearts. Could God somehow use my life in this needy harvest field?

A New Godly Influence

The sense of his call kept growing in my heart. Our move from Corona opened the door for our attendance at the Wightman Memorial Church in Oyster Bay, Long Island. This Pentecostal church was home to Long Island Bible Institute, where my father was now enrolled as a student. Rapidly I became exposed to the influence of many wonderful Christian young people and was thrilled to make new godly friends. Their dedicated lives impressed and inspired me. To this day, I am stirred afresh as I relive one particular service when all the students were standing at the altar singing and praying. I was sixteen years old, standing there too, with hands uplifted and tears flowing. My heart was aflame as I sang with them from the depths of my soul:

> I'll go where You want me to go, dear Lord,
> O'er mountain, or plain, or sea;
> I'll say what You want me to say, dear Lord,
> I'll be what You want me to be. [2]
> *Copyright: Public Domain*

Oh how I wept. Whatever the Lord wanted for me was what I wanted. There was nothing I wanted more…at least at that moment.

As the days passed, I believed I was retaining that same close relationship with the Lord, but I was not. I believe every young person becomes the target of Satan, who will do anything to distract them from the will of God. I always knew that when I graduated from high school, I, too, would go to Bible school but, by the time that day came, other interests crowded out God's plan. He was a tall, 6' 5" blonde with a Thunderbird convertible, who really liked me. That friendship almost led to marriage, but God had other plans for my life. I thought I knew what I wanted and felt upset when my father announced we were moving five hundred miles away to northern Maine, where he was to take his first pastorate. I did not want to go so far away but had no choice. How faithful the Lord is to stay on our trail, follow us, continue to work on us, to perfect his purposes in our lives.

Impossibility Defeated

We were busily packing for our big move when my father became very ill. It was unusual for him to admit to any pain, but we knew something was wrong when he stayed in bed, propped up with pillows for several days. His stomach became abnormally distended, and he began to groan. Soon he had no recourse but to go to the dreaded emergency room. Tests revealed a serious intestinal blockage that required immediate surgery. This was unbelievable! We were to leave the next day for Maine. How could such a thing be happening? As he lay on a gurney preparing for the operation, we were all at home on our knees desperately praying for his healing. It seemed like a trick of the devil to hinder Dad's desire to go pastor that church in Maine. We stormed Heaven! We claimed the promises of God:

"He sent his word, and healed them, and delivered them from their destructions" (Psalm 107:20).

"But unto you that fear my name shall the Sun of righteousness arise with healing in his wings; and ye shall go forth…" (Malachi 4:2).

"Who his own self bare our sins in his own body on the tree that we, being dead to sins, should live unto righteousness: by whose stripes ye were healed" (1 Peter 2:24).

In the meantime at the hospital, a doctor entered my father's room, verified his name from his wristband, checked an illuminated x-ray picture of Dad's intestinal blockage, and proceeded to press around gently on his stomach. He turned and checked the x-ray a second time and reexamined Dad's stomach. Next he left the room and returned with several more doctors who all repeated the same actions as the previous one. Uncertainty showed on their faces as they ordered a new x-ray.

My father had no doubt that God was working a miracle. Sure enough, the doctors were confounded at the new picture. They could find no trace of the blockage that they clearly saw just a brief time ago. They cancelled the surgery and told my father, "Mr. Wilmerton, we don't know where that blockage went, but it's gone. You can go home!"

Hallelujah! What a wonder-working God! Dad was completely healed and able to drive the big, rented U-Haul truck to Maine the next day. What the enemy meant for evil, God turned for good.

Corona, New York home where I grew up.

My brother Billy and me on Easter.

Nick the Ice cream man Dad led to the Lord on our dead-end street.

My policeman father: William Wallace Wilmerton IV, 1908-1982.

Country meets City: Jenny Thompson and my mother Helen C. Wilmerton at Jenny's farm in Medway, Maine.

A rare picture of the Wilmerton siblings together. L to R: Claire Goodwin, Bill Wilmerton, Jean Crossman, Barbara Haas.

*Final family reunion with Mom. L to R: Claire,
Bill, Barbara, Jean, and Mom in the middle.*

Claire Goodwin, Youth Director at Broadway
Assembly, Lorain, Ohio 1963-1969.

Pastor K. A. Smith and family at Broadway Assembly-1967. Back row: Grace and Keith Smith. Front Row, L to R: Kim, Rhonda, Brenda, Sandra.

Margaret McMillen - My hero.

5

MAINE—OUR NEW WORLD

Leaving It All Behind

Off to Maine these city slickers went, to a big white house with a wood furnace, a chimney and a wood stove. The firemen were at our house several times that year! We finally joked with them and assured them that we would keep the coffee ready for the next time. What amazed me most was that there were outhouses here in Maine! What? I even wrote back to my friends in New York, and told them "Can you believe there are outhouses up here, and we have one?" It wasn't hard to see that this city girl had a lot to learn.

Truthfully, I really loved it in Maine. I loved the snow. I loved the silence. We would go outside at night and look up at the beautiful stars that we rarely could see in the city. We would stand out there and just listen...yes; we would listen to the silence! No sirens, no rumbling trains or bus engines, just absolute quiet. What a wonder! I loved the woods, the deer, moose, skunks, raccoons, porcupines and foxes. I even captured a little green garden snake and kept it in a cage for awhile until it got away. My mother ran out of the house and refused to return until we got rid of that harmless little critter! What a time we had!

Our New York City accent was a novelty in Maine as we were initiated into the Northern Maine accent that made us sometimes feel like strangers in a foreign land. I remember when we went to visit Norman and Jenny Thompson, one of the church families. Sister Thompson told my mother that they had a cow and a "half-a." My

Mother quickly asked, "A 'half-a' what?" Laughing hard at her New York accent, Sister Thompson pointed to her cow and her heifer.

On my first day of work on a soda fountain job, a young boy was my first customer. His chubby round face possessed the sweetest smile. I liked him immediately, until he spoke. Was it a foreign language? He repeatedly told me that he wanted a "laahge strowbarry paawp." This was embarrassing! I couldn't understand a word of what he said. Squinting in concentration, I stared in his face and tried to mumble his words to myself. I got it! At last the light broke through my New York brain. "Ahh! He wants a large strawberry pop!" Finally understanding, I guessed I would disappoint him when I said, "I'm sorry we don't have any of them." But he hollered back, "Yes, you do. I got one yesterday." Then I realized that although pop was ice-cream on a stick to a New Yorker, it was a drink to a Northern Mainer. I gave him his request and he probably wondered what in the world was wrong with that lady behind the counter.

I made fifty-five cents an hour at that drug store but upgraded to a job as a doctor's receptionist for sixty-five cents an hour. Working for a doctor impressed me! The wage didn't matter. I now had a real job, a high class one and I wanted to do my best! As I became more acquainted with the routine I was shocked when I looked at his accounts receivable. It appeared that everyone in town owed him money. I was sure that I could help him, and with good intentions tried to rearrange his whole system. I thought it would be a good idea to develop a system of sending out bills to his patients. His face said it all when I approached him with this suggestion. There was no smile, just a serious look that quickly turned to a frown. The brief conversation that followed showed me how little I really knew about this kind man. He absolutely opposed such a plan! His compassionate policy permitted people to pay if they could, and not to pay if they could not. This short, roundish, well-dressed doctor had a heart of gold, demonstrated daily by his thoughtfulness. His pleasant personality and sense of humor delightfully seasoned my work experience with him. One morning as he arrived in the office after hospital calls, he told me a perplexing story. "Claire, we had a most unusual birth at the hospital this morning. It was part human and part animal." I was stunned, until he explained, "Yes, the beautiful baby had a dear face and a bare bottom." You never know what might turn up in one of these Maine hospitals!

Well, I had an even more humorous thing happen in that doctor's office. A mother became irate with me because I wouldn't allow her little boy to go to the basement. That was private and no one was permitted to go there. She had no idea she was dealing with a foreigner from New York who didn't know that the "basement" meant the "bathroom."

The first time we saw the little, white country church my father had come to pastor, we noticed scaffolding raised on the sides and we thought, "Oh, they must be painting or remodeling the building," but the truth is that the scaffolding actually held up the building. This small church had a potbelly stove in the middle...the first one I had ever seen. Rosie was the piano player who had never taken a lesson and couldn't read a note, but could, with hands flying, pound out the music on that old, upright piano with great exuberance, except when a song was announced that she didn't like. Then suddenly, she couldn't play. We loved these people and longed for the Lord to do a great work in their lives.

The Town Drunk Gets Saved

One little lady came to the church and turned her life and home over to the Lord. Things were difficult for her living with her husband and five small children in a little cabin partly covered with windblown tar paper and no indoor facilities. As she continued to reach out to the Lord faith began to build in her heart. Then one day she asked if we would come to her house and have a prayer meeting for her husband to get saved. We were happy to do so and, on a set date we all gathered together in that little space and began to pray. The need was much greater than any one of us could have imagined, for her husband was a drunkard who was abusive and did not work or support his family. The people of the town were well acquainted with his reputation and behavior, but we knew that our God is bigger than the sin that bound this man.

When he heard about the planned prayer meeting, he determined to be gone from the house. All the demons of Hell were out to destroy him, but we had weapons that could pull down every stronghold of Satan, and we began to aggressively use them. Powerful praying and interceding in the Spirit echoed through the place and rose higher than Mount Katahdin, the highest point in Maine, into the very throne room of God.

Somewhere, out on the darkened streets of Medway, a lonely figure plodded along, headed to no place in particular. Did he wonder what was going on back at his house? What was it that made him decide to turn around and head down that dirt road toward that unkempt abode that he often filled with terror and neglect? Near his door, his ears must have heard the sounds of praying; yet he stepped in a side door and sat down, unseen by those earnest prayer warriors.

At some point the Spirit of the Lord began to move on a young girl who stood up speaking in tongues and dancing about in the Spirit. Others just kept on praying as her footsteps took her on a God-ordained journey to the very spot where Ricky sat. Continuing to yield herself to the move of the Holy Spirit who spoke through her in a Heavenly language, she began to dance gently in a circle around that wondering man seated in his chosen spot. It makes my mind envision the Israelites marching around the walls of Jericho. Something dramatic was about to happen.

After awhile my mother rose and came upon this Spirit-charged scene---a hopeless alcoholic slumped in his seat, encircled by a supernatural work of the Spirit. She was a short little lady, but mighty in the Spirit. When she took one look at what was happening, she raised her hand and pointed directly at Ricky thundering with God's authority, "Ricky Thompson, isn't it time you fell on your knees and cried out to God for mercy?" Like a bolt of lightning, he dropped to his knees and began crying out loudly for the Lord to have mercy on him, to forgive him and save him. The Jericho wall of sin's bondage was crumbling down. The blood of Jesus Christ reached down into the depths of a sinful heart, washing it, cleansing it, renewing it, and creating a new creature in Christ Jesus. How amazing is that?

What kind of power is it that can suddenly deliver such a man from years of alcohol abuse, three packs of cigarettes a day, and a life controlled by Satan? It is the power of God! It is the humanly incomprehensible miracle of Salvation at work. It is an indisputable demonstration of the work of Calvary. "What can wash away my sin? Nothing but the blood of Jesus! What can make me pure again? Nothing but the blood of Jesus!"[3] It is Jesus, the wonder of all wonders, who made it all possible. As time went on, Ricky obtained employment, became a better husband and father, and eventually served as the Sunday School Superintendent of our church. That's what Jesus can do!

God sent a mighty revival to that church and many people got saved and filled with the Holy Ghost. Bodies were healed and problems were solved. The revival fires drew people from all over to our services. Pentecostal fire ignited afresh in my own soul. I was learning to love praying with people and ministering to them. A continuing desire grew inside of me to do more for God, but I still was not obeying his will.

The Potato Field Call

Maine is a beautiful state—bursting with many experiences for transplanted New Yorkers. When I heard that some of the church people were going to pick potatoes, my curiosity stirred up and enticed me to announce, "I want to try that! I have never even seen a potato growing!" So it was that, with the early morning fog rising from that farmland in Northern Maine, I was among those crawling on my knees gathering four or five seed potatoes in each hand, dropping them in a bucket between my knees and finally dumping them into a larger barrel that, when full, would earn me twenty-five cents. It was my get-rich-quick scheme!

But don't knock it! Do you know that God was in that potato field? Yes, He was, and what I had effectively distanced from my thoughts was dramatically and supernaturally brought to my attention right there.

Do you remember those locomotives I wrote about that were equipped with turbine powered wheels that rolled down the tracks with a rhythmic chug-a-chug-a-chug-a? Well, they must have suddenly surrounded that potato field, for that same rhythm came alive with every handful of potatoes that I swung into the basket. Each handful talked to me—"Go to Bible school!"—"Go to Bible school!"—"Go to Bible school!" I could hear in my spirit the rhythmic voice of God, calling me, reminding me, "Go to Bible school!" It was inescapable! The Spirit of God was striving with me, breaking through my clouded mind.

After that powerful demonstration from Heaven, how could a person doubt? Perhaps it was human uncertainty, or maybe a bit of unwillingness that prompted me to go to the Lord with this plea: "Lord, if that was You and You really want me to go to Bible school, let three people talk to me about it today." I wonder what God sometimes thinks about these creations of his. I will forever be thankful for his mercies and longsuffering and love. What I asked for, He did, and all I needed now was the money to go.

We went to a missionary service on that Friday night, and contrary to what some would call common sense, the Lord spoke to me to put the last of my money in the offering. That night I had a dream in which I saw my father hand me a check that was made out to a lady who picked potatoes with me. It had the farmer's signature on it, and I even saw the exact amount written on it—three times as much as I had put in the missionary offering.

When I woke up, I couldn't help but wonder what that was all about. Then on Sunday morning my father came to me and handed me that exact check. This sister had asked him to cash it for her. He did, and after he endorsed it, he gave it to me for Bible school. That day a door opened to a new, expanded adventure in my personal life—trusting God for every need, in every situation. I found myself stepping into a new phase of the future that the Lord had already designed, just for me.

6

SHUT IN WITH GOD AT BIBLE SCHOOL

Discovering A Gold Mine

Bursting with excited anticipation, I enrolled as a Bible school student! Schedules, uniforms, classes, prayer meetings, church services and studying all became a daily part of my new life at Long Island Bible Institute in Oyster Bay, Long Island, New York. It was 1958, and I had celebrated my seventeenth birthday six months earlier. This was my first time living away from home. I loved it immediately but really did think I knew so much more than I did know.

As the truths of God's word were expounded, I would sometimes think, "That's not in the Bible!" only to discover that it really was there. A goldmine of learning dangled before me like the proverbial carrot on a stick. I was eager to learn and tried to listen in on conversations of others as they discussed the scriptures. A hunger for more of God and his word ignited in my heart.

Another kind of "heart-burn" also occurred during my early days in school. Wanting to study past the "lights-out" time, I thought up a way to do it without being caught. I had a nice night light that hooked over the back of my bed's headboard, above my pillow. If I made sort of a tent over it with my bathrobe and positioned myself and my book under it, my light would not shine out under my dormitory door for the dean to see. I was safe.

It was a bad idea! The longer I read, the more deeply my mind concentrated and got buried in the subject. Then, in the midst of my intense study, I suddenly became aware of a strange smell. Something was burning! Sure enough, it was my bathrobe! I jumped up, threw the robe off of me and off of the night light and discovered that the top of the night light had melted and burned a hole in my bathrobe—near to my heart. An ugly, ragged hole with charred edges now glared out from that once pretty bathrobe. Only one thing could be worse, and it happened! Right at that moment, the dean of women walked in. Needless to say, I repented and mended both my robe and my ways.

Many life-changing things occurred during my three years in Bible school, but the greatest impact on me, then and for years to come, was that I really learned to pray. God had placed me in the middle of a treasure trove of opportunity. Bible school became my own sacred place that separated me from outside influences and involvements, and gave me time and incentive to draw near to the Lord. There I learned to discern his voice and his perfect will for my life.

The very first verse of the ninety-first Psalm became my longed-for daily experience: "He that dwelleth in the secret place of the most High shall abide under the shadow of the Almighty." That's where I wanted to be. As I sought him, He came to me. I believed what He said in James 4:8—"Draw nigh to God, and he will draw nigh to you." I believed it because it happened to me. The Lord became so real and precious to me, causing me to love my times alone with Him. What an amazing experience it became, to feel his Spirit draw me, in such a way that, even in the short times between my classes, I often hid away somewhere and prayed. When the bell rang for the next class, I felt a sense of disappointment that I had to go.

Something was happening in my life. My inner longing to get alone with God became so great that I determined to find a way to do it more often. These were busy days. People were everywhere, and places to get alone were few. Eventually, a subtle plan developed in my mind, and I hoped it would not cause a problem. I went to bed that night as usual, except for some advance preparations. I made sure my bathrobe was nearby, as well as slippers, a flashlight, my Bible, and a handkerchief. My trusty, little alarm clock was key to the whole plan. I set it for two o'clock in the morning! The room was dark and I soon fell asleep. Then one fifty-eight, one fifty-nine, and Brinnnggggg!

It blasted for only a second until my finger quickly smashed down on the button, turning it off. I saw my roommate shift positions in bed and decided to remain still until I was sure she was back to sleep. Pushing my blanket down, I slid up and out of bed, put on my robe, grabbed my pillow, a handkerchief, my Bible, and a flashlight, and quietly tiptoed out the door. Down through the quiet dormitory hall I went. My holy destination was only a few more minutes away, just beyond the dimly lit stairway.

When I marched off that last step, my heart slightly quivered with excitement, for I was about to accomplish my desire. Continuing my nearly silent trek, I whispered, "Flashlight, where are you now that I need you?" and discovered it instantly, tucked inside my pillowcase. The final passageway was dark. Just a little further and I see that door to a seldom used, nearly hidden room, piled with stacked chairs and other storage things. Somehow this struck me as a "mission accomplished!" I had arrived at what was to become a frequently visited secret place.

Chair stacks and rolled carpets were positioned in a way that created an open pathway to the back corner of the room. I did scan the room with my flashlight. It was dark and, in spite of my intentions, I wanted to make sure no one else was in this room! Satisfied, I found my spot. There I placed my pillow on the floor—it would soon become a tear stained altar. Down I went, stretching out on the floor, with my face in my pillow, where I began to cry out to God from the depths of my heart, glad that my sounds were muffled by my pillow.

What glorious and wonderful times I had with God during those times! It was my way to get alone with God. My prayer always beckoned the Lord to purge me—to cleanse me, to mold me, to make me whatever He wanted me to be. I surrendered my all to Him and prayed earnestly that He would use my life, fill me with his power, and give me souls. I often could envision the harvest field of lost souls heading for an eternity in Hell, and would weep with desire to win them. My prayer hasn't changed. As I write these words at the age of seventy, that is still my deepest yearning and desire. Oh, Lord, give me souls; use me for your glory. There is no greater joy than to walk in the center of the will of

God, to be in the ministry full-time, to feel his power move through you as you reach out to touch lives for Him.

Prayer became the one thing that would continue to draw me closer to the Lord. One evening in prayer at my bedside, God directed me to pray for Costa Rica and the missionaries I knew there. As I interceded, I suddenly had what I might call a vision. A picture came in my mind of a huge, ugly, boney hand stretching out of the sky, pointing down at Costa Rica. I knew immediately it was the hand of death and began urgently praying and interceding for those missionaries. I soon learned that, at that same time, there were devastating floods that destroyed much property and caused deaths. However, those missionaries that I prayed for and their churches were not hurt. Praise God!

We may not always know exactly how or what to pray, but Romans 8:26 assures us that "the Spirit also helpeth our infirmities: for we know not what we should pray for as we ought: but the Spirit itself maketh intercession for us with groanings which cannot be uttered." When the Holy Ghost intercedes through us, we can be sure of an answer.

My Will or God's Will

During that first year of Bible school the Lord began to repeatedly wake me at night with a clear message: "You've got to break up with Jerry."

I bolted upright, eyes barely open, and wondered, "Why, Lord?" I didn't understand. Jerry and I were engaged to be married.

Yet, I couldn't deny that this repeated awakening must be God trying to get my attention. I leaned against my pillow and cried. For some reason unknown to me, He wanted me to end this relationship. Although still questioning, I knew I had to at least try to obey God.

My feeble attempts failed, and the relationship continued. I couldn't understand the Lord's direction and struggled with it over a period of time, until one whole night of prayer that brought peace to my heart. It happened during summer break when I went back home to Maine.

Returning home around five o'clock in the evening from a part-time job, I told my mother that I didn't want to eat, that I was going to my room to pray and didn't want anyone to bother me. My heart was burdened as I brought this relationship before the Lord in prayer. The hours passed as I sought the will of God and did my best to surrender my own will to whatever God wanted. This was an important decision. It would affect the rest of my life. I had to make the right choice.

The darkness of the midnight hour passed, but I had to hear from God and was determined to stay right here on my knees until I knew his voice. I shed many tears as the battle raged in my heart. With my Bible open, my eager heart searched to find assurance of God's will. His words in Isaiah 55:8 kept prodding me—"My thoughts are not your thoughts, neither are your ways my ways, saith the LORD." I had to face it! God knew something more than I knew. He knew the future and everything in it. My understanding was finite—limited—even when I was willing to do God's will. I needed Him so much right now.

Hours passed by. Except for the ticking of my clock and occasional snoring from my sleeping family, a soothing quietness settled over the house. At around four in the morning, the battle was won. I had my answer, and blessed peace warmed my heart as I said a resolute "Yes" to God's will. Obedience is not always easy but the wisest and most beneficial choice, for now and eternity. I obeyed God. The relationship had to end, and it did. I knew I had made the right choice, and the presence of God remained strong in my heart.

When I returned to Bible school that fall, God began to test me with a new level of commitment. Sometime during my many times alone with Him, an uncomfortable notion began to dart through my mind. When I tried to dismiss it, I soon found it again, perched right in the middle of all my thoughts. It was a question, and by now I knew it was God speaking to me. "If I wanted you to remain single, would you do it?" The very essence of that idea triggered an immediate "No!" I didn't get the connection right then, but this was like the early days of God's call to me when He showed me those various difficult scenes and asked me, "If I wanted you to go there, would you do it?" Similarly, the battle began between my own desires and God's.

For about a month I struggled with that question, until I sincerely yielded my all to the Lord and said, "Yes, even if You want me to remain single, I know You will take care of me and fill me with your joy." It is obvious that He never did require me to stay single, but what

He wanted was a complete willingness on my part to do whatever He might want me to do.

Putting that issue on the altar and into God's hands kept me in peace for the years to come. I didn't dwell on getting married, as some did. I wasn't always looking for someone who might be a matrimonial candidate, as some were. I remember one girl sitting on her dormitory room floor moaning that she was twenty three and not married yet, that she'd probably be an old maid. God spared me all that useless anxiety. God kept me from distractions and put my focus on Him, and on ministry and the needy harvest field. Until I finally did marry at the age of twenty eight, I enjoyed that inner peace and assurance that my life was in God's hands and He would without fail bring to pass whatever was his will for my life. There were probably some brief times each year when that issue slipped off the altar, and I knew what I had to do. I needed to pray through and get it back on the altar. The altar is the place of peace. As Abraham did with Isaac, so we need to tie our sacrifice to the altar. To surrender means to relinquish control, to let go of, to cease to hold in the hand, to give up my rights. Surrendering is not always easy but it is always powerful! It is always God's will to present our bodies a living sacrifice to Him. We would save ourselves much distress if we would obey the wonderful words of Psalm 37:5, "Commit thy way unto the LORD; trust also in him; and he shall bring it to pass."

Learning to Trust God for Every Need

Five hundred miles away in Maine, my parents labored diligently for the Lord pastoring a small church. My brother Bill was in the Air Force, and my sisters Jean and Barbara were still at home. Financially, things were pretty bleak. Money was scarce. Dad was the pastor, but the church was unable to support him, even though they tried. The people were poor and sometimes gave total offerings of six or eight dollars in a week. With that and a small police pension they proceeded to do a work for God, eventually constructing a new church building. For the six years that I lived in Maine, I don't remember going to any department stores or buying clothes. I never did learn to be a big shopper, but to be content with whatever the Lord provided. Once we were completely out of food and got news that a cousin was coming to visit. "How will we feed or provide for him?" we all wondered. That day my father stopped at the post office for our mail. One letter was in the box. Tearing it open revealed a wonderful miracle from the Lord. Inside that envelope was enough money to buy gas for his trip to pick up my cousin. Dad was overjoyed, and we all praised the Lord! We didn't want our cousin to know of our financial condition when he arrived, so we just had toast and coffee for breakfast, and then took him for a short ride to see some of Maine's beautiful sights.

God has promised to provide all of our needs according to his riches in glory—and that is an abundant promise! We witnessed his faithfulness over and over again. When we returned from our ride, there were bags and boxes of groceries at our door, donated by Lennie, from the local market. It would be hard to count the many times we saw similar provision in answer to prayer.

This same lesson became necessarily familiar to me at Bible school—even for small things. I seldom had money and one time some of the girls went down town to get a cold drink. I stayed behind since I had no money, but just casually said, "Lord, I sure wish I had a cold drink too." Only minutes later I heard a knock on my dormitory door." Claire, while I was out I thought I'd get you a coke," were the words from that smiling classmate. Such a small thing, yet it had special meaning for me. It made me know that the Lord heard my slightest call, and cared about my smallest wish. Such a thought reminds me that one wonderful day God Himself launched a promise from Heaven's shores that awed me from the day I first learned it—"Delight thyself also in the lord, and he shall give thee the desires of thine heart." I am a living witness to that truth.

It was essential for me to learn how to live by faith, trusting God for every need. My whole unknown future would require it! I wonder if God, as our teacher, looks down with pleasure when He sees us pass his tests. You will certainly know it quickly, if you become the subject of one of his lessons in life. No one can teach like He does. Suddenly, at the end of a dark tunnel, or in the midst of some challenging situation we may find ourselves going, "Hmmmm! I think God was teaching me something!"

One day while in prayer, I experienced Heaven's great teacher in action as He brought to my mind the financial needs of the Bible school where I was a student. It was definitely a surprising challenge that He spoke to my heart that day. He asked me to give to the school, for a period of time, all the finances that came in to me, and to trust Him to literally give to me the actual material things that I might need. It was an exciting commitment, and became even more thrilling when suddenly money began to come to me in the mail, or from some person's hand. Fifty dollars! Wow! I had never had that kind of money! I needed shoes. The Dean of women had told me that I must get two more uniforms and when I told her I had no money, she had told me, "Pray them in." Well, now I had the money. What would I do? I gave all of it to the school, and trusted God to meet my needs literally. The next day a lady brought a big box to my room and told me to look through it to see if there was anything I could use. Crowded amongst the unique conglomeration inside that box emerged a brand new pair of just-the-right-size shoes, and two uniforms! I easily learned that trusting God is simply trusting in his faithfulness.

"My toothpaste is almost gone," I realized, and then prayed, "Lord, You see my need!" Before the day was over a student knocked on my door and said, "Claire, my parents sent several tubes of toothpaste to me today. I don't need all of them. Can you use some?" Another need met!

Please understand that I told no one about my financial commitment or my needs. Only the Lord knew, and more and more money kept flowing to me. This had never happened before, and I faithfully gave it in to the school, as I had committed to do. Consequently, I saw amazing answers and provisions.

One day I received a package in the mail from a book club. I knew better than to join such a thing when I had no money, but I agreed to receive their books, and if I didn't want to buy them, I had to get them back in the mail in so many days or I would have to pay for the book. I needed to pray, and I did!

"Lord, I'm in trouble. I never should have joined this book club, but I did. Now here I am with the most recent book sitting on my dresser. I need to mail it back, but all I have for postage is two cents, and I need another ten cents. Please help me once again!" (It's amazing how cheap postage was then!)

That very day I received a letter in the mail. The envelope was addressed to me in pencil. Inside was a note with the large penciled printing of a child—"Dear Sister Claire, we love you and miss you." He printed the Lord's Prayer and ended it, Love, Mikey" and at the bottom was scotch taped a dime—exactly what I needed! Several days before I even called on the Lord for that need, he let Mikey put that in the mail. He was one of the children in my father's church who I was teaching in youth service when I was at home.

Does the Lord care about our slightest need? Oh, yes! I have found Him to be faithful in both big and small things through all these years. His promise is "Call unto me and I will answer thee and show three great and mighty things which thou knowest not" (Jeremiah 33:3).

During Bible school days, I never wrote home and asked for money. I never told others of my needs. I prayed and saw God meet the need. However, one time God embarrassed me over a moment of unbelief. I had written three letters and had them standing upright on my dresser but had no stamps to send them. In a moment of silliness, I knelt down in the dormitory hallway and loudly called out, "Oh, Lord, You know I need stamps to send these letters. Please put it on someone's heart to give me some stamps!"

I knew everyone would hear me and, sure enough someone came running with the stamps I needed. My letters got sent the next day, the same day that I received in the mail an entire roll of stamps! If I had only waited and trusted God! He needed to remind me of his admonition in Psalm 37:7a—"Rest in the LORD, and wait patiently for him." No wonder the psalmist wrote in Psalm 89:1, "I will sing of the mercies of the LORD for ever: with my mouth will I make known thy faithfulness to all generations."

Powder and Beads

Saturday night arrived—the time when most students would gather in the dining hall to socialize—and I was anxious to go. Obviously, I really didn't know much about holiness at that time. There I stood posing before my mirror, looking at my face so smoothly covered with bronze powder, and the three strands of beads draped around my neck. The word "immodest" never entered my mind as I prepared to leave my dormitory room wearing my beautiful long pale green sleeveless dress, enhanced with a low neckline, and a V-back. I was ready to go!

I will never forget that evening when I strolled down the stairs from the girls' dorm and crossed paths with a young man coming from his dormitory exit. I had spent quality time getting myself ready and thought I looked pretty good, but then I saw that young man. He stopped, took one look at me, and his jaw dropped. He raised his eye brows and sighed before suddenly blurting out, "Jezebel!"

What? I couldn't believe he said that to me! I highly esteemed him as a man of God. I was horrified! Embarrassed and hurt, I ran up the stairs crying. Just one word, "Jezebel," and it preached a sermon in my heart. No one told me what to do. Just one word did it. I tore off my beads and threw them in the trash. I washed my face. I changed my dress. I even changed my shoes. How did I know that one word meant all that? God gave me another learning experience—one I sorely needed.

No one taught about holiness in the school I attended. In fact, one teacher told the girls to put on a little make up if they were a bit pale. It was one of the church officials and his family that persuaded me it was all right to go to a movie with them. Now the Holy Ghost was preaching to me through a dedicated young man. I had many things to learn and would gladly receive them, as the Lord began to open my eyes and sanctify me. Many more things would change in my life.

7

SUMMER SOUL-WINNING ADVENTURE

Compelled to Go

The end of my second year of Bible school was approaching, and the Lord began to speak to me about going back to Maine and spending the summer going door-to-door witnessing for Him. The burden intensified until I had assurance it was God's plan. Judy, a classmate of mine, committed to go with me. She was a praying person with a concern for the lost. We were persuaded in our minds that if we put in eight hours of work for the Lord, each day, He would meet our needs. It was J. Hudson Taylor[4] who proclaimed, "God's work, done in God's way, will never lack God's supply."

We had no car but were sure God was leading us. Before we left for Maine, we were in a church service with people who did not know our plans, and the Spirit of the Lord spoke through tongues and interpretation, saying that He would go before us and provide for all that we needed. It was such an encouraging promise that just confirmed all the Lord had shown us.

We arrived in Maine and stayed in my parents' house where we quickly began studying a little book called "Soul winning Made Easy" by C .S. Lovett. We didn't know what we were doing. We had never gone door-to-door before. We didn't even know what we should say, but we felt compelled to go. So we devoured that book and practically memorized the soul-winning conversation it included. We learned the scriptures and what to say with each and, after serious times of prayer, asking God for souls, we headed out. It was our desire to go to every house in this little New England town of Medway, Maine, with the gospel.

Gus and Charlotte

The first place we came to was on our way down the hill from my house. Gus was working on his falling-apart jalopy outside his dilapidated, see-through shack, with his timid wife Charlotte standing by his side. Gus had whiskers that stuck straight out and his unbathed appearance added more intrigue to the fact that every time I ever saw him, he seemed to be wearing the same clothes.

After greeting them, we simply began to quote everything we had memorized. Gus still kept working on his car. Scripture after scripture led to the final step, the invitation. "Gus, would you like the Lord to forgive you and save you?"

He raised his head for a moment and said, "Yep" and went back to work on his car.

Charlotte also wanted to be saved. We wondered what would come of what seemed to be such a disinterested response but began to pray and had them also pray out loud.

When that was done Charlotte timidly told us that she had a pain in her side for a long time and asked if we would pray for her. Pray for the sick? We were just Bible school students. We didn't expect this, but there we were laying our hands on her and earnestly praying for her healing.

When we finished Charlotte spoke so softly saying, "Thank you. It's gone now."

What? It's gone? Wow! This was amazing to us, and we left happy but not too sure what had really happened in their hearts. One thing we quickly learned was that you can't always judge the situation by the way it appears. There may be much more going on inside than the eye can see. The fact is that Gus and Charlotte were wonderfully saved and began going to our church regularly. He quit his cursing, smoking, and drinking and became the talk of the town! And this was just the beginning of our Medway adventure!

We walked from house to house giving the gospel and attempting to lead people to the Lord. One lady was so bitter because "God killed her son with lightning." We couldn't get through to her. We went up on "wicked hill" where there were several trailers and a big house that seemed to be open to everyone all the time. We prayed for an elderly couple to get saved. We walked into that big house filled with people and just began to tell them about the Lord, about the wages of sin, about forgiveness, salvation, and Heaven that could be theirs. We prayed with a couple in the next trailer. They got saved and began coming to church with their family. House after house, person after person, this was our mission.

When we went to church that Sunday and testified about all that the Lord was doing, one man stood up and said, "If you are doing all that, then I am going to give you my second car to use for the summer." We surely praised the Lord for this great provision that enabled us to go even further and to more houses.

Trapped in the Dark

In our zeal to not miss any house, we ventured down all kinds of roads just to find one more house. One time we were heading very slowly down another one of those roads hoping to find a house, when the road narrowed considerably. It was a woods road with thick trees on both sides. It started to get dark and seemed the road would never end. We had better turn back. But there was no place to turn around. Trees were on every side. There seemed to be no other option except to try to back out. That was an impossible challenge that very soon ended in disaster when my tire went off the road into a muddy rut from which I could not remove it. Now what? It was already dark as midnight. We had no flashlight. There were animals in these woods. We were stuck. We laughed at our situation, all the time knowing we were in trouble. Two young women stuck in the middle of dark woods, a long way from the only road that happened to be seldom travelled.

No, we didn't have cell phones. They hadn't been invented yet! But we did have a hotline to Heaven, and we prayed as hard as we could. That's when I felt a sudden leading to try to run to the road. It seemed crazy, but God must have given me courage enough to make me willing to take that risk. So leaving Judy in the car, I ventured out trying to stay on the path, slipping, and sliding, grabbing onto trees, and moving as fast as I could. Believe me, I prayed all the way and was out of breath when I finally made it to that dark, lonely Grindstone Road, just as I saw car lights approaching!

With a glimmer of hope, I began to wave my arms toward the oncoming car. What in the world were they thinking when they saw such a sight? Would they even stop? Or if they did stop, would I wish they hadn't? I thought I knew my answer the moment that four burly men climbed out of that car. Did I make a mistake? Surely not, if we prayed and then discerned that this was the thing to do. So I bravely told these men what had happened and how we were stuck in a muddy rut.

One of the men looked more closely at me and said, "Don't I know you from somewhere?" I told him who I was and that my father was the pastor of the Medway Full Gospel Church. Suddenly the light of recognition broke through, and he said, "Yes, I know you, and I know your father. My cousin goes to your church! We'll get your car out. Come on, guys." So I found myself following this God-sent gang of four through the dark woods where they simply lifted my car up, out of the rut, and backed it out to the road!

Phew! What a relief! We were safe, and we were back on the road and ready to continue our adventure of evangelizing wherever we could. It was a wonderful summer full of learning experiences, blessings, and souls for the kingdom of God!

A Troubling Crisis

It didn't take very long for me to learn that walking in the will of God does not exempt you from trouble. I found that to be true when I went through one of the hardest battles I had ever faced as a young person. The Bible warns us that trials will come. The Apostle Peter wrote: "Beloved, think it not strange concerning the fiery trial which is to try you, as though some strange thing happened unto you…"(1 Peter 4:12). He told us to rejoice and know that the Lord would faithfully take us through it.

I always loved the privilege of sitting and listening to godly men and women as they talked about the things of God. There were so many valuable things to learn from highly respected people, who had years of experience behind them. Then something happened that nearly overwhelmed my trusting heart. I became personally aware of seriously improper behavior of someone I respected. I was shocked and disappointed. I was thrown into the middle of a dilemma and didn't know what to do.

The situation weighed heavily upon my heart, sending me to my knees in prayer. I needed wisdom and clear guidance from the Lord. I sought to distance myself from the situation, but great pressure was put upon me by the offending party who was aware of what I knew.

It would have been a relief to share this information with a friend, but I kept it to myself, telling no one but the Lord. As a young person, not experienced in dealing with such circumstances, I thought that I had to remain silent or I would destroy that person's testimony and ministry. As I would come to realize later, that person had already destroyed their own reputation by their own actions. The Lord had kept me in peace, even though surrounded by this distressing problem.

Then one day everything came to an alarming climax. Information came to me that this person was to be very soon placed in a position of honor and great responsibility. Now I felt a responsibility! How could I remain silent when I personally knew of this individual's bold, unrepentant sin? Yet that same battle raged within me. "Lord, if I tell, will I be responsible for ruining a ministry?" In desperation, I pleaded with the Lord to show me what I should do. He is a loving and merciful God who often goes to great lengths to reveal his will. In almost a supernatural response to my cry, the Lord directed me to "make it known." It was a frightening thing to face the proper authorities and pour out my story, but I did it.

There is no doubt that my youthful decision was difficult for me, but it was biblical. The Bible makes it mandatory that a Christian leader "must be blameless...of good behavior" (1 Timothy 3:2). Christians have a responsibility to speak up against moral and spiritual wrongs. God Himself inquires, "Who will rise up for me against the evildoers...who will stand up for me against the workers of iniquity?" (Psalm 94:16).

Nowhere does the Bible tell us to tolerate sin, to be quiet, and allow it to continue unopposed. The most loving thing a Christian can do

71

when confronted with evil is to hold that person accountable, that they might be led to repentance.

The Lord was teaching me many things. He was molding my life, showing me how to be strong in the battle with conflict, to be willing to suffer to do what was right. I continued to be aware of the hand of God on my life and rejoiced in the midst of difficulties. God was still in control and my focus would remain on Him.

8

GOD'S PURPOSES SET IN MOTION

A New Level of Ministry

Back at Bible school for my senior year, the desire within me to be used by God for his service intensified. I felt stirred with an awareness of the soon coming of the Lord, and at the same time, with the greatness of the harvest. I wanted to be one of those laborers Jesus prayed for.

I still had some city starch in me and had no desire to be one of those women preachers that I had heard about, screaming into the microphone and conducting themselves in such a manly fashion. I told the Lord about it and suggested that if He ever wanted me to preach, I would want to be a "dignified" preacher.

I never should have brought up the subject, because then the Lord began to deal with me about my willingness to do or be anything He wanted me to do or be. Like I had done in the past, I gave God a challenge. "Lord, if You really want me to preach, let me get three opportunities this week. Now that seemed a clear impossibility. I had never preached before!

God must sometimes have to humor us by doing the silly things we request, just to help us to follow his will. Before the week ended, I had the three opportunities once in the midweek service at the Bible school, once on outside ministry, and one other occasion, which I have forgotten. The experience amazed me. I found myself crying out to God for messages, and for his anointing and, when He gave me the messages, I got so excited that I could hardly wait to preach them. I stood back astonished and humbled when I felt the hand of God, and his anointing, and his liberty, as I delivered my heart in those services.

It was a new experience to me and, suddenly, I wanted it to happen again. God was molding my life. He was shaping my thinking and desires. He was preparing me for his purposes, and I longed to be his willing handmaiden.

I saw God using other students in gifts of the Spirit and became hungry for gifts in my own life. What a thrill it was to have Him work through this vessel of clay as his Spirit spoke through me many times in the gift of tongues! It is his will for us to continue to grow in our relationship with Him, to rise higher, to reach out for more, and to never come to a standstill. Sometimes He worked in totally unexpected ways.

One evening as I waited for a ride to the bus station for our Christmas break, I found myself to be one of the few students remaining in the school. Things were very quiet as I sat in my room all alone. All at once the most unusual thoughts poured strongly through my mind. These thoughts were that a certain young man was going to come down the stairs from the men's dorm, enter the ladies dorm through the door next to mine, and then go into the room of his girlfriend down the hall.

I was dismayed! What would make me think such a thing? These were two honorable young people who would never allow such behavior. But almost immediately I heard that side door open from the men's dorm stairway and footsteps quietly stepping past my door. Then I heard a very faint knock on a door not far from mine. It opened, and that person entered and closed the door.

Oh, no! It actually happened. Lord, what should I do now? I fell to my knees and prayed until I Knew that I should just go and bang loudly on that door. I did so and quickly returned to my room. That girl's door opened quickly and footsteps departed back to the men's dorm stairway.

I knelt and asked the Lord, "Now what?" and felt directed to go tell that girl what had happened. She was my good friend. I respected her and was greatly disturbed that she would allow her boyfriend in her room, against all school policy. I went to her room and told her what happened, and that this was God's love, warning this couple, and preventing problems from occurring. They remained my friends and, eventually, became very active in ministry.

Sitting in class every day began to affect my back, causing pain and discomfort almost every day. Then one morning a strange thing happened while we were having a wonderful move of God in a chapel service. While seated, I suddenly experienced what felt like someone punching me forcefully in my back. It thrust me forward in my seat. I turned around and stared at the student who was seated directly behind me and, with a puzzled look on my face I told him, "Don't you ever do that again!" He looked shocked but couldn't say anything because the service was in progress. Afterward he asked me what I meant by that statement. I asked him, "Didn't you punch me in my back?"

He was astounded at my accusation and told me he had not done such a thing. "However," he continued, "I did see you suddenly thrust forward as if you were pushed."

Well, I have only one explanation for this unusual occurrence. It must have been the hand of the Lord because, from that moment onward, my back pain was gone. This I know---the Lord loves and cares for his children, and He knew I was hurting and praying for healing. Let Him use any method He chooses. Just keep on doing it, Lord!!! What a mighty God we serve!

Future Foretold Seven Years in Advance

Three years passed very quickly and soon it would be graduation time. I continued searching to discover what God wanted me to do after graduation. One day while in earnest prayer, the Lord clearly spoke to my heart from the scripture—*"And they that shall be of thee shall build the old waste places: thou shalt raise up the foundations of many generations; and thou shalt be called, The repairer of the breach, The restorer of paths to dwell in"* (Isaiah 58:12).

These words seemed to be God Himself talking directly to me. I just knew intuitively that these words pertained to my future. I didn't understand the meaning and prayed for the Lord to show me what they meant. I could only grasp that they meant that one day I would work in a Bible school. "How boring!" I thought. "Who would ever want to work in a Bible school?" Little did I realize that this was an amazing revelation from Heaven that I would see fulfilled in my life seven years later. I didn't forget that scripture but still prayed and looked for an answer, for clear direction.

I was anxious to immediately get involved in ministry, but had no idea what or where. I didn't know many preachers or churches. I was an unknown person as far as I was concerned—*just that girl sitting on the stoop on that dead-end street in Corona*. Then one day a missionary friend of mine wrote from South America, asking me to come and join her there to help her in the work. I got so excited and began telling everyone I was going to South America. The only problem was that every time I would get down to pray about it, the Lord didn't seem to be excited about it. In prayer I experienced a deadness, a blank, until I said, "Lord, if You don't want me to go to South America, I won't." I wanted God's will more than anything. However, I certainly didn't want to just go back home. That seemed out of the question. Surely somewhere there was something else God had for me. I discovered that what you sense during the time of earnest prayer is a good indicator of what God is thinking.

I was getting nowhere in finding out what I should do, and graduation was only days away. With a somewhat reluctant surrender, I told the Lord that even if it was his will for me go back home, I would go! With that decision, an amazing thing happened. The excitement I had about going to South America changed—that happy anticipation now shifted to the possibility of going home. Only God could do that, and it triggered a burst of assurance that this was his will. With thanksgiving for his direction, I readily submitted. Sometime later, I discovered how right God was, when moral issues clouded the reputation of the ones I would have worked with in South America. He sees the future before it occurs and safely leads those who will heed the promptings of his still small voice.

Unexpected Challenge In Medway

My parents were thrilled that the Lord was sending me back home, to help them in their work. Very quickly I found myself involved in ministry, teaching, preaching, singing, soul winning, and more. There was very little money available so I learned to improvise. It was the day of flannelboards, but I had no flannelboard figures to use. So I cut out pictures from old magazines, drew some by hand and used straight pins to attach them to a towel hung over a board. I brought my bedroom, gooseneck lamp and aimed it at the scene, turned the lights dim, and played music that I recorded on an old cassette recorder. Sometimes I had my sister Barbara play minor chords on the piano during the story.

What an original atmosphere all of that created! It was like wonderland. It still makes me wonder, but it worked and kept the attention of forty to fifty young people of all ages, as I dramatically presented the truths of God's Word. Some were totally undisciplined, and we had to stop them from climbing over seats and causing disruptions. The power of God began to touch their lives, and soon we had a mighty outpouring in our youth meetings. They were getting saved, getting filled with the Holy Ghost, dancing in the Spirit, getting called to ministry. You couldn't hold me back. I was thrilled. It brought great joy to my life.

I was twenty years old and felt blessed and filled with anticipation for what God had planned for my life. Although I was quite willing to do whatever He asked me to do, yet I was about to face a totally unexpected and tremendous challenge that would put me in a situation beyond what I felt were the capabilities of my young life. That's when the only option is dependency on the Lord.

It happened like this: On a normal sunny day I saw my father heading my way. He had a very sober and serious expression on his face which meant I had better listen carefully. "Claire, financial difficulties have made it necessary for me to temporarily return to New York and seek employment." At least part of the problem was that Dad had tried to help a new convert to get established and had co-signed for his work truck. Payments were short, and Dad felt the obligation to take care of the debt. He looked very intently at me and continued, "Claire, God is doing a great work here in Medway, and I don't want to just walk away from it. I want you to take over the responsibilities of the church while I am gone." I stood dazed and wondered, "Can I do this? I am just a young woman, only six months out of Bible school." There were

77

families, new converts, many children, and probably about sixty to eighty people in the church when they were all present.

My heart beat rapidly at the thought of this arrangement, but my excitement and thrill couldn't be hid. What an opportunity! I knew the Lord would enable me, and I would put my whole being into doing it well for the Glory of God.

It was settled and my family left. I had the whole house to myself and the whole church too. I knew I had to cry out to God! To my place of prayer I went, over and over, and over again. In fact, almost all I did for those next six months was pray and study, prepare and minister.

On Sunday I taught the adult Sunday school class and then preached morning and night. On Tuesday, I prepared for and spoke in the junior young people's meeting. On Thursday, I preached the midweek service. On Friday, I prepared and spoke at the older young people's meeting. On Saturday, I was responsible for having a cottage prayer meeting rotating each week in a different home.

During one Sunday morning service, we had a visiting lady with her two children. The one she held appeared about four years old and was unusual. When we attempted to pray for her she reacted with what sounded like growls. What was this? Something wasn't right. That week I did some follow-up work and drove to that lady's trailer at the end of a long country road.

The yard was neat and not far from the door was a child strapped into a small chair. Was that the same child I had seen in this mother's arms? She was staring directly at me as I approached, and when I tried to say a friendly Hello to her, she wildly threw her arms toward me as if trying to grab me, all the while emitting strange, angry sounds. What was this? I had never seen anything like it before.

Keeping my distance from her, I headed to the door and was invited inside by the mother. The conversation eventually led to a picture of two children. "They are my twins," she told me. They were eight years old. One was still at school and the other was the child outside who was half her sister's size. When the mother brought her in and held her in her arms, she did not seem aggressive, so really wanting to understand this and to help, I asked if I could hold her. All the while I was praying.

For a few minutes the little girl was fine as I held her, but then

I was startled when she suddenly threw herself down with her legs firmly wrapped around my waist and her head at my knees. I was still holding her hands and tried to pull her up but could not. "She seems very strong." I said.

"Yes she really is strong," the mother agreed. "Sometimes my husband playfully wrestles with her, and she can hold his arm down on the ground. We have problems with her when we leave her with a baby sitter. It seems she gets angry and tries to get back at us by scratching or biting herself."

I again tried to pray and felt the strong resistance from the child. Here was a desperate need; yet here was a mother who turned down the invitation to come back to church and to give her life to the Lord, explaining, "I don't want to jeopardize my marriage."

I was stunned. It is hard to imagine that a mother with a child like that would not see her need for God. The experience was another turning point for me that increased my longing for more of the power of God in my own life.

What a time of learning it was for me! I was busy. God was training me. It was his wonderful presence and anointing that made a difference. I felt his mighty power in the old barn where I would go to pray. What holy outpourings came in that sacred place! I knelt over an old tree stump that was set on top of a very old carpet. Underneath that carpet must have been an entire civilization of crawling things. I could feel them moving when I knelt there, but more important things were on my mind. I was glad no one could see or hear me when I prayed so loud, shouted, and rejoiced.

The Lord gave me messages to preach and the ability to fulfill my responsibilities for those many days, weeks and months. I was not alone. I felt the hand of the Lord yet became very aware that He was showing me that I would not be in Medway much longer. From the very beginning, I had felt this in my heart and had told my parents that I did not think I would be in Medway for long. One year had passed.

A Supernatural Rescue

Close to the end of those six months that I had the church responsibility, I was sure I would be leaving. I sought the Lord earnestly.

I longed to do his will and nothing else. I did not know what was ahead, only that my time to leave Medway had arrived. I had assurance that I would be leaving very soon. How amazing it is to experience the leading of the Lord! He has promised us, "Trust in the Lord with all thine heart; lean not unto thine own understanding; In all thy ways acknowledge him, and He shall direct thy paths" (Proverbs 3:5-6).

One morning I felt an urgency to put a letter of resignation in the mailbox, addressed to my father in New York. I also felt compelled that same day to go to my part-time job as bookkeeper at a very large automobile dealership and tell my boss that I probably would be leaving soon. He was a backslidden Pentecostal preacher, but I could not have anticipated his response.

"You're leaving? When?" he asked. "I'm not sure," I said, "but it will probably be soon. I just wanted to be fair and let you know."

His eyes narrowed as he asked, "Where are you going?"

Something about the way he asked bothered me. It made me feel hesitant about answering him. I didn't know, and I couldn't tell him at that moment.

"I'm not sure yet," I cautiously acknowledged.

Secretaries and salesmen could be seen moving about through the large showroom windows, as my boss led the way into the center of the big office. I shouldn't have been fooled by those few moments of silence, for suddenly the whole atmosphere changed. I have no idea what provoked him!

With his voice raised and the pace of his speech slowed, he spouted his taunting words. "So you're leaving and you don't know where you are going?"

I tried to refocus his thoughts, hoping to stifle what seemed like the beginning of a simmering flame. "Rocky," I said, "you were once a preacher. You know what it means to follow the leading of the Lord. I have the assurance that He is guiding me. I'll know more when I need to know."

Getting just a little louder, he directed his voice to a group of passing salesmen and continued, "Hey guys, can you believe what Claire is going to do?"

This was unbelievable to me. What was my boss trying to do?

Maybe he was remembering the times I refused to complete false sales contracts to help him win a contest. Maybe it was the times I witnessed to him about not being ready to meet the Lord. And now here are these salesmen looking this way. These men were wicked. I had often seen and heard more from them than I cared to witness. They knew better than to try to involve me in their behavior. One by one they came over and stood almost in a semi-circle around me.

"Claire says she is going to leave, and she doesn't even know where she is going." His words dripped with sarcasm. The tone of his voice and the look on his face signaled these men to follow his lead and, like those led by the Pied Piper of Hamlin, they all joined in with their own mocking words rising louder and louder.

I stood there staggered by this senseless scene.

"Why in the world would you do such a thing? That's crazy!"

"You're a young woman, and jobs are scarce, and you are planning to leave??"

"How senseless! You don't even have a place to go."

"So you say God is leading you? Do you think that is going to help?"

"Do you really know what you are doing?"

They kept at it, taunting me, until I felt so intimidated that I almost cried. Defenseless! That's how I felt, as the walls of the room seemed to close in on me. I had done nothing wrong. Why this?

I forced a weak smile through my intimidation, while fighting back tears. Then, in a moment that seemed to stretch into many minutes, my thoughts leaped beyond the looks on their faces to the secure place of my continual unfailing Help. I needed Him now, and my silent urgent prayer flew heavenward, "Lord, help me! What should I say?"

No sense of forewarning predicted what would happen next. I could feel it beginning deep inside. Then suddenly the Spirit of the God rose up from the depths of my being, and out of my mouth came a strong voice of authority that boldly declared to these men, "This day you will see what God will do!"

My hand was raised, pointed straight at them, as amazement swept over me. What had I said? Such strength had poured through me. Where did that come from? It must have shocked the whole mocking

81

bunch because, for a long moment, they just stared at me...and then slowly walked away.

I stood there alone, still shaken by what had happened. It took just a few minutes to gather my things together and take a break. I needed it. My mind tried to make sense of the whole episode as I drove back to Medway.

As usual, I stopped at my postal box to see if there was any mail. Pulling out an envelope, I looked with curiosity at the postmark— "Lorain, Ohio." It was addressed to Miss Claire Wilmerton, from Rev. K. A. Smith, Broadway Assembly. "Who is that?" I wondered. I had never even heard of Lorain, Ohio.

Quickly opening it, I was stunned. I could hardly move when I read what the letter was about. This person, unknown to me, from a church that was unknown to me—from a city I had not heard of before—was inviting me to come work with him at their church! The letterhead included the architect's drawing of this great big church. My mouth opened wide in astonishment! "Lord, look at this! What have You done? Wow! Hallelujah!" What else could a person say when such an absolutely astounding, on–time miracle occurs?

"I just mailed that resignation this morning. I just told my boss that I would be leaving. Only minutes ago your Spirit stunned those men and me with the declaration, 'This day you will see what God will do!' And here in my mailbox is this offer. Lord, this is your doing! You are so amazing, so wonderful! You are such a faithful guide. You see the pathway before us and prepare the way before we ever get there."

I could hardly wait to return to work. With great joy I walked up to my boss with that letter held out to him and said, "Rocky, look at what I found in my mailbox when I went home for lunch!"

He took the letter and read it, with eyes moving slowly over every word. He seemed speechless as his face flushed and took on a very somber expression. Then as reality revealed the hand of God, he stared at me and stammered, "That's astounding! Remember me when you come to your kingdom!" I hope he was having second thoughts about having walked away from the call of God in his own life.

The providence of God never ceases to amaze me. We sing about our "On-Time God." It was at his direction that Pastor Smith's letter was put in a mailbox in perfect time for its arrival in mine, on the very day I had sent my resignation and encountered my boss. Is this not a revelation of the love and care that the Lord has for his children? Does this not assure us again that for those who love the Lord, "all things work together for good..." (Romans 8:28)? God puts the pieces together to enable the fulfillment of his divine purposes. This truth has been firmly implanted within my heart because of the many times I have experienced God putting me in the right place, at just the right time for some significant event to occur.

Such was the time after I had moved from Maine to Lorain, Ohio, and was headed downtown to mail some church bulletins. I sensed the Lord speaking to my heart to not go to the post office I usually used but to go to one a little out of the way. I obeyed that still small voice and just as I entered that post office, the clerk was saying to a customer, "Of course, there is a God...." His eyes fell on the church bulletins I had just laid on the counter, and he continued, "Here's a church lady now." He looked toward me expectantly, "Tell him there is a God!" Just like that—a divinely prepared opportunity to witness. You can be sure that I did so!

9

LORAIN, OHIO—HERE I COME!

My parents returned from New York to Medway as I was preparing to leave for Ohio. I had purchased a little American Rambler for just $200 and was to pay it off at $50 per month. It was all packed with what belongings I had, and my mother stood at my door, worried about me making that thousand-mile trip all by myself. Certainly it was a first-time experience for me, but I was not afraid. I was so excited I could hardly wait to turn that key in the ignition. I assured them that I would not be going alone, because the Lord would go with me. Before we expressed our final farewells, I sang a little chorus to them:

> *I've placed my life within the hands of God.*
> *I've turned my will completely in his care.*
> *I know not what the future holds before me,*
> *But this I know, He knows what's best for me.5*
> *Used by permission of author Mary F. Howard*

I believed that with all my heart.

My father had prepared clear directions for my trip, and I was ready to move out into what was an unknown future for me. It was August and the beautiful New England landscape awaited me. Off I went through Maine, New Hampshire, Vermont, and Massachusetts.

My mind raced with memories of the way God had led. It was like a dream; yet I was living in its reality. I was still *that girl sitting on the stoop of a dead-end street in Corona*, but a supernatural hand was moving my life ahead faster than I could have imagined. Tears of joy flowed as I lifted my voice to the Lord. He was here, right in this car. I was not afraid, but filled with thankfulness that I was indeed in the hand of the Lord, and thrilled that He had planned all of this.

A Jewish Surprise

Five hundred miles later, I arrived at Utica, New York. It was the halfway point of my journey, and I needed to find a place to stay for the night. With very limited funds, I began to go from one motel to another, asking what the most economical room would cost. It was always more than I felt I could spend. I told one manager so and, as I was leaving, I said, "God bless you" and headed out the door.

"Wait!" he yelled. "Come back in here."

I did, and he continued: "What did you say to me?"

I told him again, "I said, 'God bless you.'"

He responded, "God bless me?? God doesn't bless people. Why God is so far away that He doesn't even know I exist."

"That's not true," I replied. "God is so close that I have been talking to Him for the last five hundred miles."

He looked at me a little strange. "Yeah, sure!" he scoffed, as if I were a little off in the head.

"My friend," I continued, "Don't you know that God is very real and that He loves you? Do you go to church anywhere?"

"I'm Jewish" was his answer.

"Jewish! Well, do you go to the synagogue?"

"Occasionally, for Bar Mitzvah or weddings."

"Oh, then you're not even a good Jew!" I nudged his unawakened conscience.

The conversation went on for a few more minutes and then I broke the news to him: "You think God is so far away and doesn't even know you exist? Well, let me tell you that five hundred miles ago, way up in Northern Maine, God knew that I would meet you. He spoke to me to put something in my purse for the Jewish person I would meet."

I pulled it out and told him, "It's a Bible that shows the fulfillment of Old Testament prophecies. It is written especially for Jewish people."

I held it out for him to receive and declared, "Here, my friend. This is for you—from God!"

As he pondered the meaning of all this, I tried to make my exit, but again he called me back. "Wait! I'll give you that room for..." and I can't remember the amount, but it was an unbelievably low price for the day and a wonderful room.'

I couldn't help responding, "You see, God does bless people!" I have often told others about this Jewish man and have prayed that He would come to know Jesus, his messiah.

"Oh No, Lord, It's Too Big!"

It was the first days of August 1962 when I finally exited the Ohio Turnpike and turned onto Highway 254 in Lorain, Ohio, for the first time. My excitement and apprehension were about equal. I was almost there. What would it be like? I have never met these people before. They have never seen me. All I knew was that this is God.

Then my eyes caught first sight of the church. There it stood, spread out over that entire corner. A creeping feeling of apprehension swept over me, and I and cried out, "Oh no, Lord, it's too big!" I had never before been in a church that size. There was no turning back now! Even the parking lot was intimidating. About sixteen church buses were neatly lined up at one end. There were so many doors that I drove around trying to decide which one I would enter, and finally twisted the knob of a door near the back. It was the right choice, near the apartment where I was to stay.

As I entered the hallway by the offices, I met my first person, Dwayne Redmond. He was friendly and immediately offered to help me to find needed hangers for my clothes. One of the other brothers called Pastor Smith's residence to let him know I had arrived.

As I stood there just a few feet from the phone conversation, I could vaguely hear the pastor's wife ask, "What does she look like?" It was tough for the brother to try to answer that question with me standing right there. A few more similar questions left him answering with "uh-hum," and "yes," and "uh-huh." They wanted to know what they were getting into by inviting me here sight unseen, and I don't blame them. I also wanted to know what I was getting into!! Soon we all had opportunity to meet and draw our first conclusions.

Pastor and Sister Smith welcomed me warmly and I was already feeling so privileged to be here. Eventually, Sister Smith asked me casually what I was going to wear the next day, which was Sunday. It was no doubt an important question about a person they knew nothing about. When I showed her the dress I had recently bought, she looked it over and very nicely suggested that there really was plenty of room to let the hem down a little and also to bring the sleeve length to my elbow. That was my immediate mini-introduction to a standard of holiness that valued sanctification on the inside and outside as well.

It was not a problem to me. I could do that. I was so happy to be here. I was ready to do whatever was needed to qualify. There were so many things that I had never been taught. It was a miracle that I was here in the first place, in this wonderful holiness church, but it was all part of God's divine plan for a young woman who longed to please Him in every way. He was launching me out into greater depths of spiritual relationship with Him.

On Sunday morning, the church was filled with hundreds of people. Sixteen church busses dropped off people of all ages at the doors. I still remember those dedicated bus drivers and bus captains, especially Raymond Fordyce, Julius Chahye, Glen Wood, Margaret McMillen, and so many more. Sunday school rooms filled up. Each department was like a little church with a superintendent and teachers. Teachers moved through the halls, greeting children, helping some find the right class, picking up attendance records from the office, smiling and happy, eager to teach the Word of God one more time.

I stood in awe of it all. It wasn't anything like our little pioneer work in Medway. I had never seen so many people in a church. My heart swelled with such joy and the thrill of having this great privilege. It surely was God who got me to this place.

How in the world did I get here? A year before this, in the summer, Pastor Smith had dropped by Long Island Bible Institute (the Bible school that I attended) just to get acquainted with it. No students were there, but he met President Willard Wilson and learned about the work there. Later, when he was in need of an additional worker, he contacted the school, asking if they knew anyone who might fit the job description he gave. I learned later that they had said they could only think of one person—that was Claire Wilmerton—but they doubted that she would be interested, because she was very active in her father's work in Maine.

It still amazes me that Pastor Smith even wrote to me after that report. He had never met me but, with that halfway recommendation, he wrote that God-ordained message. That was the most "on-time" letter he had ever written! God was in it, and here I was beginning an astounding six years as youth director, secretary, pianist and more. This was God's way of training me, teaching me, preparing me to fulfill his divine purposes.

I was offered the residence of either the guest evangelist apartment or a place in a small house with the pastor's mother-in-law. I prayed about it and was attracted to the thought of having my own place. Yet I felt a strong leading from the Lord to reside with this older sister in my own tiny room, in the little converted garage located on the church parking lot. What a decision! It was surely God!

Sister Maybelle Hance soon became "Gram" to me and greatly influenced my life. She was a prayer warrior and a soul winner. I don't ever remember seeing her discouraged. She was always the cheerful peacemaker. She taught me more than I can tell, just by her life and example. Although she was in her sixties and I was just twenty-one, we got along well. I can't remember any disagreement we ever had. I think I did make her wonder about me once when I became a bit "ornery." We had put out some traps and caught the cutest little, silky black mole. He actually just fell over dead on the kitchen floor.

Suddenly I had a "brilliant" idea. I was supposed to return a pie plate to the pastor's sister-in-law after she made us a delicious pie. I know you won't believe I would do such a thing---but I did. I placed it in a napkin and laid it in the empty pie dish, put it in a bag and brought it to church where I left it for her to pick up. The only redeeming thing about my action was that I did include a nice thank-you note. I will leave the rest to your imagination. My humor was not appreciated, but I think she did eventually forgive me!

Fully Involved in Ministry

It didn't take long for me to be fully involved in the ministry at Lorain. Brother Smith was building this dynamic church on the pillars of Pentecost, prayer, evangelism, and holiness. The prayer room was a large place, especially designed for a large body of prayer warriors. Before he would preach, he would say something like this: "When the altar call is given, how many will stay in the prayer room for at least a half-hour? He would wait for hands to be raised and then continue. How many will stay for at least twenty minutes? How about fifteen minutes, ten minutes, five minutes?" Prayer was emphasized, and it created a wonderful and powerful atmosphere with many seeking the Lord.

Visitors to the services were frequent and Pastor Smith always gave them special honor. The ushers were ready for their cue as he addressed the crowd: "If you are a visitor, we want you to know how glad we are that you came." The ushers would already start down the aisles as he said, "The ushers have a special gift for you. Please raise your hand so they will see that you receive it. We have prepared a special bookmark as a reminder of your visit. You will notice that on the side of the bookmark is a form for you to fill out and tear off. You can return that to the usher so we will know who you are."

"Now let's all stand and sing a welcome song for our visitors." And that old song would ring through the congregation,

"Smile awhile and give your face a rest;
Raise your hand to the One you love the best;
Then shake hands with those nearby
and give to them a smile!"
Author Unknown

It was a winner, and these visitors would be followed up that next week with a visit to their homes.

It was here at Broadway Assembly where I saw the Home Visitation Program in action and at its best. This was to change my life forever. Teams would gather—on Tuesday nights, Thursday afternoons, Saturday for the bus workers, Sunday afternoon for the young people—and go visiting door-to-door. Evangelism, witnessing, and soul winning were the resounding messages that stirred, motivated and sent people out on the streets with the gospel. Some gave Bible studies in homes and consistently won those people to the Lord. We would have report-back sessions where everyone told of their experiences that night. It made the flame grow brighter.

Brother Smith preached it, prayed it, and practiced it himself. He would bring people to the platform to give testimonies of witnessing, of reaching the lost. The place was on fire with passion for the lost.

Something was happening inside of me. That same passion was consuming me. It became my great desire, and every week I spent much time out evangelizing door-to-door. Little did I know that this was to become the foundation for the forty years that I would later teach Personal Evangelism at Free Gospel Bible Institute and actually motivation for the rest of my life!

I remember walking up many steps to high rise apartments on 28th Street. It was like a mission field. Young people were standing on the stairway and at the upper landing, just hanging out. I began to talk to them about the Lord and give them tracts. There were apartment doors all down the hallway. Several were wide open, so I stepped up to one entrance and saw that they were gathered around a table eating. I apologized, "Oh, I'm sorry; I'm interrupting your meal!"

"Oh no, come on in," yelled the man, so I did.

As they all listened and the people in the hall also were listening, I had my own congregation. The Lord was with me. He put the words in my mouth. I felt Him talk through me as I told them of our lost condition and of salvation that was available for all who would receive Jesus as Savior. This was a blessed experience for me, and I was amazed as I felt the Holy Ghost speak through me. It was only the beginning of what was to become years of reaching out to the unsaved with the gospel. My heart filled with joy at the experience.

Millie and Max

Our evangelism table was the starting point for soul winners. It was filled with prospect cards, family cards, salvation cards, and more. Tracts were available there, and a huge map of the city helped with directions. One day after praying, I headed for that table. I selected a stack of prospect cards and headed out to do some door-to-door witnessing.

Eventually, I wound up standing at the door of someone's "prospect" that had never been followed up. It was Millie who answered but she was clearly disinterested. Our almost one-sided conversation did inform me that she was newly married to a Baptist man but, other than that, she was more focused on the traffic that passed by than on anything I said.

I figured she was bored and didn't want to be bothered, and it was time for me to go. However, just before I took that step to leave, a strong thought occurred to me. Sensing it was the Spirit of the Lord prompting me, I simply asked her, "By the way, Millie, have you ever been saved?" It was just a simple question, nothing dramatic, but it must have been God's key to Millie's heart.

Suddenly the whole scene changed.

She emotionally confessed, "Yes, I'm a Pentecostal backslider. She then did an immediate "about-face," looked in through her open door, and loudly called out, "Max, I told you God was after us. There's a church lady here right now!"

And with that she headed into the house. Her whole demeanor changed into a person under conviction of the Holy Ghost.

Although I was uninvited, I simply followed her inside, aware that the Lord now had this situation under his control. There was no need for further talk. Evidently, God had already been talking. It was time for a response from Millie. Once inside the living room, I said, "Millie, it's true. God is after you. Let's kneel down and pray. "

There wasn't much furniture in the room. The floor was bare except for a small throw rug. A couch was against the wall by the front windows. She headed there and together we knelt.

"Call on the Lord, Millie. Open your heart to Him. He is reaching down to you right now. It's time to come back and make things right. You can settle it all now."

It was thrilling to hear her honest confession to the Lord. She earnestly told Him about her drifting, and her sorrow for doing so. "Forgive me, Lord. Please take me back again." This was no dry praying. Tears flowed onto that couch as her sincere seeking brought the power of God on the scene. I was stunned as after a good time of serious praying she suddenly began to speak in tongues.... God had poured out his Spirit on her repentant and hungry heart, baptizing her right there.

As she continued on with hands lifted to Heaven, I wondered, "Where's Max, her new Baptist husband? If he was hearing this, what was he thinking?"

To my left, there was an open doorway into a room with white walls. I guessed that it might be the kitchen. The light was on. Could Max be in there? I had to find out. I slipped away from Millie and cautiously headed to that doorway and peered around the corner. Oops! Someone else had the same idea. We almost bumped heads. It was a man holding a golf club. He was standing at the side of the stove that held the polishing materials he was using.

"Oh!" I whispered. "You must be Max."

"Yes, I'm Max," he replied as he stared over at what was happening to his wife.

"Max," I said, "look at what the Lord is doing for your wife! She has come back to the Lord, given her life to Him, and He has blessed her by filling her with his Holy Spirit. Wouldn't it be a wonderful thing for both of you to begin your new marriage with the Lord at the center? Why don't you join your wife over there, put your arm around her, and give your life to the Lord also"---and he did!

The Greek Orthodox Couple

Oh, what wondrous joys are in store for those who will obey the Lord and go out to seek and win the lost! The harvest is great…the fields are already white unto harvest. Why do you hesitate? Someone is waiting for your knock…your tract, your witness. You can be used of the Lord if you will but make that commitment to go!!

I recall the little house I visited down a side street off of Highway 254, where a husband was in bed, very sick. He and his wife had a Greek Orthodox background and knew nothing about salvation. He was particularly interested in what I had to say, as I explained how we are all sinners and that every one of us has sinned, which disqualifies us for Heaven. However, Jesus paid a great price to give to us the gift of salvation, if we will come to Him with repentant hearts.

He responded so earnestly and prayed for the Lord to save him. A short time later, I returned and was greeted by the wife who seemed very angry at me. At the door, she yelled at me and told me to go away. I felt compassion for the little lady and couldn't figure out why she was so upset. I gently tried to calm her with loving words and asked what had happened that made her so upset at me.

She tearfully cried, "You said my husband was a sinner! He was a good man. He never hurt anyone, and last week I found him outside lying on the ground dead."

Now I understood. This dear grieving woman recalled the Bible description of all men as sinners and took personal offense. With the Lord's help, I explained again what the Bible says, trying at the same time to comfort her in her sorrow. I gave her time to tell me some good memories of her husband, and then showed her how he must now be rejoicing in Heaven, because of the salvation he received. When it was all over, she was happy to have me pray with her as I had with her husband.

Many souls are wandering in darkness with no knowledge of how to be saved. Even after years of attending a church, they have never heard the true gospel of Jesus Christ. What a precious privilege it is to tenderly lead them to Jesus, our living Savior!

A Dog's Teeth Around My Ankle

Sometimes I would knock on doors in the daytime, but sometimes it was in the dark of the night, like the time no one answered the front door of a 31st Street house. I had always taught others not to give up but to try another door. Maybe they don't use that first door. So I bravely headed around toward the back of this house.

In the moonlight I saw something that startled me. A distance away was a large dog. He growled and leaped at me but was chained. Feeling safe, I stepped up on the porch, only to discover that the dog's chain was merely caught on a rock, and now that dog came flying at me, leaping past the rock, and setting his teeth around my ankle. I could not move.

"Nice doggy, in Jesus' name let me loose. Nice doggy, let go in Jesus name," I quietly intoned to his perked up ears.

When he finally did let go, in a split second, I pushed through that door into the kitchen of a very shocked stranger.

"I am so sorry," I explained, catching my breath. "Your dog had his teeth around my ankle, and this was my only escape. Please forgive me!"

We both laughed with relief. I was safe and was not a thief breaking into her house. As crazy as the situation unfolded, somehow the Lord turned it all around into a great opportunity to witness to this lady.

Danny the Rebel

Then there was Danny, a young man with deep problems, who began to respond to our outreach. We all rejoiced when he finally pulled away from his old friends and came to the Lord. His salvation was real and brought a great change in his life. He and a friend got so fired up spiritually that they would come to the church after school and pray in the prayer room. They would then take a load of gospel tracts and give them out as they walked up and down on Broadway. We were happy for them and praised God for the change.

As time went on we noticed that Danny was missing some church. He didn't come as often to pray and give out tracts. We couldn't get through to him. Something had happened. He sort of disappeared, until one night at three in the morning. There came a loud knock on my door.

I jumped up, rubbing the sleep out of my eyes, and walked to the door where I looked out at a terrible sight. Some "thing," rather someone, stood there with arms stretched out with many cuts across them. His face was terribly bruised and bleeding. What was it? I stared in horror and then heard the pathetic cry: "It's me, Danny."

I hurriedly called to Sister Hance, with whom I lived at that time, and she came as we opened the door and let him in. We sat him down and grabbed towels to clean him up and asked, "Danny, what happened to you?"

He seemed disoriented as he somberly gasped, "I think I killed my father. We got in a big fight, and when I tried to walk here, a car came from around the corner and hit me."

I anxiously called his house and was relieved when his mother answered. "Mrs. Rodriguez, are you all right? How is your husband?" I asked.

She sobbed; explaining that he was beat up but would be all right. Danny was facing a court appearance soon, and probable jail time. What a contrast with that happy, victorious witness that we had seen just a short while back! What had happened?

It's the story of the first Psalm. As he let up in prayer, he found himself WALKING back past his old friends. Then it progressed to STANDING with them, eventually to SITTING with them...in the seat of the scornful. The steps downward brought Danny miles away from Calvary and close to Hell. Although years have passed, I have never heard of Danny coming back to the Lord. How sad!

Those Great Young People

I loved our Friday night youth services. We called them Teen Club and gathered in a separate building. We had great fun and fellowship, but most of all we did some serious Bible studies, learned scriptures, studied how to witness, and had some Holy Ghost prayer meetings. It thrills me to remember how many of them eventually went to Bible school and into the ministry. I still remember Bob and Bill Stewart, Pat and Bob Sutter, Harold Sid Griffith, who later served as campus pastor at Evangel University, the Sultzers and their great trio, Glenda Kincer, the Fordyce boys, Delbert Watson, Dennis Drew, Gary Goss, Wendell Layne, Judy Rice, Diane Hardwick, David Griffith, Ed and Linda (Prince) Machan, who have pastored for years, Roger Griffith, the Russell girls, Mary Bowmar, Janet Duley, Sharon Pettry, Darwin and Lynn Hayes, Liz Ramos, and so many more. That is nearly 50 years ago now, and names have slipped by, but I still can see so many of their faces. They just jumped into my heart. What a great bunch!

One time we took a select number of the young people on a soul-winning crusade to Peelee Island, Canada. After driving about thirty miles to Sandusky, Ohio, we took a ferry across to the island which was a vacation hotspot for many. In the evening we held street meetings at the downtown square with everyone testifying and letting the people know that we were there and planned to come knocking at their doors to talk to them about the Lord. We asked them to please welcome our teams. The next day, we dropped off teams at different points around the island.

My partner and I were about to approach a house, when three men sitting on the porch of the next house yelled over to us, "Yeah, be sure to go in there. She really needs it!"

I yelled back to them, "Okay, we will, but don't you run off, because we're coming there next!" She was a Catholic lady who responded well to the gospel and prayed with us.

Then we headed to the next place. There they sat, waiting for us. When I discovered they were all retired college professors, I began to feel a little intimidated. I quickly prayed, "Lord, you know who they are, and I know who You are. Please put your words in our mouth!"

In the midst of the conversation, one man told us that he believed in Jesus and that He was a great man, but that the idea of Hell seemed a bit absurd to him. The others agreed, and there we stood. What do you say next?

Then it suddenly came to me. "Sir, I think you are mistaken about Jesus. How could he be a great and honorable man when he was such a liar? Many times he told people that there is a Hell and even described it in detail, explaining that those who inhabit it are tormented by the flames. How can you respect a man who lies and deceives like that?"

The logical facts could not be denied. They didn't want to say Jesus was a liar, so now they had to choose. Would they call him a liar or believe what he taught?

"Okay, I get your point," one man sheepishly mumbled. The others grinned, realizing that they were in a predicament. Truth always wins.

A Revolting Remedy

It was during my time in Lorain that I became seriously afflicted with bronchial asthma. At times my strained breathing would be so loud that you could hear the deep wheezing when you entered my house. If I turned over too quickly in bed, an attack might start. If I just got up too fast, or walked too fast, I would feel an attack coming on. It was work to breathe. I was conscious of working at it all day long until the muscles in my back, chest and shoulders would be sore. Some nights "Gram" (Sister Hance) would be kneeling at my chair praying for me to get my next breath.

I used inhalers, and tried other "remedies" sometimes not too willingly. For example, a couple of loving missionaries came from Australia to hold services. They were wonderful people who inspired me with their accounts of reaching souls. Well, they took special interest in me and my asthma problem. They had the cure for me. It had worked on their daughter Ruth, and now her asthma is all gone.

First Sister Hance and I had to split the cost to buy a juicer from them. Then came the action! The dear sister, dedicated to her task, prepared a glass of 100% pure onion juice for me to drink. She was convinced that it would burn out the cause of the asthma and cure me. First of all, I hated raw onions but, as dreadful as it was—with her watching me—I sipped little by little until it was all gone. Three days later I was still burping onions, and I still had asthma! And I still dislike raw onions almost 50 years later.

I still loved those special people, but I needed a better cure and kept praying to the Great Physician to deliver me from this cursed affliction. I surely have learned to never give up until the answer comes. Mine didn't come quickly, but then one day as I walked outside, it suddenly dawned on me that I wasn't working at breathing. I was breathing normally. Hallelujah! I shouted at the revelation that the Lord had healed me. The asthma was gone—all gone—and it has never returned. How I praise the Lord for this great deliverance! God cared about me and was still preparing me for his purposes.

10

MEET MY HERO

A One-of-a-Kind Ministry

Lorain, Ohio, became a place of unique discovery for me. It was there that I observed and recognized one rare person whose life greatly influenced mine. She is my hero, Margaret McMillen. It is doubtful she could hit a home run, but she could show people how to get home to Heaven. She never studied acting or starred in a movie, but she was dynamically directed by the God of Heaven and will surely gain many stars in her Heavenly crown. She had no degree in astronomy and never looked through powerful telescopes to discover planets but, with a burdened heart and a God given vision, she searched for and found lost souls needing a Savior.

For the nearly 50 years that I have known her, Margaret has been a prayer warrior and has had a one-of-a-kind ministry of evangelism and soul winning that has never died. This small, humble lady daily makes her way to the throne room of Heaven to petition the King for lost souls. I have seen the pages of her huge prayer list taped to her living room wall. I was glad my name was on it. Her prayer list goes around the world as she intercedes for individuals and for unknown people groups that have never heard the gospel.

In February of 2011, when Margaret was in her nineties, I talked to this dear hero on the phone. All I could do was pray for her, for she was severely injured from a sudden fall in her home. She had five broken ribs, and five fractured ribs, and was in an emergency room getting care. How I wish I could have been there to comfort her in her pain!

It was amazing to hear her speak with such a positive spirit, in spite of her great discomfort. What a lady! She is "true grit" personified, although she would humbly reject that badge of courage! Her strength of character and steadfastness are all born out of her close relationship with the Lord.

I have always been fired up all over again after talking to Margaret. It is astonishing to realize that when she was ninety-two, she continued to be a bus worker at Broadway Assembly, Lorain, Ohio, where Rev. Matt Jones is pastor.

When Margaret turned ninety, her church had a special birthday celebration for her. I'm sure she was ready to leap for joy when she saw the amazing gift they got for her. She had been diligently working the bus route with their 30-passenger bus, and one day Margaret told her pastor, "Brother Jones, I have been turning kids away! Today I had to turn away 9 people. What can we do?"

That did it! Something had to be done, and it was. On that 90th birthday, they gave her an extraordinary gift of a brand new 60-passenger bus!! Soon afterward, she excitedly told me on the phone, "We filled it on Sunday!"

On Saturdays, she was busy knocking on the doors of the people on her bus route, giving out tracts, looking for children on the playground or teenagers hanging out on the corner, always inviting them to church and arranging to pick them up in the bus. They have no idea that they have just been claimed for the Lord!

Margaret's heart bursts with joy as she tells of incidents like this: "I saw one girl on the sidewalk and talked to her and then knocked on her door and asked the mother if she could come to Sunday School. She came, and then later the mother came and got saved."

She saw a girl up in a yard chasing butterflies and talked to her and then to the mother for permission for the girl to come to Sunday School. They picked up the girl faithfully for 5 years (she is now 10 yrs old), and the mother finally came and she got saved.

Margaret sometimes does medical transports for senior citizens and was waiting for a lady in the doctor's office when a woman came in with a twisted ankle. Margaret talked to her and found she had six children. She asked if they went to Sunday School.

"No, but I want them to," the woman replied.

Margaret arranged for them to be picked up on the Sunday School bus. After awhile, the mother came too and got saved. In an earlier conversation, she excitedly reported, "We had three bus mothers get saved this year so far." All that was in four months time. Do you want to know how to build a church? Just follow Margaret around and do what she does!

Margaret has also faithfully picked up bakery items twice a week for the Love Extended ministry and, showing her humor, she says, "I distributed it to the poor, the needy, and the greedy. I don't want to miss anyone."

One day a man and his sister came to church looking for her. Their mother had sent them to see if Margaret McMillen was still alive because "at all their family reunions, everyone talked about her." Margaret was told and she went to the church foyer to see who it was. Although she did not remember them, they told how she had brought their mother and father to church on her bus 50 years ago, and they got saved. Then both children grew and came on the bus and got saved, and now they and their whole family are serving the Lord! Imagine 50 years of bus ministry and soul winning!

Uniquely Led by the Lord

God is not willing that any should perish, and He will lead willing vessels in unusual ways in order to reach some lost soul. One time Margaret knocked on a door, and when there was no answer, she looked in the window and saw something cooking on the stove. She then figured someone was in there, but started to leave anyway. She felt a "check" in her spirit and turned back.

Feeling directed by the Lord, she quietly opened the door and walked in, where she found an elderly lady lying on a stretcher. It seemed she was being prepared for transport somewhere, but no one was around. Margaret quickly knelt beside the woman, told her about Jesus and how she could be saved. The lady began to weep and readily responded, praying and asking the Lord to forgive and save her. Seeing no one else there, Margaret then quietly and quickly left, closing the door behind her. Her mission was accomplished. Perhaps it was that woman's last chance to get saved.

On another day, Margaret started out letting the Lord lead her as she went witnessing. She came to a house where the lady said she already had someone inside giving her a "Bible study," someone from Kingdom Hall. As a former Jehovah's Witness, Margaret understood their destructive beliefs and asked nicely if she could join them for the study.

It wasn't long until her pointed questions drew out answers that convinced the lady of the house that the Jehovah Witness doctrine was definitely not something she wanted. Defeated, the Jehovah Witness left, and Margaret was able to give the true gospel to the lady.

Days later, asking the Lord to direct her, she came to a different house and found that the same Jehovah Witness was here giving another "Bible study." Much to the Jehovah Witness' dismay, Margaret again was welcomed by the lady of the house and invited to join them. As you can guess, the "Jehovah Witness teacher" was soon on her way, and Margaret was again giving the true gospel to one more soul.

This may seem hard to believe, but shortly afterward, the exact same thing happened on a third occasion, when Margaret had absolutely no idea that the same Jehovah Witness was in the house where she was knocking. When she saw Margaret at the door, she stood, and accused her of following her, and bellowed, "If she comes in, I'm going out," and she did. It was not Margaret who was pursuing her but the Lord who warned that false prophets would arise and deceive many.

Her First Visit to a Pentecostal Church

Soul winning, prayer, holiness, and Pentecost were not always part of Margaret's life. Her mother told her, "Never go to that Pentecostal church. They are crazy!" She was busy indoctrinating them into her own unbiblical beliefs. But God had other plans and sent another notable saint of God knocking on their door inviting them to church. It was Maybelle Hance, who was then the Pentecostal pastor's wife!

Margaret and her sister Rose dared to go and, once in the service, they soon convinced the people really were "crazy," but there was no way out...they were seated in the middle of a row. All of a sudden, a lady seated behind them stood and gave a loud message in tongues. Some thought these visitors would never come back again! However, that anointed Holy Ghost message and interpretation had a powerful effect on Margaret. She was shaken and convicted, and the next night surrendered to the Lord, and then led her sister Rose to the Lord. God was already preparing to raise up a woman whose life would influence many hundreds for Him.

Sister Jean Fordyce tells of a day "when Margaret was visiting and the man became angry and chased her down the street with a broom." He was a rejecting lost sinner, and Margaret was running down the street away from him, yelling back to him, "It is appointed unto men once to die, but after this the judgment" (Hebrews 9:27).

For three years, she tirelessly continued to knock on the Jeffreys' door every Saturday. They always knew she would be there to invite them to church and responded many different ways but would not come. Then one day a change came. Opal Jeffreys came and got saved. Then her husband came and got saved. Then all of her five children came and got saved. Now all of them serve the Lord together. What positive evidence this is of the strong promise of God in Psalm 126:6—"He that goeth forth and weepeth, bearing precious seed, shall doubtless come again with rejoicing, bringing his sheaves with him."

When Pastor Keith A. Smith resigned, after 20 years of ministry at Broadway Assembly, he and his family relocated to Corpus Christi, Texas, where they began a church. Margaret went along with them to help with the outreach. She met a Christian Spanish lady, and they began making trips to Mexico taking Bibles to the people. She also began to have a Bible study in this lady's house. This neighborhood evangelism brought 13 women to the church. Yet there was still one more person who desperately needed to be reached.

Her life was hanging in the balance, and God seemed to keep her alive long enough for Margaret to come all the way to Texas to knock on her door. First, it was her mother who came with a neighbor, but then Margaret discovered this exceptionally needy one Jessica, a daughter with cerebral palsy.

Margaret began to bring her to church in her wheelchair, pulling it up the steps and into the church. She got saved the first night. It was just like God's great mercy to give this needy woman a final opportunity to prepare for eternity. She was saved, baptized in water, and was faithful to the Lord for one month, and then victoriously went to Heaven.

Margaret had knocked on her door just in time! Numbers of others were led to the Lord, with several now in the ministry. Can you imagine what would happen if each church had a dozen like Margaret?

Recently, I learned that Margaret has moved to a high rise apartment and, due to some minor auto accidents, has lost her driver's license. What a distressful dilemma for Margaret, who almost daily had driven the streets to reach out to souls! Now what would she do? I couldn't help getting a big smile as I was told that she just walks out of her apartment and downtown witnessing to people on the streets. Nothing seemed to stop such a woman who was filled with a love for the lost. She is now twice my hero and surely in God's Hall of Fame!

Another person like Margaret was Brother Julius Chahye, who in his 90s was still actively winning souls. One day he went looking for a prospect and found the lady in the back yard hanging up wash. Right there he began to talk to her about the Lord and her need of salvation. She was somewhat responsive, so he helped carry her laundry back to the house and asked if he could come in and talk some more. Inside, it was wild! Children were everywhere making noise. The television was on; the radio was on; the children were running and playing. All of that chaotic clamor and commotion did not detract dear Brother Chahye from his purpose. He stuck to the message and led this lady to the Lord. Sister Julia Carter truly got saved that day and became a faithful member of the church.

11

AWAKENING TO BIBLICAL HOLINESS

The Whole Counsel of God

One powerful highlight of my time at Lorain was the emphasis on biblical holiness. My eyes were opened to the truths of God's Word that were previously not known or understood by me. When we first went to Maine, my father told me, "Claire, you need to stop wearing jeans, because the people up here don't believe women should wear them." I thought that was odd but stopped for the sake of the ministry. It was stranger yet to discover they didn't watch television. "What kind of people are they?" I wondered. "Maybe it's a cultural thing here in Maine."

Now, a thousand miles away from that northern place, I began to hear a similar message. I noticed how good the people in the church looked. They were dressed fashionably, but modestly, with no pants on the women. Neither did I see makeup or jewelry on the women, or long hair on men. Instead of having the appearance of Hollywood, they looked godly.

Not only did they look holy, but these people knew how to worship God and pray. They were Pentecostal in every way. What a thrill it was to hear them earnestly seek the Lord and to testify about exciting soul-winning experiences.

Pastor Smith's powerful preaching built me spiritually. He didn't preach only part of the Bible but, with burden and anointing, he presented the whole counsel of God.

My eyes were opened to many truths of the Bible that I had ignored and had never heard preached before. As I listened, searched the scripture for myself, and prayed, I experienced a spiritual awakening...to holiness. It was a turning point in my life.

I looked at 1Peter 1:15 with new eyes: "But as he which hath called you is holy, so be ye holy in all manner of conversation."

The command of God in Hebrews 12:14 came alive to me: "Follow peace with all men, and holiness, without which no man shall see the Lord."

Holiness certainly started in the heart, but scripture surely showed God's interest in the outside as well. God had much to say about outer appearance as in 1Timothy 2:9—"In like manner also, that women adorn themselves in modest apparel, with shamefacedness and sobriety; not with broided hair, or gold, or pearls, or costly array."

It was evident He wanted a clear distinction between outer appearance of men and women. The moral law of Deuteronomy 22:5 set the pattern for some of those differences: "The woman shall not wear that which pertaineth unto a man; neither shall a man put on a woman's garment: for all that do so are abomination unto the LORD thy God." There were ceremonial laws in the same chapter, but it was the moral laws of the Old Testament that were carried over into the New Testament. God's holy, moral nature is unchanging.

Even hair would declare God's determined distinctions between men and women, as seen in 1 Corinthians 11:14 and 15: "Doth not even nature itself teach you, that, if a man have long hair, it is a shame unto him? But if a woman have long hair, it is a glory to her: for her hair is given her for a covering."

My greatest desire is to please God. He was changing me. Yet, at that time, one of my biggest battles was something that millions take for granted—mixed bathing. I had grown up in New York spending much time swimming in the ocean, at pools, and rivers, and loved the water. No one knew it, but when I first went to Lorain, I used to drive around with a bathing suit and towel in the trunk of my car, searching for some place where I could swim in private but found none. I had not given a thought to the immodesty of a bathing suit and had never associated it with God's instruction to dress in "modest apparel." I was desensitized by my lifestyle and associations. Now the Word of God was piercing through my spirit and my soul. I had to wonder, "When you seriously consider it, what is really modest about a bathing suit?"

I remember hearing about one preacher who received a special invitation from another preacher. He said to the brother, "I would like to invite you and your wife to our swimming party for all the preachers and their wives."

This brother looked at him and replied, "Thank you for your kind invitation. I would like to make an offer to you. We will come to your swimming party, if you will accept our invitation to an underwear party."

"What? Brother, how can you say such a thing?" protested the stunned preacher.

The holiness brother replied, "I believe that, at our underwear party, there would be more covered than at your swimming party."

What a shocker! How can it be that a little sand and splashing water suddenly make immodesty acceptable? To be blunt, most people would be horrified at the thought of walking before the public in their underwear. Forgive my plainness, but most run for cover if anyone approaches while they are not properly covered.

Our God is holy. He dwells in a holy Heaven. His angels are holy. His Name is holy. His prophets are holy. His Word is holy. His Son Jesus is holy. He is coming back for a holy people. God wants us to be holy. Holiness is purity of heart and life. What begins with inner sanctification continues as sanctification of body, soul, and spirit, as expressed by the Holy Spirit in Paul's writing: "Abstain from all appearance of evil. And the very God of peace sanctify you wholly; and I pray God your whole spirit and soul and body be preserved blameless unto the coming of our Lord Jesus Christ" (1Thessalonians 5:22-23).

I am so thankful for the opportunity I had to work with Pastor Keith A. Smith. My life was forever changed because of the influence of my time in Lorain. It was my privilege to be there when Brother Smith began the Call to Holiness conventions across the country. The first one was held in the large prayer room there at Broadway Assembly. People came from many areas.

Brother John Rettinger had come from Michigan and, for the first time, was exposed to a gathering of this nature. I still remember him standing and tearfully telling how thrilled he was to find brothers of like-precious-faith. He had felt all alone, not wanting to subject his young people to the monthly rallies in his area that had become so worldly. He didn't want to take his precious young people to hear "Christian rock" with flashing strobe lights, or to take them to the bowling alley, or roller rink, where the other churches were taking their young people. He didn't want them to be influenced by the worldly dress of so many of the other young people. Brother Rettinger rejoiced in this newfound fellowship, becoming a strong supporter and eventually one of the Call to Holiness evangelists who helped with the conventions across the country. I was part of the crew that helped put together the Home Bible Studies and the Call to Holiness magazine that was sent out to hundreds. God surely used this movement to stir many churches and call wavering and wandering people back to the old paths of righteousness.

Newfoundland Experience

One day Brother Smith told me he wanted me to go with him, his wife Grace, and his four girls—Sandy, Brenda, Rhonda, and Kim—on a trip to Newfoundland, Canada. We would conduct holiness conventions and teach evangelism. I was thrilled! We all crammed into their car which was pulling a pop-up trailer capable of converting into a tent with several sleeping areas.

With great excitement, we started out driving for hours, with a map, a schedule, and planned stopping points. I was chomping at the bit, anxious to take my turn driving in Quebec! The narrow, winding, tree-lined roads were a challenge to navigate, but I could do it. Holding firmly to the wheel, I drove down a very steep hill and, at the same time, noticed I had to cross a railroad track at the bottom. Things were fine until the road leveled off briefly and then headed straight up again. That's called a dip—a bad one! I heard an unfamiliar noise and then yelled, "Oh, no, the trailer is coming past us!" Sure enough it had popped off the hitch and headed in its own determined direction. Thanking the Lord that no serious damage was done, we continued on.

One morning we stopped at a park rest area to refresh and had to deal with no lights inside. But we managed to find what we needed in our travel bags, clean up, brush our teeth and head back out. Later that day, my face began to burn terribly. It felt very hot and kept getting darker red. That night we were in a holiness convention in Houlton, Maine, but my problem became unbearable. I could hardly participate. In the bathroom, I soothed my face with cool water. I thought I had somehow gotten a severe sunburn, but it didn't take much longer for me to discover that, in the dimly lit park rest area, I had mistaken my little shampoo container for my face moisturizer. No wonder! That shampoo was literally burning my skin!!! It was a minor catastrophe, but I survived!

The next day we drove to Nova Scotia and boarded a big ferry, along with our car and trailer. We each had our own room on board the ferry where we slept overnight, as the ferry sailed seven hours toward our destination. When I looked outside in the morning, it looked like another land, and it was. Long rows of rock formations peered out of the water. Fishermen were adjusting nets and boats as we pulled to shore. This was our introduction to Stephenville, Newfoundland, where I was able to stay for only the first convention and then had to fly back to Lorain to take charge of the services until Brother Smith returned.

It was my privilege to stay with a church family that owned the local taxi service. This sister made fresh homemade bread every morning, and it was there that I learned to eat and enjoy orange marmalade. They treated me royally. The people had British accents, and the women all wore head coverings. They were sincere and on fire for the Lord. When the pastor gave the invitation for testimonies, everyone who planned to testify stood and waited their turn. It seemed that each one preached their testimony with fervor. Here I taught on evangelism and took teams out on the city streets witnessing. It was a great experience.

Open Doors of Ministry

After flying back to Lorain, I immediately returned to the work of the ministry there. Spiritual hunger was growing in my heart, along with a longing to be used by the Lord. Before me were doors of ministry that I couldn't have previously imagined. Alone with God I often poured out my heart to Him, praying in the Holy Ghost and experiencing his hand upon my life. Joy and excitement filled my heart as I realized what He was putting in my hands to do.

Often Pastor Smith had me preach in the Thursday night service. He gave me the privilege of instructing Sunday school workers in our weekly worker's conferences. I assisted with the local radio broadcast. It was on-the-job-training ordained by God, and I learned and experienced much. As superintendent of the teen department, I had oversight of over eighty teenagers, aged fourteen through sixteen. What a treasure! It became part of my responsibility to help create Sunday school loyalty campaigns and enlargement campaigns from scratch and help integrate them into all age groups of the Sunday school. I guess the one thing I never thought I would do was build a rocket ship, but I did. It was big enough for someone to stand next to on a float, in a community parade.

Yet there was one even more unusual thing that I wound up doing. For one campaign, we used a sheep theme. There were three teams— red, black, and white. (Why do some pastors have to be so creative?) Pastor Smith actually brought in three, live little sheep, and I had to lift two of them into full tubs of water and dye their wool—one red, one black, and one just stayed white. (That was not in my job description!) We let them stay in an enclosure in front of the church, to promote the campaign, and then, at night, I had to get them into a sheltered area.

Oh, what fun! Can you imagine the absurd scene as this lady from the streets of New York City, who had never even seen a live cow until she was ten, now attempts to herd three sheep to a shelter! "Here we go, little sheep...up into my arms." How do you hold a sheep anyway? I surely didn't want to hang his head over my shoulder and carry him like a baby. He was a resisting armful. This was going to be a tricky trip! "Just a little bit farther, little sheep, and we will be there." He (or was it a she?) began wiggling harder, and then it happened. "No! No! Come back here!" It was too late! That rascal slipped right out of my arms, and I had to chase it all over the parking lot. It's a wonder I didn't just decide to have roast lamb for supper! Eventually all three were tucked away for the night. Do you suppose that is what the Lord sometimes has to do with some of his wandering sheep?

Each morning I headed to my office at 8:30 and met with Brother

Smith and the staff to review our work list and plans. Often I headed out knocking on doors, visiting prospects, visitors, or absentees. I did a lot of secretarial work that involved creating and printing newsletters, handbills, announcements, and posters from scratch, with stencils and a mimeograph machine. That was one of my favorite parts of the office work. I just accepted the fact that much of this work would take me up some steps to a very hot attic-like room where I would ink the mimeograph machine, apply the stencil to the drum, fill up the paper holder, hand-turn the first copies to make sure the printout looked good, start the motor, and watch carefully as the hundreds of copies flew out the other end. It was a sense of accomplishment to finally carry that pile of materials down for use in the ministry of the church.

Frequently my office was packed with youth department officers as we worked together planning for the upcoming meetings. These were sharp, dedicated guys and girls, with great ideas and, as we prayed together, we saw the Lord use these plans to affect many young people.

Life was very busy, sometimes including helping to paint walls in the new Sunday school addition, gathering used bricks from a construction site, loading them in a truck, and using them to lay out the original "Lantern Lane," when Camp Blessing in Lorain was newly purchased and in the development stage. We all worked hard to see the Lord's work advance. I loved it. There was nothing else I wanted to do. It was my life and my love.

When the big tent went up near the entrance to the camp, everyone was excited. It was campmeeting time! A whole month was dedicated to camp ministry and divided up into Kids' Kamp, Youth Camp, and Adult Camp. How great it was to see all these boys and girls, young people, and adults seeking God at the altars. I played the organ on the platform and could see how the Lord was touching people. It was a time of great evangelism with Holy Ghost conviction sweeping through the tent and souls coming to the altar for salvation. The power of God fell night after night, sanctifying and changing lives, baptizing with the Holy Ghost, calling people to the ministry.

Many Preachers from Many Places

Pastor Smith brought some of the finest preachers to Broadway Assembly for revival meetings. His heart was focused on reaching the lost, and he used every possible opportunity to do so. Coming from a small church background, I had not been exposed to many big evangelistic campaigns and campmeetings, so I was filled with anticipation and excitement when such meetings were scheduled. It is sad to note that some of those ministry groups eventually became very liberal and, thankfully, others maintained a standard.

Now, after years have passed, I get a subtle delight in seeing the response from people when I tell them, "I played the piano for Jimmy Swaggart!" Then I have to break the news: "It was only for two weeks, during the altar call." He was the camp meeting speaker for two weeks under the big gospel tent at Camp Blessing. It was prior to his loftier days and before the tragedies that would come into his life.

He preached powerfully, drawing the full attention of the crowd of four to five hundred. I sat in the congregation with his wife Francis, and she backed her husband like an old-time Pentecostal, shouting "Amen!" speaking in tongues, raising her hands in praise.

When the altar call was given, he called me to the piano and shouted out with his preacher voice, "Sing it, Claire!" I wasn't even a singer but I sang, "Coming home, coming home, Lord, I'm coming home."

"Sing it again, Claire!" his strong voice echoed through the speaker system—and I did. And people would stream down the aisle to seek the Lord.

Their son Donnie was youth camp age, and his hair was too long by camp regulations, so he had to get it cut so he could come to Camp Blessing as a youth camper. We were happy to have him there where the Lord could work in his life.

Those days have passed us by, and much "water has gone under the bridge" since then, but the memories remain.

I remember when we had Tommy Barnett, who was then a fiery young, single evangelist. He chose a tall stool for his seat on the platform as he sang, "I'm Gonna Walk Them Golden Stairs." After preaching dynamically, he gave an altar call differently from any I had ever heard before. It was like a countdown to decision: "Ten...now is your opportunity; nine…step into that aisle; eight…Jesus is reaching for you right now; seven…Come now and surrender to Christ!" As he urged people to respond, the Spirit of God drew them to that altar where many were saved. His long-play recordings were big sellers in that day. I recall when he stood behind me in my office, dictating a letter about one of his new recordings to Word Record Company back when it was located in Waco, Texas.

Missionaries came and awakened in us the call of the harvest. Rev. C. G. Enticknapp from Australia stirred us toward practicing "Every Believer Evangelism," the title of one of his books.

William Hull, a Canadian Pentecostal preacher with many years as a missionary in Israel, stirred us with his story. Hull was spiritual counselor to Nazi war criminal, Adolph Eichman, up to the time Eichman was executed, and wrote about his experience in his book, The Struggle For A Soul.

Some others that I remember and had the privilege of meeting and associating with are: The Sunshine Party, headed by American Indian Evangelist, Chief Bruce Thum, who created and presented the drama, Heaven's Gates and Hell's Flames; The Lowell Lundstrom Team; The Klaudt Indian Family; Ken Gaub; Loren Cunningham from Youth With A Mission; Tommy Reid; John Bedzyk; and John Rettinger.

One young evangelist, who will remain unnamed, was invited to our little house to have lunch with Sister Hance and me. At the conclusion, he nonchalantly began to list for me his requirements for a wife. First of all, I wasn't interested and, secondly, I couldn't believe that he was telling me that his final requirement was that his wife would bow down and call him "Lord Edward"(Not his real name).

I told him, "Well, I hope you find her soon." That was years ago. I wonder if he found a wife who would give him his wish. Poor lady!

One older evangelist, L. K. Dodge, set up a prison cell on the platform and dressed with a striped prison suit, and ball and chain, to preach his message of deliverance from the chains of sin. He was also a great promoter of prayer—real prayer. As I worked in my office, I could sometimes hear him praying in the prayer room for hours. When others gathered there to pray, he was there too. Once there were two brothers lying on the floor face down for a long time, supposedly praying… but awful quietly. Brother Dodge came by and kicked them gently with his foot and told them, "Get up! It's time to pray, not to sleep!" At a Call to Holiness convention in Goshen, Indiana, I saw him go to preachers who had gathered in the foyer to fellowship during the prayer time at the altar. He asked them strongly why they were not at the altar praying with the other preachers; it was time to pray! And they went!

12

"I KNOW WHO YOU
SHOULD MARRY"

A Shocking Statement

Evangelist William K. Wilson was notable for many reasons, but mostly—in my mind—for the strange announcement he made to me one day. While I was a Bible school student, he was president of the school. He also spent many years as a pioneer missionary in Africa and was a man of God. I knew him and his wife well and considered them to be spiritual mentors for me. The incident I mentioned occurred when he came to Broadway Assembly for a series of meetings. As I worked in my office one morning he appeared at the door and walked in. He looked at me with his usual grandfatherly glint in his eyes and, instead of greeting me, he asked me a question. "Well, Claire, when are you going to get married?"

What a question to ask a 22-year-old young woman! I looked at him with a grin and replied, "I have no idea."

He then said, "Well, I know who you should marry."

What a shocking, bold statement! I knew the natural and spiritual character of this man and respected him highly. Slightly stunned, I replied with a grin, "I've heard that before. Tell me, who should I marry?"

I couldn't believe this conversation was taking place. Brother Wilson then proceeded to tell me about a person named David J. Beam.

"Who is he?" I asked, and he told me that he pastored a church of 300 in Youngstown, Ohio, and was president of Free Gospel Bible Institute in Export, Pennsylvania.

I had never heard of him or the school but, simply because it was Brother Wilson who had said this, I wondered, "Lord, what is that all about?"

Now I suppose some girls would immediately begin a search to find out more about David J. Beam, but I didn't. In fact, I merely slipped this unusual conversation away to the back of my mind where, on a rare occasion, I thought about it. Yes, I was curious but smart enough to commit what was said to the Lord. This was a part of my life that I believed was in the hands of the Lord.

This subject makes me recall the invitation I had to eat dinner with a fine family. The wife was a Christian but, at that time, her husband was not. We sat at the table and, just before we ate, the gentleman began, "Claire, we had a special reason for inviting you here. We are concerned about you. You are getting older and, with the Viet Nam war, there is a shortage of men, and we think a lot of you and are concerned about your finding a husband."

He continued expressing his well-intentioned feelings as I listened and wondered, "Lord, what am I going to say to these good people?" When he finished, I said, "Well, I think I agree with you. What would you suggest I should do?"

Unprepared for that, he stuttered around a bit and said, "Just make yourself available."

"Okay," I replied. "I am youth director in a large church surrounded by many people; I go to youth rallies; I am in camp meetings. What else do you think I should do? Should I advertise in a newspaper or stand on a street corner with a sign that says, 'I'm available'?"

No, he didn't think so.

I then replied from my heart, "You see, a long time ago, I committed my life to the Lord. I gave him everything, and He has faithfully directed my path through these years. He has promised that if I commit my way to the Lord that He would bring to pass what was his will. I really am not worried about finding a husband. Yes, I would like that to happen, but I want the will of God. I appreciate your sincere interest and concern for me and want you to know that I have perfect peace and confidence that the Lord will continue to guide my life."

I don't know if they expected a mini-sermon like that, but it didn't hinder our enjoyment of the meal or the fellowship.

I Want You to Leave Now

As time passed, in a gradual sort of way, I began to get this feeling that I would be leaving Lorain. It was such a wonderful place and had been such a tremendous experience for me but, inside, something was happening. Days and weeks went by and I still felt it. I loved this work and was very loyal to Pastor Smith. It seemed disloyal to have this lingering feeling and not share it with him. After all, if I did leave, they would need to search for a replacement. Not in any sense of boasting do I say this, but I knew all the work I did—all the responsibilities I had—and had sense enough to know that finding replacements isn't easy. At least that is what my young mind was thinking. But I was in for a shock!

When I was sufficiently sure of my feelings and found the courage, I asked to talk to Brother Smith. There I opened my heart and explained this lingering feeling that I might be leaving.

Pastor Smith's response was not what I expected. He looked at me and simply stated, "Then I want you to leave now."

What? Did I hear that right? Was he telling me to leave now? I was stunned.

He continued with his explanation: "I have learned that when anyone starts feeling like leaving, they have lost the vision and, if they stay around, they often cause trouble. I want you to take a month's leave of absence without pay, and come to a decision."

I was almost speechless as I left the office, wondering in my mind what I would do. Yet there was also a sense of anticipation inside me, knowing that this would force me to seek the Lord and discover his will.

Puerto Rico: Ministry and Decisions

As I prayed about where I would go, I thought about my missionary friends in Puerto Rico. I loved Spanish and had always wanted to visit there. Soon we communicated and the arrangements were made. I was able to cash in some insurance dividends and put it together with my few savings to buy an airplane ticket to Puerto Rico. It was an exciting time flying over the ocean and seeing the beautiful shades of turquoise and blue surrounding the Bahamas and other islands. I was filled with wonder when we landed in San Juan and entered a world of Spanish everywhere.

My friends, Vic and Sue Coetzee, met me and took me to their house in Carolina. It was a grand reunion. Sue had been my Bible school roommate, and Vic had been the one to call me "Jezebel" on that historic evening when God dealt with my heart. They had come to this island with a vision to build a church and had started out with this house.

They went door to door inviting people to the church that they were beginning in their house. One-by-one they came, until the house couldn't hold them. They rented another house and made it into a church. When I arrived, that house was packed to overflowing with people, and they were in the process of expanding to another house. That's what evangelism will do. What services!

Almost everyone had an instrument of some kind—accordions, concertinas, drums, and many homemade instruments, some made from gourds. They sang from the depths of their hearts. It was wonderful as the gospel was preached and lives were changed.

Vic and Sue were so hospitable and kind. Vic arranged for me to speak almost every other night in churches around the island. What an unforgettable experience it was! One night I preached in a little church that had a Satanist church directly across the street. The doors and windows were open and the gospel was preached to those inside and outside. Only God knows what was happening at the altar as many came to pray. My Spanish is not good enough to fully grasp the results, but Heaven has recorded all of them.

On one of the trips around the island, I stayed with a family that knew very little English. It surely was a learning experience. They set my meal before me at the head of the table and sat on the side, waiting for me to eat, before they would touch the food. It was their way of honoring me. I didn't know what to do when the bottle by my plate had a label that said "beer." I chose to leave it untouched.

The food on my plate was interesting. Some things were foreign to me, like the light green thing on the side of the plate. As a "good missionary," I did try to eat everything, except the "beer." When I finished, they asked me, "Did you like it?" I told them it was good, although some of it was different for me. That's when they expressed surprise.

"Well, that is the first time we ever saw someone eat the skin of the avocado!" They laughed at me and also laughed at my concern about the suspicious bottle of "beer," assuring me that it was just a common beverage that in no way was alcoholic or like the "beer" I was thinking about! Well, at least I attempted to be a "good missionary"!

These were days of earnestly praying to find the will of God for my future. I was willing to go or stay but needed an assurance of what the Lord wanted. It is hard to believe that, in all this time, I couldn't get over the feeling that I would be leaving Lorain.

I stayed in Puerto Rico for a whole month before returning to Ohio and bringing Brother Smith my answer. "I still feel the same, Brother Smith."

"Where will you go? What will you do if you leave now?" he asked.

(Strangely, this conversation seemed almost identical to one that took place when I was leaving my job in Maine! It appears that arriving and leaving positions must open the door for unique situations! I'm glad that the Lord is in control!)

I did not know, but I felt in my heart that the Lord would direct me. I believe Pastor Smith was concerned and did not want to see me make a mistake so he suggested this: "Why don't you continue here until the Lord opens the door for you elsewhere?"

I should have quickly heeded the wise words of this man of God but, self-assured, I left saying, "I'll pray about it." I had not walked very far into the parking lot until I almost heard the voice of God telling me to read the book of Proverbs. I was about twenty-six years old and felt that I could hear God's voice for myself. I guess I had a lot to learn, and the Lord was about to drive a few sharp points home to me.

"Where no counsel is, the people fall: but in the multitude of counsellors there is safety" (Proverbs 11:14).

"The way of a fool is right in his own eyes: but he that hearkeneth unto counsel is wise" (Proverbs 12:15).

"Hear counsel, and receive instruction, that thou mayest be wise in thy latter end" (Proverbs 19:20).

"Speak not in the ears of a fool: for he will despise the wisdom of thy words" (Proverbs 23:9).

God's Word is quick and powerful, and sharper than a two-edged sword. He surely pierced me with chastisement and revealed to me a principle that would be valuable to me for the rest of my life. I didn't understand everything that was happening, but I was certain of one thing: I needed to heed the counsel of Brother Smith. He graciously allowed me to continue in the ministry of Broadway Assembly. I was about to learn that sometimes God really is revealing his will to your heart, but you may be jumping too quickly, before God's time. What happened soon afterward proved that to me.

A Letter to Rev. David J. Beam

It was soon after my trip to Puerto Rico, and about five years after Brother Bill Wilson's statements to me about David J. Beam, that Brother Smith called me into his office and said, "Claire, I want you to send a letter to Rev. David J. Beam."

It hit me like a ton of bricks. That was that name! I hadn't heard it since Brother Wilson's conversation. What could this mean? The letter invited Brother Beam to bring a student ministry to the church and informed him that Brother Smith would be away, but that Sister Claire Wilmerton would show him around and give him any needed help.

Incredible! Could Brother Wilson have been right, and could this be some kind of providential working of the Lord? What would happen next?

When that Sunday morning arrived, I was nervous enough to want to be well prepared in advance. I headed to my office, unlocked it, walked in, and was stunned by a totally unexpected sight. It was occupied by a group of strangers! Brother Beam was sitting at my desk with his feet up on it, and students were crowded all around on the available seats! Talk about shock!

Brother Beam's feet flew off the desk and he jumped up, apologizing and explaining that they had come early, and a board member had let them in, and that they would leave so I could have my office.

It was a flustering and embarrassing moment that I tried to quickly calm by introducing myself and telling them how welcome they were and that it is no problem that they are in my office, and that I would simply use Brother Smith's office since he was gone. Settled! It was a wonderful day with some powerful preaching and ministry.

Brother Beam joined Sister Hance and me for lunch at our little house, and we had an enjoyable time of fellowship until he went to rest in the church evangelist apartment. Before the evening service, I needed to talk to him about plans for the students' participation, so I made my way across the blacktop parking lot toward the church.

As I opened the big glass doors and stepped into the long hallway of the educational wing of the building, my thoughts wandered to his anointed preaching that morning. I wondered how old he was. I had noticed that he was beginning to bald a little. I still flinched at how some of his students had done a good job of embarrassing me before the service. As I had walked in through the front sanctuary entrance a group of them were huddled to the side watching me come in. They surrounded me and quietly, in a sing-song manner, began to chant while pointing at me, "You and Brother Beam...You and Brother Beam!"

"Stop it! Stop it! Don't say that!" I immediately insisted, looking around, hoping no one else had heard. I laughed with them but felt embarrassed. I was in charge of the services and didn't want anything to distract my thoughts or anyone else's.

Now as I approached the evangelist apartment, those student words began to drift through my mind like shadows floating past. "Stop it, Claire! Stop it!" I firmly told myself as I did my best to exert a proper official attitude.

I always thought it was a good choice to locate the evangelist quarters right across the hall from the wonderfully impressive, fully carpeted, and often-filled prayer room. I am glad that I spent much time on my knees in that place and walked daily with assurance of God's direction in my life.

When I knocked on his door, Brother Beam was quick to answer. I began to tell him about the service plans, but he seemed more interested in telling me all about his life. With his hand leaning up on the door frame, he stood in the doorway looking down at me, speaking like a man with a vision who was thrilled with the way God had worked in his life and in the Bible school. What was this all about? This was the first day we had met and here he was pouring out the story of his life to me. I was impressed by his testimony. He seemed to be a real man of God. I began to wonder if the Lord was beginning something pertaining to a future that was as yet unknown to me?

About two months later it happened again. Pastor Smith was to be gone and, once more, invited the Free Gospel Bible Institute ministry to come for services. Of course, Brother Beam came with them and, of course, I was again responsible for the services. I suspect that Pastor Smith was not aware that Brother Beam was single---and I didn't tell him.

This was also the beginning of a year and a half of letter writing between Brother Beam and me. As the letters continued, I could not help but sense where this was leading. Sometimes I would lie on the floor with the letters in front of me and cry out to God: "Lord, You see these letters. If this is of You make me to know, but if it is not of You I don't want anything to do with it. Lord, keep me in the center of your will."

I was determined not to appear forward or aggressive. If David took two weeks to answer my letter, I took two weeks to answer his. Our letters were filled with accounts of our work for the Lord and what He was doing in each of our lives.

All of this was kept confidential. For that year and a half, I told no one about the letters except the Lord and one other person who was praying with me. I intercepted the mail each day, so no one knew what was happening. I didn't want this to become a public issue. I wanted to hear from God. We were both cautious and wanting only God's will. It even took awhile before we stopped calling each other Brother and Sister.

The first time he signed his name "David," was a memorable moment. But the first time he signed his name "Love, David," I knew that we were travelling on a serious journey. I would read his letters over and over, and then do my best to read between the lines. There was no doubt that something was happening to me. I was so excited and filled with joy. What would happen next?

We had never yet been seen together in public. In fact, all of this was a pretty well kept secret until the day David called me and said he was coming up to Lorain to go to the camp meeting. He would be coming to see me. Oh, now what would I do! Brother Smith didn't even know about this.

I knew I had to break the news to him, and so I made the big announcement in his office that day. I sighed, "Brother Smith, there is something I need to tell you." He settled back into his chair, crossed his arms, and looked intently at me. "Brother Beam is planning to come up today, and I just want you to know that we will probably be seen together. You see, we have been corresponding for a year and a half."

His jaw dropped slightly and his eyes grew big with surprise. I can still see the shocked look on his face. Then came the stream of questions. Well, when it was all over, the news was out, and I felt relieved.

In the day time, we had youth camp. Campers had arrived and all of the staff was fully involved in the work. I had no idea when David would arrive. The sun beat down on us with tremendous fervor, as we rushed from one task to the next. Then, about mid-morning, out of the corner of my eye, I saw a car driving up past the tent. I turned quickly, but couldn't see inside. It had an Ohio license plate. It was at that moment that David emerged from the car, along with Brother A. C. Wilson, who was Superintendent of the Free Gospel Churches.

My hair was a mess and I was hot and sweaty from working, but my excitement at seeing David far outweighed that concern. It didn't take long for all eyes to be turned toward us as we casually talked and walked together.

"Who is that with Sister Wilmerton?" It was like a wave that swept through the campground. It quickly became apparent that something was going on between this David Beam and their Sister Claire as we drove off together and then sat together in the evening service under the tent. Well, the word was out and it spread like wildfire.

I saw him two more times, when he came to Lorain with a student ministry group, and about three more times through the summer, but the letters continued. So did my praying and sensing what God was doing. Then one day, he asked me to meet him half-way, since it was almost one hundred and seventy miles from Export to Lorain. I knew in my heart that he was going to ask me to marry him. I told that to Sister Hance before I left on that unforgettable journey.

Meeting at a restaurant in Youngstown, Ohio, David and I were enjoying what was actually the first time we were alone, without any other friends or associates present. Neither of us was interested in what to eat. Something else was in the air. Yet, as we searched the menu, I assumed that he was ordering a meal, so I went ahead and ordered one. When the waitress asked for his order, he simply requested a cup of soup. How embarrassed I felt.

David talked casually, yet with a sense of nervousness, fiddling with a spoon in his cup of soup. It was apparent that he was having a hard time eating. What goes on in the mind of a man who is thirty-six and about to propose to a woman? Whatever it was that was going on in David's mind didn't interfere with what God had put in his heart. By this time, we both had the assurance that the Lord had directed our lives and it became an exciting and joyous occasion when he proposed to me at Boardman Park, near Youngstown, Ohio.

That was August third and, in David's mind, there was no good reason to wait a long time for a wedding. While I still fulfilled my responsibilities at Broadway Assembly, I also planned our wedding in one and a half months. We were joined in holy matrimony on September 20, 1969, at Broadway Assembly. Pastor Smith and Rev. Chester Heath from Export conducted the ceremony. David was thirty-six years old, and I was twenty-eight. You see, God really was speaking to me a year earlier about leaving Lorain, but it was not God's time then. Now my departure was on God's divine schedule. We had a wonderful honeymoon at Niagara Falls, and then slowly made our way back to Pennsylvania and to our new life together at Free Gospel Bible Institute.

13

THE PRESIDENT'S BRIDE AT F.G.B.I.

Married! I walked through my little apartment examining every corner. "I am married!" It was a stunning reality that was still sinking in. "Rev. and Mrs. David J. Beam," I'd whisper, overjoyed at the sound of those awesome words. A new life had begun for this twenty-eight-year old young woman. To my delight, also unfolding before me was a whole new world.

About one week after our wedding, Free Gospel Bible Institute opened for another term and I was officially the President's new bride and a faculty member. I felt so honored. What a great privilege was mine!

At that time, we were praying for fifty students. The school consisted of only the main three-story, red brick building. On the third floor, the ladies dormitory was separated from the men's dormitory by a block of rooms, including the school office, a classroom that also served as our first library, and storage space. At the opposite end from the school office was the apartment where David and I lived. It faced Italy Road and stretched across almost the entire width of the building. This was our "honeymoon cottage." I loved fixing it up. It was now my home.

The second floor was sometimes called the big black hole. It would someday become the main auditorium but was unfinished then, except for the platform that was partitioned into two classrooms with a prayer room between. The downstairs level was half chapel and half dining hall and kitchen. The historic little white cottages spread across the campus held within them amazing memories of campmeeting days for many years past.

Faith and Dedication at F.G.B.I.

The birth of Free Gospel Bible Institute, in 1958, introduced the kind of life that became a tremendous adventure in faith. In answer to strong prayers, God continually revealed Himself in miracles of provision, enabling the day-to-day maintenance of his work. There were also many struggles, sacrifices, and unending hard work, out of which grew great fruit for God's kingdom.

In the earlier days, before David and I got married, David's brother, Gordon Beam, and his wife Naomi lived on the campus, full time sharing responsibilities with David. They faced the hardest days with much sacrifice, giving of their time, strength, energy, finances, and leadership, with great dedication.

At that time David was still pastor of the Free Gospel Church in Youngstown, Ohio, and would commute to Export to teach and carry out the responsibilities of president. This continued until he resigned the Youngstown church and moved onto the Bible school campus, several years before we married.

Sister Florence Shoemaker was the determined, very precise, elderly English teacher that he would bring with him on these trips. She is the author of the original F.G.B.I. Alma Mater and diligently labored to teach students correct English. She especially abhorred double negatives and was ready to gently chide practicing preachers on how few times they mentioned Jesus in their sermon. However, she was not your usual English teacher! She once came to class and declared, "Someone is going to receive the baptism of the Holy Ghost in this class today!" The Spirit of God began to move in that class and before it was over, Matthew (our first student from India) was speaking in tongues as the Spirit gave utterance—baptized with the Holy Ghost in an English class!

Another faculty member was George Baker, who taught Cults and more but was also an accomplished piano and organ player. Sometimes the Spirit of God would anoint him so that he would jump up off the piano seat, prophesy, or dance around the auditorium.

It was no secret that he began to wear a hairpiece after baldness set in. On one occasion he was eating with a group of faculty members and their families when several became curious about that hairpiece. He had no qualms about flipping the front of it up to show how he attached it. Underneath was his bald head. My tiny daughter Becky's eyes opened wide in terror as she began to wail with a terrible scream. It took a little explaining to convince her that the top of his head had not come off.

Salaries were very small in those days; yet through the years, God gave us wonderful faculty who were there, not for the money, but because of the call of God. Their abilities and dedication far surpassed their remuneration on this side of life, but ahead will be rewards for eternity.

It was a thrill to see students come from across the country and around the world. A great highlight in David's life was finalizing Pennsylvania Department of Education paperwork in granting F.G.B.I. the right to educate foreign students. Our school scripture was a reflection of the burden of his heart: Psalm 2:8—"Ask of me and I shall give thee the heathen for thine inheritance, and the uttermost parts of the earth for thy possession." The many flags that hang around the walls of the auditorium represent the fulfillment of that vision...for God had sent students to us from all of those countries.

Faith isn't learned in our comfort zone, but often in times that are uncomfortable for the flesh. It was a test of faith each week to see necessary food come in to feed a school full of students, to pay the bills, and especially the mortgage payment. Once when the money wasn't coming in and the bank was about to foreclose, David and Brother Chester Heath went to the bank officials and suggested the unimaginable: "The answer is for you to give us another loan."

It took a lot of faith to even suggest such a thing, and even more astounding was the voice of the bank president telling his men, "I feel that we should do it!" Banks just don't operate that way, but God knows how to work the impossible to meet the need of his work. Money was provided, payments were made, and the building was completed, enabling more students to enroll, increasing the financial base that would help pay the mortgage each month.

David would frequently declare, that "Free Gospel Bible Institute stands as a monument of what faith in God can do." Prayer and more prayer was the continuous need, and God heard and answered in miraculous ways. After all, how do you maintain a work and feed a body of students, families, and faculty members, when there is no student charge for room, board or tuition? Faith in God, prayer and trust, and much work made it all happen as part of his divine plan.

On one occasion a bread truck broke down on the road in front of the school. The driver came in and announced, "You can take all the bread you want!" Oh yes, bread was exactly what we had prayed for. Another amazing work of God was a tough little lady in Ohio, who went to turkey farmers and declared to them, "If you want God to bless your work, you need to give some turkeys to that Bible school in Export." And the turkeys arrived! Then she went to the potato farmers with the same message, and the potatoes came—once an entire tractor trailer load.

In those days God sent live chickens, not frozen and nicely wrapped chicken parts. Oh, what a time! Students killed, plucked, cleaned, and packaged them. The clucking, and squawking, and the jumping headless chickens surely created not only a stir, but lots of unforgettable smells and memories that are still talked about. Some of those earlier students may even confess to holding hands with their girlfriend or boyfriend as they reached into opposite sides of the chicken to clean it. Such shenanigans! (Go ahead and look that one up in the dictionary!) Can you believe Bible school students would do such a thing?

Joseph Dutka is a name that resurrects many memories. He was David's "right-hand man" for twenty years, until the Lord took him home to Heaven at the age of forty four, after a battle with cancer. He was such a blessing as he gave of himself in so many ways to minister and help. No one will forget his song-leading or his strong personality, his "favorites" who would get the special treats from his own house, and his readiness to always press onward in the work of the Lord no matter how difficult the task.

His wife Virginia, better known as Ginny, (now Mrs. Paul McGechie) continues to be a best friend of mine. She and I took turns preparing a big Sunday dinner that both our families shared together in each other's home. We looked forward to that time of fellowship with all of us around the tables. It was a welcome relief from the stresses of the week and a special highlight.

We hardly ever varied that special Sunday menu consisting of roast beef cooked in the oven with onions and carrots, creamy mashed potatoes, broccoli and cauliflower covered with melted cheese, corn, and Pennsylvania Dutch noodles over the potatoes and drenched in gravy. Those noodles became such a memorable part of that meal that, occasionally, one of the little children would enter and anxiously ask, "Does the cook have noodles?" and, of course we did!

The name of Rev. Chester Heath is very familiar at F.G.B.I., for he faithfully and humbly served the Lord beside David, from the beginning of the school. He was David's good friend who then stood with other ministers at his bedside in his dying moments. Brother Heath's unshakable devotion and commitment have kept him laboring for more than fifty years of service at the Bible school, also as director of Free Gospel Missions, and for many years as Superintendent of the Free Gospel Churches, Inc.

Administration of a Bible school inherently produced many pressures and occasional differences of opinions. There were times I saw Joe and David openly discussing some hot issue that grew in intensity until I wished they would move out of sight of the students. Perhaps witnessing the weight of decision-making by God's appointed leaders was an unplanned way for students to understand and share in the burden. Many were the times we would take the accumulating bills into the chapel service and have everyone lay hands on them as we cried out to God for the needs to be met. We had no natural way to pay those bills. It was humanly impossible, and that's why we rejoiced so greatly as we saw the supernatural hand of God meet the needs time after time.

The Little White Church

In the early days we had only six acres of land. Adjacent to our property was a little white church, a parking lot and a small cemetery that was community-owned. Different preachers would come to preach the services. They had their services and we had ours at the Bible school. There always seemed to be some kind of friction between those folks and the school. But God saw that land and planned for it to become part of the work of Free Gospel Churches and Free Gospel Bible Institute. How would such a thing happen? God knew how, and worked amazingly to accomplish it.

One day David was out in the parking lot with some of the people from that church, and one of the young ladies was standing there dressed very scantily. David was sure she knew better and began to speak with her, admonishing her that she ought not to dress that way. He reminded her of the scriptural injunction to dress modestly. As another evidence of the providential working of God, one of the trustees of the property happened to be standing nearby and overheard the conversation. He immediately stated, "That is the kind of man we need for this church." He proceeded to contact every trustee with his thoughts and eventually persuaded them to sign the deed over to Free Gospel Church and make Brother Beam the pastor. That is how God works!

That church became the place for our church services and daily chapel for many years. It was also the early location for our summer campmeetings. Commitment to righteousness always pleases God! That little church on the hillside is now weather beaten and worn, and has become a storage building waiting for a big storm to knock it down. The Lord works in amazing ways his wonders to perform.

The Providential Workings of God

When I began my life at Free Gospel Bible Institute I was awed by the realization that this was a fulfillment of what God told me seven years before. Here I was standing before students from all over the country and around the world, teaching them, preparing them to go into all the world and preach the gospel. During the last days of my own Bible school preparation in New York the Lord had told me that I would someday work in a Bible school and now it was happening. He had told me, "They that shall be of thee shall build the old waste places: thou shalt raise up the foundations of many generations...." (Isaiah 58:12). These students were the foundation for generations to come. They were already building and rebuilding churches.

What a God! He has promised, "In all thy ways acknowledge him, and he shall direct thy paths" (Proverbs 3:6). I have experienced it and know it to be true. I am amazed as I look back and see his chosen pathways for my life. How blessed I have been! I have loved what God put in my hands to do. I was thrilled with it. I loved the students. I loved the privilege of standing before a class and pouring out my heart to them, pouring into them what the Lord had poured into me. These were not just students.

These were preachers, pastors, missionaries, evangelists, youth workers, children's workers, teachers, Christian school administrators, radio preachers, Christian writers, witnesses, soul winners. God had put them in my hands to help mold them for his service. I loved them and prayed earnestly for them and still thrill when I see them in my journeys across the country and around the world. There they are in the harvest field for the Lord! It makes my heart swell with great joy!

What Rev. A. N. Trotter Knew

In my earlier years, I had never heard of Free Gospel Bible Institute or the Free Gospel Church of Export, Pennsylvania; yet I grew up in a church called the Free Gospel Church, in Corona, New York. The identical names were a curious mystery until one Free Gospel Campmeeting when Rev. A. N. Trotter and other preachers were gathered at my dining room table after a service. Brother Trotter was like a walking encyclopedia of Pentecostal history in the United States. He filled the lively discussion with amazing recall of names, dates, times and places. It seemed that he knew just about everyone associated with the Pentecostal movement. Thoughts began to fly through my mind and mount up with increasing desire for an answer. I waited for an appropriate lull in the conversation and addressed him.

"Brother Trotter, did you ever hear of William K. Bouton from Corona, New York?" (William K. Bouton was my father's uncle and the pastor of the Free Gospel Church where I grew up.)

Without delay Brother Trotter replied: "Old Bill Bouton? Of course I knew him. He used to ride the train with E. S. Williams and others, and come here to this camp, and sometimes preached in the meetings."

What a revelation! My father's uncle, who held me in his arms and dedicated me to the Lord as a baby, had a connection to this very place where the Lord would send me many years later. His feet and mine would walk the same holy ground. What an awesome connection, a providential working of the Lord. Evidently, Uncle Bill went back to Corona and named his church after the work in Export—Free Gospel Church. That church still exists but is now located in Flushing, New York.

A mighty move of God was evident in those early Free Gospel Church campmeeting days. Many shook with conviction, as they ran down the old sawdust trail to the altar of that sacred wooden tabernacle. There they wept their way through to genuine salvation at that tear-stained altar bench. Many were saved and filled with the Spirit. God called hundreds to preach and to go to the mission field.

A well known former speaker for the Assemblies of God Revivaltime radio broadcast, C. M. Ward, was baptized in the Holy Ghost in this campmeeting. Years ago, he verified this fact to Mark Brand. who once happened to cross paths with him at an airport. Rev. E. N. Bell was also an attendee at the camp and was honored with the best available housing—the first of the little white cabins that eventually became part of the campground.

I did considerable door-to-door evangelism in Export and found countless people who would respond, "You mean that old campground up on Italy Road with all those little white cottages? My mother took me there as a child." One man acknowledged that he and a young friend would sneak up the hill from Export, through the woods, and lay down hidden behind tree branches, while they listened to the singing and watched the people shout and dance in the tabernacle straw. He never forgot the impact of that preaching.

A Mighty Move of God in Corona

The Lord has given special promises to those who are spiritually hungry and thirsty. "...I will pour water upon him that is thirsty, and floods upon the dry ground..." (Isaiah 44:3). William Bouton was one of those with a deep hunger for God. He often said to his congregation and to anyone who would listen, "God is about to do some strange thing in our midst, but what it is I do not know." Heaven was ready to show him that "strange thing."

It is because of God's work in the life of my great uncle William K.

Bouton that I am Pentecostal today. It is an amazing story, for he was not always Pentecostal. The church he pastored was Methodist until revival came.

By his unique planning, God brought Aimee Semple McPherson to Corona to hold evangelistic and healing Meetings. She came in response to the God-ordained plea of a dear saint of God who lay on her face before God for several years, crying out to Him to send revival to Corona. When Sister Aimee arrived, this lady was the only person she could find in the area who had received the baptism of the Holy Spirit.

Searching street after street, she could not even locate a hall where she could preach, until a Swedish Baptist church said she could hold her meetings there. It was the fall of 1916, and the local pastors all warned their people to stay away from those Pentecostals because it was "all hypnotism." Of course, they went anyway and the Holy Ghost was poured out.

Dismayed at the effect upon his people, Pastor Bouton headed to her meeting intending to tell her to get out of town but, instead was persuaded of the truth of her message. It was a life-shattering conviction of truth that led him to actually invite Sister McPherson to his own church to preach. Excerpts from her writings report what followed:

He knelt at his own pulpit and peered through his fingers at *"the strange proceedings taking place in his dignified congregation."* His own people were swaying and falling and speaking in tongues. It was incredible. *"Sinners broke down and wept their way to Jesus' feet. He had never heard such praying before and feared that his people might be arrested for disturbing the peace....The third night nineteen received the baptism of the Holy Spirit. Down they went right and left, between the seats, in the aisles, in front of the chancel rail, up on the platform."*

Desire began to burst within him until he made his way back to his pulpit and bowed, praying simply but in earnest, *"Oh, Lord, fill me. Oh, Lord, fill me...After some time he began to sway from side to side, and soon fell backwards under the power and rolled off the little step and lay under the glorious power of the Lord."*

"Someone spoke to his wife, who had been sitting in the audience, and exclaimed: 'Oh, there goes William!'"

"*This was too much and with one bound she was in the aisle and ran to the front sobbing imploringly: 'Oh, Will, Will, speak to me. Speak to me.'*"

"*She believed he was dying, but just at that tense moment, when the congregation was gathered round in breathless circles, leaning over the chancel rail, some even standing on the pews to see over the others' shoulders, Pastor W. K. Bouton was filled with the blessed Holy Spirit.*"

"*People fell to the floor here and there through the audience. Strong men sobbed like babies, and when at last the Pastor rose to his feet he walked up and down the platform, and cried out: 'Oh, friends, I have to preach!' And preach he did, under the inspiration of the Holy Spirit, telling the people that 'This Is That,' commanding them to be filled with the Spirit, to get oil in their lamps and prepare for the coming of the Lord.*"

"*In the two weeks that followed practically the entire congregation from pulpit to the door, besides members who came in from other churches, were baptized with the Holy Spirit and were afire with the Spirit of Evangelism*"8

That was the wonderful beginning of my Pentecostal heritage. Because of that outpouring of the Holy Spirit in 1916, that Methodist church was transformed into a Pentecostal church—and was my church, when I was growing up.

David and Claire Beam- married 1969 until
his death October 15, 1998.

My precious children: Rebecca Claire (1971)
and David Joseph Jr.(1973) Beam.

Free Gospel Church Group-Corona, New York- Front Row, second from left: Pastor William K. Bouton; Fifth and sixth from left: My mother's twin sister Anna Becker and her husband Burtis Becker.

David Beam honored for 40 years at Free Gospel Bible Institute. L to R: Rev. and Mrs. Chester Heath, Rev. and Mrs. David J. Beam.

Claire Beam in middle of wonderful senor class girls from the last year I taught at F.G.B.I.

Academic Dean Claire Beam Goodwin congratulating a graduate at F.G.B.I.

My daughter and son-in-law Jim and Becky Hawk.

Briana and Jessica Hawk, my granddaughters.

My grandsons- Front to Back: Wesley, David, and Andrew Hawk

14

BLESSINGS FROM HEAVEN

Baby Rebecca

In February 1971 God blessed our home with a beautiful baby girl, Rebecca Claire Beam, our bundle of joy. She was a precious gift to us—and what a change she brought into our lives! I learned quickly that while you are changing the baby, she is changing you. Well planned days just didn't happen anymore. Suddenly a tiny little bundle helped shape our days. It was a brand new experience that required loving and patient learning every day.

Motherhood was serious business, and as a new mother, I wanted to do things perfectly. I read every book I could find on the subject. I determined in my heart to be a good mother. No charge of neglect would come near my name. So when David and I went on our very first ministry with our little darling I had it all figured out. In our car went the high chair, the stroller, the baby bathtub, a playpen and plenty of clothes for Rebecca. How in the world did we ever fit all that into one car? And the poor pastor and wife where we went had to tolerate all of this being moved into their small parsonage. What an experience it was! Well it didn't take too long to figure out that I really didn't have to take everything but the kitchen sink, and we survived.

I remember the time poor little Becky (as she came to be called) was limp as a rag, her body so hot with a high fever. She lay on the couch so still. The doctor took a culture to see if she had some sort of infection, but the results were not back yet. Looking at this tiny little bundle in such a condition caused great concern in our hearts. About that time came the sounds of music wafting upward from the chapel service beginning downstairs, beneath our apartment. David and I looked at each other and instantly knew what we should do.

We wrapped Becky in a soft blanket and carried her downstairs. Students and faculty were already singing as we entered the auditorium and walked straight to the altar. It was evident that we wanted prayer for our child and everyone present responded, praying in unison. They stormed Heaven believing God for an answer and God heard. He reached down his great healing hand and healed her. The fever left immediately, and she began to improve from that moment. What a mighty God we serve—and what a tremendous lesson in faith had been learned. We would need that faith many times in the days ahead.

For children to be raised in a Bible school atmosphere is a tremendous privilege. They are surrounded with students who are saved and good examples (usually!). They are blessed to be in great Pentecostal services with the move of God and wonderful praying at the altars. Becky was not quite three years old when we were creating a list of things we are thankful for. It was Thanksgiving time and I would do the writing as she would tell me things to write down. She was thankful for a house, her parents, lions and tigers, dressers, doorknobs, birds....and the list grew...and then she said, "...and I'm thankful that Jesus saved me and took my sins away." I wrote it down just as she said it and always was amazed that, at such an early age, she expressed such a testimony without any prompting. Little did I know that my sweet little darling would someday be a pastor's wife and mother of five homeschooled children.

I still remember little David, behind the closed doors of his bedroom, preaching his heart out about Jonah! As a young boy he made a poster for his dad that said, "When I grow up, I want to be a preacher just like you."

Camps that Changed Lives

We taught classes from September to May and then filled the month of July with family camp, youth camp and kids' kamp on the same F.G.B.I. campus. I loved those opportunities to teach and present the gospel to many young people who came from all kinds of neighborhoods and backgrounds. We saw many get saved and baptized with the Holy Ghost. We had water baptismal services during camp that were glorious testimonies of lives changed by the power of God. I have heard wonderful testimonies from young people who were called into the ministry right there in youth camp. Today these former campers are missionaries on foreign fields, pastors, youth workers and other kinds of Christian workers in churches. Although many campers were Christians, we also had some from ghetto-like areas who had never been in services like these.

One of those years we experienced what some called the "demon year," because so many arrived needing spiritual deliverance like this boy. A knock came to our apartment door. It was a male counselor leading a 16 year old camper. "I found him walking the campus acting like he was in a trance." His blank stare, as he slowly shuffled his way into our apartment, certainly convinced us that something was wrong. We began to pray for him, not knowing if his problem was physical or spiritual. We soon found out when he suddenly began thrashing about, falling on the floor, and then slithering down the hallway like a snake. Three men were holding fast to his legs as, with super strength, he thrust his whole body forward, without using his arms. He appeared driven by some invisible force.

Our prayers turned into warfare as we continued to rebuke and take authority over the devil. He had slithered halfway down the hall, to Becky's bedroom door, when he came to a sudden stop and dropped as if he were dead. We kept praying as he laid there not moving. In a few minutes he lifted himself up on his elbows, looked around confused and asked, "Where am I? What happened? How did I get here?"

We told him that the Lord had just set him free from demonic powers and that now he needed to repent of his sins and ask Christ to come into his heart and take control. With great emotion he did so, until his face changed to one of peace and joy of newfound salvation. That night he received the baptism of the Holy Ghost on his dormitory bunkbed.

How did he become demon possessed? He told us the story of how he had gone into a Spencer Gift store in a mall and bought a large poster with strange looking half-human and half-animal creatures around

145

the borders. In the center was an evil looking spider-like creature. He hung it on his bedroom wall and at night would stare at it. One night something gave him the idea to shine a black light on it. When he did he saw the creature's eyes moving. The next night as he stared at it again he heard voices coming from it. Startled, he quickly asked "Who are you?"

The voice stopped as if unwilling to identify itself.

Later as he again tried to talk to the voices, they began to tell him things to do, bad things. In the process of time, this young man came under the control of a demon. The power of God delivered him at camp. We instructed him to go home and burn that poster, to renounce all association with the spirits involved with it.

This was the same year that a young woman about 25 years old came to my door saying she needed to talk with me. It seemed obvious that she had a problem. I invited her to sit on the couch with me, and I waited for her to give her reason for coming. She was strangely silent, so I implored, "Lillian, why have you come? What is your problem?"

She was still silent but got a strange look on her face and it seemed as if she began to stiffen up.

I turned my face to her and asked again, a bit stronger, "Lillian, tell me what your problem is."

In a tortured kind of a voice and a twisted face she forced out the words, "I can't."

"What do you mean, you can't?" I asked, sensing that this was becoming more of a problem than I had expected.

"I can't tell you..he won't let me," she blurted out again with great effort. Her eyes had become fierce looking and her arms and legs began to stretch out.

I knew now that I was dealing with a spirit. "In the name of Jesus, tell me what your problem is!" I commanded.

The words forcefully came out, "Gluttony!"

This woman was skinny as a rail. "You are a lying spirit!" I declared.

"No, I am not!" she screamed. "The spirit tells me where there is food and I go and get it. I hide food all over in my room, in the cracks in the stairwell. I can't help it."

"You evil spirit, I command you to come out, in the name of Jesus!" I demanded. The battle was on and demonic forces were manifesting in my living room. Although we gained some victory then, the real confrontation came in the night youth campmeeting when she fell to the floor as she was prayed for. She rolled back and forth on that hard uneven wooden floor of the old white church building until I was sure she would be black and blue. Her eyes were fierce and she refused to call on Jesus. As we battled in prayer demons finally came out. How pathetic it is to see how the entrance of sin can take a person much farther than they ever wanted to go! I am glad that the bondage of the devil is broken by the power of the name of Jesus.

I remember one youth camp under the gospel tent when Evangelist Jerry Matney was preaching with great power and anointing. The Spirit of the Lord broke through in that service with someone suddenly jumping up and giving a loud message in tongues. It so shocked some of those campers who were used to drive-by shootings in their neighborhoods that they threw themselves down on the floor in fright. We assured them everything was all right, that they were safe, and told them to just sit up and listen because the Spirit of God was speaking to them supernaturally. The word of the Lord got through to them that night causing many to come to the altar for salvation. There never seemed to be a dull moment at Export.

Echoes of Faith Radio Broadcast

For over twenty years David and I did a radio broadcast that grew from once-a-week recordings, to 30-minute live radio broadcasts—five drive-time afternoons and Saturday mornings each week. It was David's daily delight when that phone would ring with listeners on the other end. After a busy day in the office and teaching classes he would come home just after three o'clock and drop into his favorite recliner. With eyes closed he prayed and meditated in preparation for the broadcast. About four o'clock he would rock himself out of that chair and call to me, "Claire, it's time for broadcast" and off we would go to the auditorium.

At 4:30 sharp you would hear the opening song, "Someone is Praying for You" and then David's voice announcing, "Welcome to another Echoes of Faith radio broadcast." It was a divinely appointed time to reach beyond the campus of Free Gospel Bible Institute into the surrounding communities. "Our phone lines are open right now for you to call in with your special need or testimony" was heard many times throughout the broadcast and the calls would come in and we would pray and minister to the needs of listeners. Listeners would call from about twenty to thirty cities each week. The gospel went out to many Catholics, to elderly shut-ins, to people with marriage troubles, some on the verge of suicide, to nominal churchgoers and many were turned to the Lord.

It was amazing how many Catholics listened and were touched by the Lord. One Catholic listener called very often and we would pray for her. She even sponsored numerous broadcasts. One day I decided to try and track her down. I knew she lived locally so I searched for her apartment and found it. When I knocked on her door I greeted her by saying, "Hi, I'm Claire from Echoes of Faith."

Her eyes opened wide and she grabbed my arm, pulling me inside as she pleaded, "Oh, don't tell the priest that I listen!" Fear filled her heart, but Jesus was breaking through that bondage and reaching for her soul. Although she had so little understanding of Biblical truth, she felt something powerful when she listened to the broadcast. As soon as it would begin, she explained, she would stand right there in front of her radio the whole time it was on, with her hands clasped as if in prayer. She didn't understand what it was that she felt but was so excited to tell me all about it.

What a joy it was to explain the gospel to her and to pray with her! We never did see her come to the church, but she continued to listen. Often we wondered how many more there were out there hearing the truth but afraid to step out from their dismal forms of religion.

It was always a blessing to meet people in stores and in other businesses, who would tell us how the broadcast had helped them. I still recall the day I was in a gas station in Greensburg, just eleven miles from Export, and I casually greeted a man who was getting coffee. I spoke just a few words when he said, "You sound so familiar. I have heard that voice before. Who are you?"

What an interesting occurrence! I just said, "My name is Claire Beam and I'm from Export."

"Oh," he burst out, "Are you Claire Beam from Echoes of Faith?" I was amazed and told him I was.

"Oh, I can't believe I'm standing here right next to Claire Beam! I listen to you all the time."

Imagine that! Well, it stunned me, for I realize that I am nothing except what the Lord is in me, and to hear someone exclaim like that was amazing, but fulfilling, for I could see that people really were listening! People really were being affected by our daily radio ministry. I just praised the Lord.

Another Beaming Baby

It was during one of those early Saturday broadcasts in 1973, presented live from the Apollo WAVL radio station that I told David it was time for me to go to the hospital. I was in my ninth month of pregnancy with our second child and it was time for little David Joseph Beam, Jr. to join our family.

Brother Chester Heath quickly arrived to take over the broadcast as we headed to the hospital and soon afterward we brought our tiny baby David home to our little castle in the sky. Two year old Rebecca sat expectantly on the couch, with arms stretched out and so excited, as we carefully placed her new baby brother in her arms. Our home was now buzzing with more sounds of life than we had ever heard before. God had blessed us and we gave Him thanks.

Soon after little David was born we moved. We had watched and listened to the construction of the new men's dormitory with a growing sense of anticipation, knowing that inside it would be our new apartment. While the structure was still unfinished, we took a little tour, stepping into our apartment space that was yet without walls. The planned layout of rooms was marked on the floor. We didn't need walls to envision what was soon to be our beautiful home. How thrilled we were! It would be an abundant blessing to enjoy three bedrooms, a bathroom and a smaller powder room, a kitchen, dining room, and living room. We were really going to live now! To top it all off we would be on the ground floor with place for the children to play right outside our door.

This was my little palace, and I fixed it up the best way possible without spending much money. One price to pay was the fact that we were over a classroom. During the school year the children forever heard me saying, "Don't pound the floor." "Walk quietly." "No, you can't play the piano now." I would vacuum and do other "noisy" things during the ten minute break between classes or at non-class times. We got used to it and it didn't bother us too much.

The children were growing and they were beautiful. Little David had the most beautiful eyes and big eyelashes and Rebecca's long blonde hair framed her pretty face. David was so pleasant and always smiling, but new mothers really do have some interesting concerns. When he was first born, I was so used to having a girl that I worried about how to make sure he would know how to act as a boy! My worries ended the moment that tiny tot picked up a little Hot Wheels car, knelt on all fours, and shoved it across the floor while loudly crooning, "Brrrooooooom!" He revved that engine and it flew like a thunderbolt! Some things just come naturally!

Rebecca was at my side, always wanting to help with whatever I was doing. I guided her little hands as she picked up fragile things from soapy dishwater and followed her closely as she tried to push the heavy vacuum.

It was a special outing to visit the public library and bring back ten books for each one. Then came the fun of reading to them and observing their growing interest in books. They soon became excellent readers.

Years later my husband and I were hurrying from our house, across the lawn toward the auditorium to do the radio broadcast. We saw David, Jr, now about twelve years old, coming stumbling toward us crying. He had crashed his bike, and we assumed he just had a fall and would be all right, so we hugged him and comforted him and told him to go lay down on his bed until we finished the broadcast. We also sent Sister Virginia Dutka over to stay with him.

When we completed the program and headed home, we learned how mistaken we had been. The bike he rode was borrowed and was much too big for him. Attempting to go around a sharp curve too fast, he drove into the side of a garage, making impact with his hands first; then he bounced off and hit a tree.

The devastating hospital report was that he had two broken arms and other bruises. It was terrible! The doctor said that if he had not hit with his hands first—if his head had hit first—he might have been critically injured. We felt awful for not taking care of him immediately. He came home with two casts, his arms stretched out in a position that made it impossible for him to use them to eat or do anything else, so he needed much help and care. Our poor David! In spite of it all he stayed cheerful. It was a great day for him and for us when his injuries healed and his casts came off.

There were many occasions through their growing up years that the Lord blessed them greatly. Both gave their hearts to the Lord and were baptized with the Holy Ghost. One time when David was about twelve years old he was so blessed and speaking in tongues for so long at the altar that some of the students picked him up and carried him over to the men's prayer room, still praying in tongues. Those are memories that are precious.

Finances were tight, but sufficient. God met all of our needs. We made good use of thrift stores. Prices in other stores were just too high for us. I prayed that the Lord would help us find good clothes for the children and felt so happy when we did. On bag sale days we could fill a big brown bag to the top and stuff it down, all for a dollar. We had to say, "Thank God for Friends Thrift Store in Export!"

My husband David was a great grocery shopper. He knew how to find the bargains and bring them home. One problem was that when he saw better sales on quantity purchases, he would buy several of the same items. One time we had fourteen boxes of cereal stuffed into our little kitchen cabinets and a huge carton of toilet paper stored in our book closet in the hall. It was just a little harder to get down on hands and knees to search behind all the boxes to find the Captain Crunch.

I had no complaints! David was an excellent manager of our meager finances. I never had to worry about bills getting paid. He usually paid early and built a good credit rating. He wisely saved money, even when that limited what was available for use.

We were not able to go on vacation very often but when we did we had a great time. We just fell in love with Niagara Falls and several times were able to enjoy its beauty and wonder. Yet, in the midst of relaxation, we always seemed to find people who desperately needed the Lord.

15

WITNESSING TO THE LOST

The Tallest Man in the World

One unforgettable experience occurred as we walked down Clifton Hill at Niagara Falls, Canada. The Guinness World Book of Records Museum had a special guest who was greeting visitors. He was the "tallest man in the world"—8 feet two inches tall Donald A. Koehler. As I looked through the window I saw people lined up shaking his hand. One thing I noticed was the emptiness in his face as he robotically said "Hello" to each person. I thought of the unusual life he must live. He can't ride in a normal car. He couldn't sit at a table in McDonalds. If he walked out on the street, no doubt many would stare. My heart was touched with a feeling of compassion for him and I sensed the Lord leading me to go inside and meet him.

Reaching into my purse, I found a suitable gospel tract and folded it up until just a red heart on the front was visible. I joined others in line and when it was my turn I reached up and shook his hand. It was so huge. I looked up at him and told him I was glad to meet him and that I had something I wanted to give him. I handed him the tract and urged him, "Don't open it now. Wait until everyone is gone and then take it out and read it."

He looked down at it and with a grin he said, "Okay" probably thinking it was some kind of love letter.

I watched him through the window later as he unfolded that tract and carefully and slowly read each panel, stared seriously out into space, then folded it back and returned it to his pocket. I was praying, "Lord, save him." I don't know what happened that day, but I do know that this tallest man in the world died within the next year. Maybe when I get to Heaven I will see a big tall man coming jogging down Glory Avenue toward me, shouting, "I made it! I got saved that day!" What a great moment of rejoicing that would be!

In addition to Niagara Falls, we once toured Washington, DC and were deeply stirred as we toured the Holocaust Museum. Other times, the children simply built tents out of couch cushions and blankets. No one ever wanted to tear them down! Our family fun and entertainment often were the inventions of a mother's mind: hikes in the woods, hot dog roasts in the field, waking up in the middle of the night to go out in freezing temperatures and lay on a picnic table watching meteor showers in the sky. Library trips and playground adventures were loved. Both children were reading books before they even enrolled in their first classes in a Christian school. We had family altar with Bible stories and scripture memorization. What an awesome responsibility was before us!

Life was very busy. There were family responsibilities, classes to be taught and lessons to be prepared. David had his own office space for his work, but our house was my office. Our dining room table was filled with my Bible, concordances, commentaries, papers and other study helps—alongside my trusty typewriter (before computer days!)—while toys were scattered everywhere.

I studied earnestly and prepared every class with purpose. Each year I revised the lectures, adding updated material and praying again before each time to teach. This was urgent. These classes couldn't be just plain old teaching. God had to be there to instruct and prepare these young people for the greatest mission of all—the ministry. I would hurriedly clean it all up in time to prepare a delicious meal for my husband and family.

Personal Evangelism Class

Books filled my arms as I stepped outside my apartment door and headed down the stairway to the freshmen classroom. I was ready. My heart and mind were both prepared. A yearning swelled inside me to impart to this class what the Lord had poured into me. It was the anointing of the Spirit that I hungered for as I poured out my heart to them. Undoubtedly, this was a different generation. Laptops were raised and ready. I was standing before the hope of Pentecost, the hope of the church, the hope of the world. What a responsibility! What unimagined possibilities were settled into these classroom chairs!

My eyes met their eyes as I urged them to take up their cross, to answer the call of God, to take the gospel to the lost. They were with me. It was visible on their faces. I pressed forward with an urgent call for preparation. Their response ignited a fire inside of me as I heard the whole class thundering forth the soulwinning scriptures, rhythmically in unison—Romans 3:23, Romans 6:23, Acts 3:19, John 1:12, Revelation 3:20. Could there be any sweeter sound of music than hearing their voices reverberate with vibrant passion—"Lord Lay Some Soul upon My Heart?"

As I looked into their faces, I saw tears, the glow of dedication, and desire to be the instrument through which that soul would be won. Something was happening to them. Just weeks earlier they came to this class like open books ready to be written upon and so quickly many of them have experienced a spiritual transformation as the pen of the Word of God engraved his will and passion upon their hearts. It was my intense joy to see such growth of soulwinning vision that would soon be displayed in evangelism activities.

This was my favorite class from the beginning and the place where the Lord increased the fire in my own soul for witnessing and winning souls. It was not enough to just teach it—I wanted these students to do it...and I wanted to do it! I had heard the passionate call from Jesus, urging all of us to move out beyond the four walls of the church. My voice echoed his words to these young people to "...Lift up your eyes, and look on the fields; for they are white already to harvest" (John 4:35). I could see some tremble when I revealed that requirements for successful completion of this Personal Evangelism course included going beyond the four walls of this classroom, out into the streets, and knocking on doors to take the gospel into surrounding communities.

The inexperienced and timid gained confidence in witnessing workshops where student teams interacted with each other, as the Christian team practiced witnessing to the "sinner" team. The Christian team demonstrated how to approach the door, introduce themselves with friendly conversation, and move from a transition into the gospel presentation.

The Pentecostal witness doesn't merely give the good news, but he reaches for a verdict. This is the vital moment when it is not enough to get a "fish" to bite the "hook", but also to do as Jesus instructed and become an actual fisher of men, by pulling in the catch. His promise is "Come ye after me, and I will make you to become fishers of men."

The process of becoming a real soul winner could be compared to the development of a butterfly. As Christians we must all begin with the "Egg Stage," simply living the life and being an example, as Timothy instructed—"be thou an example of the believers" (1 Timothy 4:12)

Although all Christians begin as an example, we must not stay there but grow next into the "Caterpillar Stage." Now we become more than just a silent witness. We begin to give out gospel tracts. Hudson Taylor, John Bunyan, and John Huss were all saved through reading a gospel tract. Literature evangelism is a powerful way to win souls. Many Christians have never even entered this stage. Some of my students were already active witnesses before coming to school, but many had never distributed even one tract. This was fast becoming a new adventure in commitment and courage for them.

Yet there is more as the believer transitions into the "Cocoon Stage." This adds words to example and action. It propels that maturing Christian into a verbally witnessing tool in the Master's hands. Speaking the good news tremendously extends the possibilities of success in witnessing. Here is where most Christians finally stop and dwell comfortably. It is thrilling to speak the message of the gospel to the unsaved. It is exciting! Many are the encouraging and motivating testimonies from on-fire believers who have just come back from witnessing to a sinner. However, this is not time to stop. Allowing this to be the final resting place of your evangelistic endeavor creates a great crisis!

Just imagine all of those "hooked fish" dangling on the end of all those "spiritual fishing rods!" The same Savior, who sends us forth to be his witness, will also equip us with everything we need to "reel in those fish." He promised, "ye shall receive power, after that the Holy Ghost is come upon you: and ye shall be witnesses unto me" (Acts 1:8). Paul the apostle expressed his grand purpose as he wrote in Second Corinthians 5:11, "Knowing therefore the terror of the Lord, we persuade men…" Realizing that judgment day is coming, he not only pleaded with people to come to Christ, but he convinced them to do it.

If we go witnessing in the power of the Spirit, we will see more persuaded to make that vital decision to repent and be saved by faith in the Lord Jesus Christ. This is the "Butterfly Stage." Usually within three to four hours after emerging from its cocoon the butterfly is constantly seeking opportunities to reproduce. Evangelism is much more than simply presenting the gospel to sinners. We have a mandate from Jesus to persuade sinners to accept Him as Lord and to follow Him as reproducing disciples.

It wasn't an easy task to organize evangelism teams, arrange for their transportation, and get them on their way stocked with an assignment, report sheet, and literature, but the event was dynamic! It was on-the-job-training. It was "do or die." Some may have felt like they would die when they had to knock on the first door they had ever knocked on for witnessing purposes. The next class would be explosive with student witnessing reports that simply could not be restrained. He that winneth souls is not only wise, but very happy.

One team knocked on a lady's door and began a series of visits to her house that resulted in her freedom from a cult and her genuine salvation. Her atheist husband strongly resisted her newfound life, making things very difficult for her. However, the end of the story is that when he was stricken down with cancer, this precious lady graciously led him to Jesus. He lived to testify of his conversion and died ready to meet the Lord he had so long denied.

The Personal Evangelism syllabus included a series of studies on evangelizing those of varying beliefs. We delved into the doctrines of Roman Catholicism and taught how to present the Gospel to a Catholic. My personal preparation led to some interesting anonymous phone conversations with Roman Catholic priests. One example follows:

When a male voice answered my first call I asked to speak to Father—and waited. I'll try to replicate that interaction:

Priest: Hello, how may I help you?

Me: Hello, I have a question that I'm hoping you can help me with. Have you ever heard of the book, The Glories of Mary by Cardinal St. Alphonsus DeLigouri?

Priest: Yes. He is one of the greatest devotional writers of the Catholic Church.

Me: Since it was written so long ago, in 1852, is what he wrote still okay to believe today?

Priest: Yes, definitely. He is a highly esteemed writer.

Me: Well, my question has to do with something the cardinal wrote in his book. He said that if a person does not turn to Mary as the route to Heaven, he would be lost. Also, on another page, he explains that the reason Mary is called the gate of Heaven, is because going through her is the only way to get into Heaven.

I wondered about that and would like an answer from you. What if I respect and honor Mary but set her aside and instead place my full attention on Jesus, because he died on the cross for me. What if I only put my trust in Him to save me? Can I be saved?

Priest: (There is a long pause of silence before he speaks in a very harsh voice:) You ought never to even consider such a thing!!

I assume he thought I was a straying Catholic. However, I got his message.

What joy it is to have the assurance of genuine salvation through Jesus, who is the way the truth and the life. He made it clear that no man cometh to the father but by him (John 14:6).

The millions Roman Catholics in the United States represent a vast harvest field lying in the web of a different gospel. When the actual doctrines of this Church are revealed, what is seen is a massive organization that is not Christian at all but a vast political and unscriptural religion.

The field is the world and Jesus has sent us to it with his Word. Our course studies also included evangelism of Jewish people, Atheists, the unconcerned, people whose excuses have kept them from God, the soul winner's personal life, and so much more.

During some years, each student was required to develop a personal mission field, which was defined as a section of a local town that they would claim for the Lord and work by door-to-door visitation and evangelism. A required record of their project was evaluated academically.

Then came the day I walked into class and asked, "Are the unevangelized really lost?" This is the question of the college campuses, the skeptic and the agnostic. Until you personally and biblically research the subject your mind will never be satisfied with the answers of others. This became an intellectual and spiritual challenge for the class that was to be met in the writing of a 3,500- word thesis. As students diligently involved themselves in research, their intimidation by the topic soon faded and was replaced with burden for the lost. I recall one year when I taught the subject that the Spirit of God brought such a burden for the lost into the class that many just dropped to their knees beside their desks and wept before the Lord. Graduates still talk about how that paper changed them.

Believe me that paper also changes the teacher who must now read and grade these fifty or sixty theses of 3,500 words! It was quite amusing to hear the statement of one graduate during a special meeting of the Alumni Association that had been planned to honor me. They passed a microphone around to former students for their comments. Most brought tears of appreciation to my eyes. But I will never forget the one who admitted, "I didn't believe that Sister Beam actually read all the way through those 3,500-word theses and decided to test her. Somewhere in the middle of the thesis I wrote 'Mickey Mouse'. Guess what! When I got my graded paper back, there was a red circle around

'Mickey Mouse' with several red question marks around it." It is so true that grading papers took a whole lot of time but was a necessary part of teaching. So often it was a reverse test, showing the teacher how well she/he had conveyed the material.

"Evangelize!" is the pulsating heart cry of Jesus. "Untold millions are yet untold" has now become "untold billions are yet untold." I urged students, "Allow the Spirit of God to impress your soul with the magnitude of Christ's Great Commission." World population has now climbed above seven billion people. Such a number boggles the mind. Can we even grasp the concept of just one billion souls for whom Jesus died?

Do you know how many a billion is? "Counting non-stop, one number per second, it would take you 31 years, 251 days, 7 hours, 46 minutes, and 39 seconds to count to 1 billion"[5] (mathforum.org).

Multiply that by seven and attempt the impossible: grasp the greatness of the world to which Jesus has sent us. Now take a deep breath and say it out loud: "This is the whitened harvest field that is waiting for laborers—waiting for me!" Multitudes wallow in the valley of decision, most falling headlong into the flames of an eternal Hell. I have often wept before the Lord for their souls. The call for laborers has burned deeply in my heart, compelling a frequent prayer to ascend to Heaven pleading, "Lord, raise up a whole army of soul winners!"

The overwhelming magnitude of the harvest field must not hinder even the smallest effort to reach one more soul. To the person who says, "I can't go into all the world," I say, "Then begin with one square mile around your house. Do all of your neighbors know that you are a Christian?"

Pittsburgh Witnessing

Friday evenings were times some men students would go to Pittsburgh to preach on the streets, witness, and give out tracts. What happened one night brings to mind the theme of one of Pastor Michael Shaffer's missions conferences in Roanoke, Virginia—"The Duty and Danger of Missions." That theme was demonstrated on the streets of

Pittsburgh one night when a senior student, whom I will call Nick, went preaching with a group of students carrying a burden for the lost.

Parts of Liberty Avenue are dangerous and no place for the fearful. At some point Nick got separated from his group and was unexpectedly surrounded by some big, rough-looking guys. They took him into an alley where their demands made him think, "I could die in this alley." It all happened so fast. They put him on the ground and as one bent over him—like a flash of lightning—Nick threw his fist upward as fast and hard as he could, hitting his target and drawing blood. Just as fast Nick, leaped up and ran for his life. He survived and is today a dynamic soul-winning, fearless pastor.

Keep the Vision Alive and Active

Life is busy. Responsibilities multiply. Priorities get shuffled. How easily vision for souls can dim and be replaced with other things. Weeks slip by and then you notice that you haven't given out a tract lately; you haven't spoken to anyone about the Lord in a while. You justify yourself by citing your hectic schedule. Tragically, prayer also slips until you are so occupied with the Master's business that you have no time for the Master Himself. It's time to hit the altar again and pray through. There were times that I would hear the echo of Pastor K. A. Smith's voice declaring that any preacher or teacher that preached or taught about witnessing and didn't do it himself wasn't worth anything. I didn't want that to happen to me and continually called on the Lord to lead me to souls, to open the way for me to reach the lost for Him.

Threatened by a Dying Woman

One day I received a phone call from a lady named Isabella, who wanted me to come to visit her elderly, dying mother who lay in a bed, crowded into their little kitchen area. I told her I would be happy to come. Then she warned me that her mother was not saved and didn't want to hear about it. This frail little eighty-something-year-old had threatened, "If she comes, I'll kick her out of the house!" Well, that was like saying "Sic 'em!" to a bulldog. The Spirit rose up in my heart with the determination, "I've got to win her to the Lord!"

I prayed and sought the Lord for his direction and way to reach her and felt led to take my accordion with me. As I walked into her house I said a friendly "Hello!" to the dear lady in the bed and said, "Look at what I brought for you!" Opening my accordion case, I lifted the instrument to my shoulders and began to play some music.

She just stared but as I continued, her face changed to one of interest. I had no idea that she had been a concert pianist and loved music, but God knew the key to her heart! I began to add words to the music, singing the gospel to her—Amazing Grace, He Was Nailed To The Cross For Me, The Old Rugged Cross, and What Can Wash Away My Sins- Nothing But The Blood of Jesus.

In between some of the songs I began to exhort her about Jesus and Salvation. When it finally came to the end I told her I was going to sing a prayer... "Come Into My Heart Lord Jesus"...and if she would like Jesus to come into her heart, take away all her sins and be her Savior, she could pray those words from her heart. To my great joy I saw her lips moving in prayer. I took her hand and prayed with her as she did receive the Lord Jesus as her Savior. It was a comfort and delight to know she had overcome her resistance to the gospel, and surrendered to the pull of the Spirit, when she slipped off into eternity just a few days later.

Charles Spurgeon said: "I say it solemnly...that unless souls are converted by you, you had lived in vain; unless you personally are, in the hand of God, the instrument of bringing souls to Christ, you have not answered the end (purpose) of your being.."[6]

I was knocking on doors in Jeannette, Pennsylvania and came to one duplex that had a big dog standing loose at the front door. I stayed back at the sidewalk and prayed, "Lord, let that dog move away." He was vicious looking.

Just then a girl appeared and I called to her, "Is that your dog?"

"Yes," she said.

"Could you take him around the back so I can knock on the door?" She was glad to do it, and I stepped up to the door and knocked.

A lady answered and I began to introduce myself. "I'm Claire Beam...." and hardly got those words out of my mouth when I heard someone yell from inside.

"You mean Claire Beam from Echoes of Faith?" Looking further into the room, I saw about twenty-five women seated, looking toward me. "Yes," I affirmed. "What's going on in here?"

They explained that they were having a "Plant Party" and invited me in. Some said that they listened to the broadcast. Wow! There I stood with a golden opportunity, and I took it. For the next several minutes I had a congregation of twenty-five women listening to the gospel! It was great!

You never know what kind of a reception you will get when you go knocking on doors for Jesus.

One man answered the door in an apartment building and when I gave him my usual introduction he declared sarcastically with a wave of his hand, "Oh, I'm a heathen. You can't help me."

Acting as excited as I could, I replied, "Really? Well, I am so glad to find you, because you are the very one Jesus died for." He did stand there and listen to the gospel after that.

Dead Five Minutes Before

I had finished my rounds from room to room, as a volunteer hospital chaplain, and was about to leave, when I heard this announcement over the speaker system:

"Code Alert - Emergency Room; Code Alert – Emergency Room."

Just a few minutes earlier, a man by the name of Jon had been brought into the hospital by ambulance, having chest pains. His wife was with him in the emergency room (ER) when, suddenly, he experienced cardiac arrest. His heart stopped beating, and he was dead. The ER doctor immediately called for the code team as he worked on Jon.

As the code alert announcement was made, the medical team, that was spread out all over the hospital immediately came racing to the ER.

I thought, "I've never gone to a CODE ALERT. I think I'll go and see if there is any way I can help." So I joined the running staff and while the medical team headed behind that ominous curtain, I headed straight to the ER desk and said:

"Hi! I'm Claire, a volunteer chaplain, and I heard the Code announcement. Can I help? Are there family members here?

The nurse said, "Yes… Over there is the wife," and so I hurried over to her and began to comfort her, and pray with her.

In the midst of this, she suddenly cried out, "But he's not right with God. He's not ready!" and I thought, "Ah! She knows something about the need to be right with God!"

I said, "Then we need to pray for a miracle," and we did.

Soon the ER nurse came in smiling and said they were able to bring him back, but he was very unstable, and they didn't know if they would lose him again.

We thanked the Lord for this miracle, but the wife said again, "But he's still not right with God, and they could lose him again…"

Then she told me how her husband was a backslider who had been to Bible school and had been in the ministry.

I said, "Well, you're the wife. Go ask the nurse if I can go in there and pray with him."

I had never done anything like that before, but the Lord had opened this door for me, and I needed to step forward for Him. She asked them and they said "Yes," so I stepped into a situation I had never experienced before… I didn't know if I had 10 seconds to talk to him, or 30 minutes or a whole day, so I had to talk quickly and effectively.

As I walked behind the curtains the medical staff stepped back and let me approach Jon.

I bent close to his face and his opened eyes, and said, "Jon, I'm Claire, a volunteer chaplain, and your wife has told me about you. God has just given you a miracle and brought you back, I know that you know what it means to be saved. Would you like to pray with me right now, and come back to the Lord, and make everything right with Him? "

With great earnestness he said, "Yes!" and we prayed. He smiled and thanked me, and I quickly stepped away, letting the medical team return to his care.

Three weeks later, I was back visiting patients and walked into my last room, and there he was. It was Jon, and he looked at me and excitedly said, "It's YOU!" and I said, "It's YOU!"

"Yes," he said. "It's really me, and I'm still alive and I'm still saved! Praise the Lord!"

Think of it! Here is a man who was dead five minutes before and, five minutes later, he was truly alive and redeemed by the grace of God. What a thrill that was to my soul! I cannot help but give this testimony everywhere I go. It thrilled me to witness the mighty hand of God drawing a man from death to eternal life.

Everywhere we go there are people on the edge of eternity. If we make ourselves available, God can use us to win them for Him!"

A Neglected, Bedridden Lady

The mission field is never far away from where you are. I had to only go down a slight hill, past our old white church, and make a right turn down a steep little hill, and turn left into a slightly wooded area... (about a 3-minute ride) to see a dilapidated house hidden behind the trees. Inside was a bedridden lady who was neglected.

One day I took a few ladies there with mops, buckets, brooms and anything else we could think of to be some kind of a help to Ella. She welcomed us as we came in and told her we came to help her. The ladies set to work amongst the piles of debris, buckets of human waste, and unbelievable disarray. Her husband was gone, as usual, doing his own thing, as Ella was left with perhaps one egg to eat for the day.

I took on Ella as my personal project. I wanted to do whatever I could to help her. When I offered to bathe her and wash her hair, she whispered, "That would be so nice" and continued to tell of some long-ago time when someone else was so nice to do that for her. I began to remove her heavy socks, but they would not come off. They had grown to her skin. I filled two buckets with warm water and put one foot in each to soak, while I bathed the rest of her body. Washing her hair and winding it around pink curlers made her smile. Her socks did come off and we completed the job. Then I asked if I could wash her sheets and blanket.

"Oh," she inquired, "do you wash blankets? I've had this one thirty years and never washed it."

We persuaded her that it would be alright to wash them, and replaced them with newer ones. As I drew the bed clothes open, many black critters scurried around to escape. We stuffed laundry in a garbage bag, and had to wash the things three times to get even a semblance of cleanness. Poor Ella! Our hearts went out to her for such pathetic living conditions.

When I returned the next day with her "clean" sheets and blankets I also combed out her hair. She looked in the mirror and sighed, "Oh that looks so nice. Thank you so much!" But I wasn't finished yet. More important matters had to be taken care of. I was privileged to present the gospel to Ella and pray with her to receive Christ. She was so happy. I later did my best to get social services to bring assistance and food to her, but her husband refused to sign the necessary papers. It was only about a month later that Ella got pneumonia, and the doors of Heaven opened to receive her. Little did we know that her time was so short! What a joy it was to have participated in such a sacred event.

Witnessing in Cyberspace

When I was over fifty, a remarkable thing happened. The Lord gave me a desire to learn computer. That is amazing, because I was even intimidated by little children who would come around, talking about files and directories and folders, when I didn't even know how to turn on a computer. With a little persuasion I convinced my husband to buy a used computer for me and it opened up a brand new world. I knew nothing, and I tried everything.

From my little office space in the house I would yell, "Look at what I just did!" "Wow! Look at what I just found on this computer!" "Oh, no, I think I broke it! What is that blue screen?"

Sure enough I would mess it up and have to have someone come and straighten out what I had done but by trial and error and then a few college courses the Lord allowed me to learn something that has become such a tremendous benefit for the ministry. At that time there were only two computers on campus, mine and one set up in a back storage room that Brother Chester Heath did his best to figure out and use. What amazing changes would come to F.G.B.I. in the days ahead, when computers would be everywhere—in offices, homes, a computer lab in the library, and on student desks! God knew that we would need the help of technology as the school grew and was now preparing us for those days.

As I gained a little more knowledge of computer and internet I became challenged with the tremendous mission field that existed out in cyberspace. I began to explore ways to take the gospel to people online and found multiple opportunities.

"Anarchist" was the screen name for an individual I purposely interacted with. Such audacity! What kind of a person would use such a screen name? I knew I had to reach out to him. His first question to me was, "Do you know who Marilyn Manson is?" I thought the name belonged to a woman and he quickly informed me that he is a he not a she. So it began and continued as I dug into his attitudes and poured in the gospel. I finally uncovered his cover. He was a backslidden, sixteen-year-old homeschooler on the computer when he was supposed to be doing schoolwork. I prayed for him and did my best to direct him to repentance and salvation. He is only one of millions lost in cyberspace needing the contact of a true Christian.

At one point I infiltrated an online group called Suicide Holiday. These were people who supposedly really wanted to kill themselves. My sister Barbara actually drew my attention to these people. I read their posts and did my best to find the ones who were open to help. The lost souls in this group posted the easiest ways to kill yourself and all kinds of devilish encouragement to those who wanted to die. But there was Claire.

They called me a troll; they insulted me; they told me to get out of the group, but I kept looking and listening and finding those I could help outside of that group. I communicated with one particular girl who lived in New York. By God's help I was able to persuade her to not kill herself and then to get away from her abusive live-in boyfriend, and finally I directed her to help from a church in her area.

The Lord has ways and means of getting the gospel into places far beyond your reach, even into "Caesar's household," mentioned by Paul (Philippians 4:22). I once had an astounding, long-term witnessing experience with someone in high places. When I asked an online question about nursing homes I could not have anticipated that one of the four people responding would be a man from the Netherlands who was a spokesperson before the United Nations. I only knew that he was a stranger with some knowledge of nursing homes, due to a relative's situation.

I replied to each of the four like this: "I appreciated your response to my question about my mother. You have helped me to think more clearly about this, and I believe you are right. Thank you so much. During times like this, we need the help of the Lord and wisdom from above. May God bless and strengthen you."

One person replied to that mail by saying, "I'm not a very religious man. I would like to have strength that comes from the Lord."

In one email after another, I inserted bits of the gospel until finally he wrote: "I am a hard-boiled realist, someone who believes in nothing but the 'laws' of nature—which are still in the process of being discovered—and therefore I seem to be an unlikely person to be converted."

This witness continued for months, during which I had to get out my bible and my best apologetics books to deal with him. Gradually the wall was crumbling. At one point he remarked:

"If you can forgive my unbelief, I would be very thankful. And I promise to follow your religious admonishments: I need them, although I, regretfully, remain a skeptic."

Later he acknowledged that he began to read a religious book. "…the book is intended to get lost sheep back to the herd. Will it work with me, I wonder? I'm interested—but in doubt."

God was working. Eventually he wrote: "I will try and pray tonight."

He soon involved his wife in the communication. She was about the same as he but was reading my messages and was opening her heart.

He wrote: "I'll be praying again tonight, Claire," and he now admitted to having two Bibles at his bed and reading them each night. What a change! He was now searching for spiritual truth.

Who is this man? He is from the Netherlands and works at the Dutch Ministry of Education, Culture and Science. In his positions, he is a spokesman before the United Nations

It is astounding that I, from my desk in Export, Pennsylvania, was giving the gospel to a stranger who stands in such a prestigious position. My communication with him ended when I was able to contact a Pentecostal pastor in the same city and arrange for a Pentecostal man who works on the same floor as he, to make contact with him.

There are scales of blindness to remove, walls of unbelief to tear down, hardened, sinful and skeptical minds to soften and open. Will you be that one whom the Lord can work through to reach into the darkness and pull men and women out, into the glorious light of Salvation?

Jesus came to seek and to save that which was lost. The Comforter, the Holy Ghost has come into the world to do all of these things: "And when he is come, he will reprove the world of sin, and of righteousness, and of judgment..." (John 16:8). He can work through you!

16

WORKERS TOGETHER WITH GOD

After the death of Joseph Dutka, Ken and Connie Roles stepped into God's appointed place at Free Gospel Bible Institute and enriched the work in so many ways. Laboring as a servant, Brother Roles was another God-send for David. He shared administrative responsibilities as he worked side-by-side with him in the office. He taught, preached, led singing, and served as Dean of Men. Voluntarily, Ken almost became his official chauffeur. He sometimes cleaned or repaired our car and, in many ways, was like Elisha who "poured water on the hands of Elijah" (2 Kings 3:11). He was dependable, capable, and dedicated and for a while became the Administrator of the school after David's death.

God Makes the Impossible Happen

In the early days it was difficult to picture the construction of a brand new men's dormitory building—that also included three faculty residences, a prayer room, the office complex, a campus store, and a small library. God not only gave us that building, but also a second men's dormitory after that, built by the volunteer labors of many, including a team brought by Brother Lee Strickler from Virginia. What a blessing those men were! That second building was completed debt-free because of the generous gift of a godly Pentecostal ministry. My son-in-law, Jim Hawk, will not forget those days under the hot sun, mixing and hauling the cement for the bricklayers.

Bigger yet and more unpredictable was the construction of a large 7600 square foot library. Some of David's last days were spent walking up to that library construction site each morning to watch the progress. He would come back to the house grinning from ear to ear with joy over what he saw happening on the F.G.B.I. campus! Brother Kenneth Roles would already be there on a ladder or inside trying to continue moving the work forward.

In one of my positions as librarian, I eagerly pursued the selections and purchases of the new library carpeting, lighting, shelving, and furnishings. I was thrilled with the library and dreamed of having a beautiful circulation desk. Pastor Jim Suits and Pastor Rick Binkley from Hodgenville, Kentucky had offered to build one for us but had no idea what I had in mind. I researched and studied library furniture catalogs and selected a beautiful design that included multiple connected units. After cutting out the pictures from the catalogs, I prayed and placed them in an envelope to mail to these two unsuspecting pastors. When they opened that mail I think they nearly fainted. My dream was far more than they had anticipated!

If you know Brothers Suits and Binkley, you know that after their initial, nearly speechless reaction, they went to work diligently laying out plans, purchasing supplies, and building that beautiful furnishing that greets you upon entering the library. Brother Binkley even added more to the initial challenge by pursuing another project. He sized, cut, finished, delivered and installed beautiful full-length wood panels at the end of each of the many steel book shelves. God bless you, my treasured brothers!

When the library was completed it was dedicated as the David J. Beam Memorial Library. It was beautiful and became my responsibility. As librarian I saw God help us gradually fill the shelves with 25,000 volumes. God sent Jim and Teresa Stewart to provide and set up computer technology for the library and the offices. They worked late into the night hours along with their son, installing and programming computers. Fiber optic lines were used to connect a network of computers that set F.G.B.I. on a new path. What a tremendous blessing they were and continue to be. Over the years they were always ready to advise and help where needed. May God bless them richly.

Does Anyone Wear Size 10 Shoes?

Previously I had no knowledge of library science but in God's good planning He permitted me to do some volunteer library work at a local Christian school. The process was an education that helped prepare me for what was ahead. God gave me an amazing answer to prayer one day while meeting with some of the volunteers at that school. I had been praying for some new shoes and, in this planning meeting, a lady stood up and asked if anyone there wore a size ten shoe. I was somewhat a newcomer at that time and felt too backward to respond. She then repeated her question. "Isn't there anyone here who wears a size ten shoe?"

This time I spoke up and said, "I do."

She continued, "Well, if you can use some shoes, just follow me after the meeting."

Following her in my car took me to her home where she showed me a wall that had many shoe boxes piled up and leaning against it. She told me that a wealthy lady had given all these shoes. She only wore them a few times and if I wanted them, they were mine. I went away from that place with not just the pair of shoes I was praying for, but with twenty pairs of very expensive shoes!! What a generous, prayer-answering God is mine! I let that generosity work in me also and gave many of those shoes to others. Over and over, the Lord has shown Himself mighty to meet my every need through the years. I love Him and praise Him with all my heart.

17

GOD'S MAN WITH A VISION

Anointed to Preach

My husband was elated to see all that God was doing. For almost forty years David gave himself wholeheartedly to the ministry of Free Gospel Bible Institute. He started preaching in the streets at sixteen, went to Zion Bible Institute in Rhode Island for three years, and began to pastor a small Free Gospel Church in Scienceville, Ohio. God gave him a vision of a church so filled with people that there was standing room only, even on the platform.

That very thing happened when the Lord brought that church a powerful revival. Thrust forward by God's direction, they purchased a large, historical landmark church that became the Free Gospel Church of Youngstown, Ohio. Salvation, healing, and deliverance services grew the church to about 350 in the Sunday night services. His church work was combined with the Bible school work in Export. He was part of Free Gospel Bible Institute from its inception in 1958 and became president in its third year of operation.

Can this Church Grow?

When he left the Youngstown church and settled at the Bible school, there were few people attending the local church. He regularly visited the homes of attendees and visitors and gradually, one person at a time, one family at a time, it grew. With prayer and patience, we began to see a move of God in the services. People were drawn to the old-fashioned Pentecostal preaching and altar services. After a while the

Lord helped him build the Export Free Gospel Church up to a summer attendance of over one hundred, not including the Bible school students. In those days we ran two buses and reached out to the surrounding communities. Bob Seaman and Bill Kerr were some early assistants that kept those buses on the road.

My daughter Becky and her husband, Jim Hawk, had already graduated from F.G.B.I. and were now working at the school, teaching, preaching, doing office work, maintenance, and working with the church. They often went door-to-door looking for more children and parents to pick up on the bus. Sometimes they found them at the playground or down the street, and they would keep going back, following up faithfully with a passion.

One day they visited a home in Jeannette, Pennsylvania, trying to reach the family for the Lord. An older daughter in the house just didn't seem to act right. As they continued to converse, she left the room and went to another room and closed the door. Suddenly they heard a gunshot from the room and found that she had shot herself in the head and died. It was a dreadful experience with such a sad ending.

Those were also the days of souls getting saved regularly in the church services. Unsaved people came—some by church bus, others on their own. David grasped that microphone in his hand and preached up and down the aisle, sometimes inviting those with needs to form long lines down the center aisle. He began with the first one in line, anointing them with oil, laying hands on each one and earnestly praying for healing and deliverance. The power of God was manifested and brought many testimonies of victories. We saw whole families get back to God and begin to live changed lives.

I had a young people's class of from twenty to twenty-five, from local areas. Some rough neighborhoods were reached and brought needy young people into my class. What a challenge it was! It excited and motivated me! I earnestly prayed and prepared lessons to pull them to the Lord. The Holy Ghost faithfully brought conviction on their hearts and eternal decisions were made for Christ. Some were called to Bible school and ministry. Sadly, some rejected the Lord and wound up bank robbers and murderers.

One day there came a knock on my door from a man just out of prison. He had been one of my students but had already served thirty years incarcerated in different facilities. His sister, also a past Sunday School student, was convicted of murdering their own mother who had backslidden and become involved in all kinds of sin. Such a dark picture points out the terrible danger of turning one's back on God. "...sin, when it is finished, bringeth forth death" (James 1:15). "There is no peace, saith the LORD, unto the wicked" (Isaiah 48:22). That is why my deepest desire is to give the gospel to the lost and to see them saved.

A Dreadful Diagnosis

David was a man with a calling and vision that continually moved him to do more for the Lord. For sixty-six years he served. Then God called him away. It was right after his much loved trip to the Free Gospel mission work in Sierra Leone, West Africa that he was diagnosed with Chronic Myelogenous Leukemia. It was a shock to each of us to discover the large sign "CANCER INSTITUTE" at the door we entered for an early appointment. The seriousness of the situation had not yet sunk in, but soon a quiet sadness began to drift over us like a fog growing in density.

We could tell when the heaviness of realization gripped us. It was on a day that we faced each other in the kitchen and our eyes locked in such a look that we were immediately drawn into each other's arms. Spontaneously, tears began to flow as we cried on each other's shoulders. It was during that emotional surge that we began to come to our senses. "We can't go on like this. We have always trusted the Lord, and we will continue to do so now. We have to commit this thing to Him and go on walking forward with his victory." From that day, God gave us a peace that passed understanding, in the face of every battle.

When his white blood cell count began to mount higher and higher, different treatment became necessary. I injected him with Interferon five days a week and this fatigued him terribly. There were times that this physical weariness opened the door to some dark feelings of discouragement in David. He came to a point when he spent much time resting in his brown recliner or laying on the couch.

During one such time, a most unusual thing occurred. Around

eight o'clock in the evening, there came a knock at our door. When I opened it, two strangers stood there—a man and a woman. They apologized for disturbing us and asked if Rev. David J. Beam lived here. They claimed they were on their way to Michigan and got lost on our road. That is hard to imagine, but as they passed the tall, illuminated sign for Free Gospel Bible Institute and saw the words, Rev. David J. Beam, President, the Lord spoke to their hearts to stop here and go in and find him. I hardly knew what to think about this, but invited them in.

David got up from the couch to meet them and before there was much conversation these people began to speak encouraging words to David that they said the Lord wanted him to hear. It turned into a wonderful, encouraging time of prayer, after which they soon left. David then told me what I had not known. He had been laying there, talking to the Lord and telling Him, "Lord, I just need to hear from you." God heard that deep yearning and directed a couple of his servants right to our doorstep with the answer. What a wonderful, caring Lord we serve! No wonder First Peter 5:7 directs us to cast "all your care upon him; for he careth for you."

When the burden gets heavy and things seem uncertain, there is no better hiding place than in the presence of the Lord. I had a similar time when the Lord made this so real to me as well. I had gone out into the open field and woods of our property and told the Lord that I was not going to leave until I heard from Him. There was a special place I would often go to when I wanted to get alone with God. In a little hollow place in the woods facing the field was a fallen tree where I would sit and talk to the Lord.

As the hours passed, I kept praying in that place and then began walking and wondering if I would hear from God. I began wandering down a wooded path that led to an oil pipeline and eventually stopped and sat down on a musty-looking, leaf covered log. "Oh, Lord, I need You today!" I cried. My hands were resting on the log where I sat and just then, as I looked down to my right I was stunned to see words carved into the log, right where my hand rested. They said, "He careth for you." Tears flowed as I worshipped my Lord who surely saw me there and just as surely was speaking to me exactly what I needed to hear. Whoever carved those words so long ago had no idea how God would use them on that needy morning. We can never praise Him enough for his loving-kindness and tender mercies.

Eternity Called Him and He Went

Doctors determined that David would only live three years, but he stayed with us for six and continued his daily responsibilities to the end, although fatigued. On the day that I took him for a midnight trip to the hospital, he had taught all his classes, completed responsibilities in the office, and had stood in the auditorium, holding onto the back of a pew, as he leaned forward to teach his night class. He came home in pain.

During this same time, my mother was dying in a hospital in Latrobe, Pennsylvania, about twenty miles away. It was already dark outside, and here I was facing two crises, each of them tearing at me emotionally. My poor husband was in pain. My mother could die at any time. I had to make a quick decision.

With difficulty, I decided to risk taking a quick trip to visit my mother, not knowing what condition she might be in. It was a difficult choice to leave David and I did my best to return home quickly. When I arrived David was still in pain, but now it was much more severe. We rushed to the emergency room. It was midnight, Monday, October 12, 1998. I did not know it, but Heaven was calling.

Surgery was performed to fix a twisted intestine that was causing the pain. It was a minor problem but David never spoke to me again. His blood clotting factor was acceptable prior to surgery but, due to the leukemia, the number dropped during surgery, and his blood would not clot. He continued to bleed internally and all efforts to help were futile. A code was called and although an emergency team resuscitated him, he continued to sink fast.

I stayed by his side as Tuesday passed and Wednesday passed. David was not conscious but at times squeezed my hand. Then came the time when eternity called the loudest at 6:30 Thursday morning. My children, David and Becky, and my sister, Barbara, were with me as, together, we dealt with this difficult time. David's brother, Gordon Beam, Rev. Chester Heath and Rev. Kenneth Roles were some of the ministers present with me in that intensive care room when we watched his heart monitor race rapidly upward to what seemed to be its highest registration and then sink so slowly and so surely to the bottom to form a long straight line. I had been quietly singing in his ear, "What a Day That Will Be When My Jesus I Shall See."

David's God called him, and he left us. Heaven's door opened and David entered. He opened his eyes in a new world that he had waited for so long. I am sure he started immediately to rejoice on the streets of Glory. If they have microphones in Heaven, David might have grabbed one and begun to spin around in a holy dance, switching that microphone from one hand to the other as he turned, like so many saw him do in church. His suffering was ended. His greatest joy burst forth into eternal reality.

Yet on that October 15th morning of 1998, I walked out of the Forbes Regional Hospital thinking for the first time, "I am a widow!" My house was empty when I returned to it. A hollow feeling wrapped itself around me. Shock! It is really true. David is gone. My gradual but intense recall of the last three days brought a flood of tears.

It soon became obvious that death keeps the bereaved moving. There was no stopping. I had to meet with the funeral director, pick out a casket, choose clothing for David, and provide obituary information. How can one think logically at such a time?

The hours of this first day without David crept by slowly, giving me much time to ponder my situation and adjust my thinking. Four o'clock was approaching. It would soon be broadcast time. Should I do it? How will we tell the listeners? I knew that I didn't want anyone else to do it. I had to be the one. The Lord would have to help me. We had faithful listeners who had been praying and would be waiting and wondering. By the grace of God, I prepared a statement and the first segment of the broadcast and planned for Ken Roles to take over after I completed my part.

Nine and one half hours passed since David left us. It was now four o'clock, October 15, 1998, as radio station WAVL Apollo opened the lines to Export. The Echoes of Faith program intro, "Someone is Praying for You," gently rolled out over the sound waves into the homes of listeners in many cities. Now it was my turn and I began.

"Thank you for joining us for this Echoes of Faith radio broadcast.

This is Claire Beam, and I want to tell you right at the beginning that today's will be a very significant broadcast, unlike any others that we have ever done. For today I am sitting at the microphone in my husband David's chair. That is not too unusual, except that this time he will not be returning to this chair.

Yesterday morning I sat in another chair alongside my beloved husband's bed, in the Intensive Care Unit of the Forbes Regional Hospital in Monroeville, Pennsylvania. I sat there as David's physical condition rapidly deteriorated. I took his hand and leaned close to his ear, and sang quietly to him: "What a day that will be when my Jesus I shall see! When I look upon his face, the One who saved me by his grace. When He takes me by the hand, and leads me to that promised land, what a day, glorious day that will be!" It wasn't too much longer until Heaven opened and my beloved husband David was transported to his Heavenly home."

"It is a sorrow and loss to all of us who are left behind but, as for David, He has WON the race. Please reach out and worship the Lord as you listen to this very moving song:"

SONG: I'VE WON

"How different it is for the child of God at the time of death. Natural grief and pain are present; yet the Lord pours in his wonderful all-sufficient strength and grace. What would we do without Jesus? Thank God for the great Comfort of the Holy Spirit. Perhaps you are going through difficulties right now that have left you in turmoil or grief. You need the Lord. You need his help, his strength, and his grace. If you would like to call in to our phone lines with your prayer request or comments, our phones are open right now.

"When all of your life is over, will you be ready to meet the Lord? I know my husband was, and I have thought about how he may now be rejoicing with his mother, his father, and with his co-laborer Joseph Dutka, but most of all, with Jesus. The most important goal of your life needs to be that you will live in such a way that when you face eternity, the Lord will say: Well done, my child."

SONG: Well Done My Child

I left the auditorium studio desk with Brother Roles handling the rest of the broadcast. It was all that I felt I could do that day.

Hundreds came to the funeral from many parts of the country with words of comfort, honor and tribute. It brought great consolation to my heart as so many shook my hand, hugged me, expressed love, and promised prayer. David was buried in the Free Gospel Cemetery, located on the campus he loved and lived for. My name is engraved on the same beautiful granite headstone but without a final date. Some day we shall all meet together in the air, to dwell forever with the Lord.

On Sunday following the funeral a man walked up to me and handed me a stack of hundred dollar bills to fully pay for that headstone. His life had been greatly impacted by David's ministry. I knew the Lord was showing me that He would continue to take care of every need in the days ahead.

Two weeks later my 88-year-old mother, Helen Clara Wilmerton, went to Heaven. Two weeks later we learned that, during those stressful days, the unborn child within my daughter Becky Hawk, also died. I was glad we all knew "the God of all comfort." I was upheld by God who was my refuge and strength, my very present help in trouble. How blessed I was to be surrounded by people who loved me! I learned through it all that his grace is sufficient for even this. And the peace of God, which passeth all understanding kept my heart and mind through Christ Jesus.

The Day After Yesterday

Your yesterday is that time when you came face to face with grief. Your yesterday may have been a long time ago or just recent. Right now, you can be assured that the Lord who saved you will turn the sorrows of your yesterdays into the victories of today. God has provided loving words of assurance to those who have felt the sting of sorrow. He knows what it is for his only son to die a cruel death. With loving arms outstretched to us he assures us that:

- "...weeping may endure for a night, but joy cometh in the morning" (Psalm 30:5).
- "...in all of these things we are more than conquerors through him that loved us" (Romans 8:37).
- "...thanks be to God, which giveth us the victory through our Lord Jesus Christ" (1 Corinthians 15:57).
- "I can do all things through Christ which strengtheneth me" (Philippians 4:13).
- "The LORD will perfect that which concerneth me..." (Psalm 138:8).

God's plan for our lives doesn't end when crises appear. The next months became times of grieving, hours of intensive prayer and recommitment of my life to the Lord and his will, for this new phase of my life. I was fifty-seven years old. Things could never be the same for me. Grief and sorrow, adjustment and change found their sufficient counterpart as I bowed my knees in my living room and met with the King of all kings. The difficulties of life faded in his presence and I soon returned to teaching and other responsibilities. I was blessed with God's peace. Inner joy sprung to life again coupled with anticipation of what the Lord might have planned for me.

F.G.B.I. Moves Forward

During the next years, many changes occurred. The leadership of Free Gospel Bible Institute moved into the hands of Rev. Kenneth Roles and then to Rev. Garry Smith. God had a purpose for the ministry of each of these men at the school. He used them to fulfill those purposes and bless the work of God.

I had been a widow for about three years when Rev. Thomas Peretic and his wife Donna came to Free Gospel Bible Institute to serve as President and President's wife. Their world suddenly changed as they left behind an active church and a history of pastoring and ministering for years. They walked onto a campus that would become their "sacred ground" and to a school that would become a living extension of their lives.

I observed them as they adjusted to the unique work before them, where the day never seemed to end and the morning always came too soon. They gave themselves without reserve to the work of the Lord. As I listened to him preach, I sometimes wept with thanksgiving for his passionate vision and burden, for his anointing and courage to do whatsoever God put in his hand to do. They became God's hand extended to Free Gospel Bible Institute and also to me.

After the death of my husband, David J. Beam, my world changed too. By the time the Peretics arrived I still was uncertain as to where I fit into the scheme of things. I was faculty member and librarian, and tried to help wherever I could. I had always worked behind the scenes, always carrying a burden for the school. It was at this time that the Lord, through Brother Peretic, established me in my own office within the administration offices. It was my joy to be in that office and to be a greater part of the work than I had ever been. As time passed I became very aware of the hand of the Lord directing my steps, involving me more in the work and responsibility of F.G.B.I..

Mike and Luann Petit had been an integral part of the Bible school for many years, teaching, going on ministry—Luann serving as Dean of Women, Mike serving as Treasurer and eventually Academic Dean. Then the day came when the Lord called them to go to the Philippines as missionaries. They would leave behind positions to be filled.

In the absence of an Academic Dean I offered to review Brother Petit's office files to determine the responsibilities of an Academic Dean so I could help prepare whoever would step into that office. I did so with great interest, searching out old files, compiling notes and instructions for policies and procedures for the next Academic Dean. Then came the day when Brother Peretic entered my office and stated that I knew the job so well now, and was already fulfilling many of the responsibilities, that he would like for me to now become that next Academic Dean. With Board approval it became a thrilling opportunity. The Lord knew the silent growing desire that He had caused to grow within my heart. He privileged me to work more closely with many aspects of the work.

The work of God increased and moved onward. My responsibilities gradually increased. I was blessed to teach more subjects and loved it. Personal Evangelism was always my favorite and then Christian

Counseling. Pentecostal Dynamics was a powerful course when the truths of Pentecost and Gifts of the Spirit put a fire in the hearts of seniors and teacher alike. I loved the challenge of Apologetics and the studies in Biblical Anthropology. Some years I taught General Epistles, Introduction to Christian Literature and Fundamental Theology. I spent many hours studying and preparing to teach, building courses that would benefit young men and women who would someday go into the ministry. It was exciting and also hard work. I loved it and acknowledge it to have been a tremendous privilege.

I will never forget the mighty moves of the Spirit that came through the years. One time it began as a senior's breakthrough that filled the class with Pentecostal praying and dynamic responses to God's touch. The sounds of Pentecost got louder and louder until the juniors in the downstairs classroom came outside to see what was going on upstairs.

In a short time the outpouring spread outside…then came the freshmen across the patio already shouting and praying. Seniors came out their classroom door to the top of their steps where one after another began to preach powerfully to their congregation that was now spread out across the campus. It was campmeeting time everywhere with people shouting and praying, running, dancing in the Spirit, praying for one another, getting filled with the Holy Ghost. The call of God came strong into many hearts.

Another time I remember how the Holy Ghost moved like a wave through the auditorium that was filled with people. As people were worshipping, suddenly the Spirit of God moved on those on the platform and almost as one, they began to dance in the Spirit. Then it almost visibly moved to the first rows in the front, where people were slain in the spirit, some shouting. Like a mighty wind the Spirit continued sweeping from the front pews to the rear until the entire sanctuary was alive with Pentecostal worship. It was moves of God like that and the powerful preaching, plus the intensive studying of God's Word that shaped and molded generations of students and resulted in great men and women of God going forth into full time ministry.

18

THE ROOM CALLED "ORDINARY"

Early one morning God spoke to me as I prayed in the Holy Ghost. I was telling the Lord all over again that I wanted Him to use my life and that I was willing to do anything He wanted me to do. Down deep in my spirit the voice of God asked me a question that would affect the rest of my life: "Are you ready to step out of the room of the ordinary and step into the room of the unordinary?" It was a powerful question. God was speaking to me. His presence was so real. I wasn't sure what God had in mind, but I was very willing to follow his plan for my life and told Him so. It was such a significant moment in my widowed life. It excited me and made me know something more was ahead for me.

Because of all the mighty works of God, I am sure no book could hold all the history and stories related to my life at F.G.B.I. I was there in God's will, in God's time, and was thrilled with the awareness of his continual presence with me. There were times when family situations drew me to my knees and even flat on the floor in intercessory prayer. I had learned how to battle against principalities and powers and rulers of the darkness of this world, against spiritual wickedness in high places. I was not afraid of the devil. God had filled me with his Spirit. I knew that the Third Person of the Trinity dwelt within me. By his power I prayed and in his Name I saw God pull down strongholds, cast down imaginations, and every high thing that exalteth itself against the knowledge of God. I saw Him bring into captivity every stray thought to the obedience of Christ.

Many years before, I sat on my couch alongside a great woman of

God, Sister Jane Daoud, who drew my attention to Luke 9:1—"Then he called his twelve disciples together, and gave them power and authority over all devils, and to cure diseases." She related accounts of the power of God working mightily though her. Once in another country, she visited a place that was either a hospital or an insane asylum. A demon possessed woman was kept behind bars because of her uncontrolled violence. No one would go into that cell. The workers simply put her food through the bars. Everyone had great fear of her.

Sister Daoud asked them to let her into that cell. They refused, saying the woman would kill her. Sister Daoud insisted and at her own risk they quickly unlocked the door and let her in. The demon possessed women lunged at her with a fierce and eerie scream. Sister Daoud pointed her finger at the woman and commanded, "Come out, in the name of Jesus." The woman dropped to the ground and Sister Daoud went over and picked her up. The demons were gone. She was a different woman. The two of them walked out of that cell arm in arm to the utter amazement of the staff.

On that couch in my living room, Sister Daoud spoke in my ear, "Did you read that? What power did Jesus give his disciples? Power and authority over what? How many devils? ALL devils." She almost shouted it in my ear, "ALL DEVILS. REMEMBER THAT!" It did something to me. I felt God impart a new kind of faith in my soul.

A New Fire in My Soul

As I sought the Lord He filled me with a passion to pour out my soul and by his design, I began to receive invitations to speak at ladies retreats and conferences, and mother-daughter banquets. I will never forget those focused events when women of God joined together in fellowship and spiritual pursuit. Usually such gatherings were geared toward Christian ladies, but I clearly recall the wonderful move of God in one retreat where a preacher's adult daughter listened to the preaching of the Word. She had been backslidden for a long time, but God was getting her attention. The Spirit of the Lord dealt with her heart in such a way that she fell to her knees at the altar, weeping with great conviction and repentance. How glorious was the shout of joy from everyone who witnessed her upraised hands praising the Lord for restoring her relationship with Him!

In Castleton, Virginia, I spoke at two mother-daughter banquets. God had an interest in these ladies and drew them together to receive from Him. Sister Shirley Savage and other dedicated ladies led the way to a time of great blessing.

My return to Lorain, Ohio, for two different women's conferences awakened a million memories of my years there as Youth Director. Although time had passed, my love for the people was still alive. That's what made it so special to again minister to this gathering of ladies and to the whole church that Sunday. "For Such a Time as This" and "Women in Pursuit of Excellence" were the themes of those unique days.

Broadway Assembly is a beautiful church, blessed with a wonderful, caring pastor, Brother Matthew Jones. It was my privilege to stand on that same platform from which he preaches so well. There I looked out at the faces of all those registered attendees and prayed, "Oh, God, You know the need of each life. Please direct me!" What a blessing it was to pray with people around the altar and witness the work of God in their lives. Some important commitments were made during those days.

I never stopped feeling awed and thrilled when asked to be a speaker at these kinds of events. How would you feel if you were invited to preach at the Pentecostal Ladies Retreat in Kimberling City, Missouri; and the Blue Grass Ladies Retreat in Lebanon Junction, Kentucky; as well as at the Christian Retreat in Carlinville, Illinois? Believe me, I was humbled to be asked and full of joy at the opportunity. I took each challenge very seriously. During preparation, nothing was more important than earnestly seeking the Lord for his will and anointing. "Lord, let me be emptied of self and filled with You" was my prayer. When I arrived at these places I was ready and excited to give what the Lord had poured into me.

Do you know what kind of woman is most valuable in the church? Not the fashion icon or the social media addict; not the lover of the world or the "perfectly-hair-styled, too-proud-to-shout" woman. In this day of compromise and lukewarm experiences, there is an urgent need for godly women who are filled with the Holy Ghost, who know how to pray in the Spirit and live holy lives. These are the church's treasures! A revival of repentance and Pentecost in the women of the church can result in a needed, last-days' move of God. Lord, let us experience it soon!

Doors of opportunity for ministry were increasing. Occasionally, I took student groups to churches but usually was home staying "with the stuff." Eventually I began to go on more student ministries, sometimes preaching in a service. Then came a change that really excited me. Brother Peretic asked me to be the summer representative to the various camps and churches. I travelled about 3,500 miles each time and was thrilled to have opportunity to speak in many of these places. It put a new fire in my soul. It was a life-changing experience for the next several summers. It thrilled me to see people saved, filled with the Spirit, and called to ministry. I saw numbers of people respond and become students at F.G.B.I. What a great joy it was!

Was this the beginning of what the Lord meant when He spoke to me shortly after David's death when I was earnestly praying? He asked me if I was ready to step out of the room called "ordinary" and step into the room called "unordinary." Back when I was in Medway, Maine, I preached no less than four times a week. During my time in Lorain, Ohio, I preached almost every Thursday night, but the next phase of my life, at Export, was different. I had to get used to not being out knocking on doors and witnessing every day. There were student preachers by the handful, ready and anxious to preach. This was school. There were classes to teach and the responsibilities of a school to be fulfilled seven days a week. Some aspects of my life had to be adjusted.

It is important to have the ability to adjust to each phase of ministry that the Lord might place you in. Someone once correctly quipped, "Blessed are the flexible, for they shall not be bent out of shape." For the next years I rarely preached, except for Mother's Day or some other special times. That was not hard for me to adjust to. I still had the joy of teaching my classes and expounding on the truths of God's Word Monday through Friday, but now something was changing.

I wasn't sure what was happening, but I felt an excitement within and an anticipation of God working out his plan for me. It was not necessarily preaching that I desired, but rather any opportunity to reach lives for the Lord and win souls. That desire burned within me. Many times I saw God work in people as I prayed with them around the altar. Sometimes it was from a pulpit. Many times it would be in ordinary places like a mall, or a hospital, or a home. I just longed for God to use my life for his glory.

Once I had preached in a morning service at a campmeeting in Arkansas and when the night service concluded with people praying at the altar the pastor motioned to me. When I went to him, he pointed out a particular lady and asked me to go pray with her. He indicated that she might need deliverance. I simply walked up behind that lady who was standing with many others at the altar, laid my hand on her head and with prayerful authority uttered the words, "In the name of Jesus!" That's all I said, and she fell to the ground. She began to thrash about, and others gathered around to pray for her. I knelt quietly behind her head and began to pray quietly so she could not hear me. I didn't want to put any suggestions into her mind. I said, "In the name of Jesus, if there are any demons involved here, Jesus gives me authority over you." She thrashed more. Continuing to pray quietly I said, "In the name of Jesus, I command you to come out!" Next, I experienced something I never had experienced before. I know that lady could not hear what I was saying. There was too much other loud praying all around her. But my voice was heard by that which possessed her.

Out of her mouth, in a strange voice, came the clear words, "No we won't."

It stunned me, but I quickly responded, "Yes, you will. Come out NOW!"

It was a strained and long drawn out "Noooooooo!" that came out of her this time.

It may strike you as unusual, but when I heard those voices of devils, I had to smile. They were afraid of me. It was evident by the way they responded. It encouraged me on. "In Jesus Name, you cannot stay. You will come out NOW!"

"No!" it continued.

This went on for about ten minutes, until finally that woman stopped her jerking and screamed. Then she lifted her hands and began to cry out, "Jesus!"

I knew the victory was won and instructed her to repent of her sins, to ask Jesus to cleanse her from all evil, to come into her heart and save her now. She responded positively and earnestly prayed. It was amazing to me. When I questioned her later I learned that she had suffered with voices in her head continually, but now they were gone. What a mighty Savior is Jesus my Lord. No power is greater than his.

I will always remember an afternoon service at Russellville, Arkansas youth camp, when I was privileged to preach. The message was burning in my heart and, with great Holy Ghost liberty, the Lord filled my mouth with his message. It is difficult to find words to describe that experience, except to say that when it happens you are motivated by an exciting and bold zeal that is not your own. By the Spirit's anointing words flow from your mouth with power and continuity that thrills you and accomplishes God's purposes. You just know it is God and not you.

At the altar call, a great movement of young people swept to the front committing their lives to do the will of God. Some got saved. Some were refilled with the Holy Ghost. I believe some were called to ministry. It is just one of those special memories in my heart.

The first time I went on this 3,500-mile circuit, my journey began by plane, then continued with a rented car, and finished with a return flight. What an experience! I took with me the great big display board promoting Free Gospel Bible Institute. I had suitcases with not only my own belongings, but school CDs, catalogs, applications, and more. What an interesting event it was to pick up my luggage and then try to make it out of the airport! I finally found a cart and balanced the big display board on it as I went.

I was so excited. I had never done this before. I had never even been inside Oklahoma and certainly not to that famous Bristow holiness campmeeting, and now I was going! I'm sure they had no idea how amazed I was when they permitted me time to say something in the youth service. I was thrilled and felt the Lord as I testified and urged young people to give their all to Him—to answer the call of God. I hoped my invitation would bring them to visit the Free Gospel Bible Institute display table in the camp bookstore, where I intended to show up and talk to whomever would come.

When the meeting was over, I observed various young people gathering around the display that was filled with pictures. Some chatted happily as they came across photos of some student they knew. Hands reached to pick up the yearbook on display and flash through the pages. Some stood at a distance, just staring and listening, before joining the investigating crowd.

"What do you think God is going to do with your life?" I inquired of one girl.

Looking serious she replied, "I'm not sure, but I want to do his will."

"Have you ever thought about going to Bible school?"

One young man answered that question with, "Never! I'd never go to Bible school!" He was enrolled the next year!

"I've been praying about it" was a more common answer.

Many young people are anxious to do something for the Lord. They have heard good preaching and have surrendered to whatever the will of God is for them. They are ready for the next step. It was rewarding to watch those who did come to school, as they grew spiritually and became wonderful servants and handmaidens of the Lord.

It may have been two more years that I made this journey and was blessed beyond words with the opportunity. A burning desire for God to use me wherever He wanted and in any way He wanted, filled my heart and influenced my life.

That September 2004 brought more new students to join the juniors and seniors. A great move of the Holy Ghost came almost like the sound of a mighty rushing wind into that opening welcome banquet. It was the start of another year, with God supernaturally preparing young men and women to become anointed preachers and laborers in his harvest field.

An Unforgettable Alumni Convention

As autumn turned to fall it was time for another Alumni Convention which was always on the first Thursday and Friday of October. It was a thrill to see former students arrive and gather with testimonies of what God was doing in their lives. I looked forward to seeing them once again, after having taught them for three years. They were "my children" and I loved and prayed for them.

As I entered the auditorium for the evening service I was amazed to see such a crowd. There were many more present than usual, and they seemed to come from so many of the earlier classes as well. My smile just wouldn't leave as I greeted one person after another. This was surely going to be a memorable convention.

Brother Gene Garrison (the alumni president) was opening the service when he suddenly walked away from the pulpit, came down the aisle to me, took me by the arm, and led me up to the platform to sit on a seat that looked like a throne decorated with beautiful flowers. At least, that's what I think happened. I was in so much shock that I hardly knew how I got up to the platform. How in the world did they keep this secret from me? The whole thing was a planned night of honor for me.

Realizing what behind-the-scenes planning and organizing had been done, I was astonished. What an honor! Tears filled my eyes as I looked on the faces of so many of "my treasures" filling the auditorium. You know they can't do something like this without a PowerPoint, putting half of your life on public display. I loved it! Where did they ever get those pictures? I soon discovered that my lovely daughter Becky was the biggest culprit. How sweet it was of her to dig around and find all those memorable scenes. I sure did look different when I was seventeen. The whole thing was very moving and emotional for me.

They soon passed the microphone around in the congregation to various graduates who said such nice things about me. Do you know what it felt like to be seated up on that throne, listening to all these words? My heart swelled with love for my Lord. I was overwhelmed with thanksgiving that He had blessed me with the indescribable privilege of influencing all these lives. I couldn't hold back the tears or the smile that became an extension of my heart. "Thank You, Lord." "I praise You, Lord." How could I help but be overjoyed at this scene? Then more words flowed from those on the platform, concluding with the presentation to me of a beautiful plaque and lovely flowers.

Brother Garrison began to dismiss the people. He said there would be food and fellowship, and they all streamed out. I thought it was odd that everyone left and no one came to shake my hand or talk to me. Brother Garrison delayed me "for pictures," he said. Several were taken, and gradually he led me out the back door toward the patio.

I thought we would be going down, into the dining hall for the fellowship. Why are we going outside? What were all those people doing over on the patio? He was moving me quickly now and as I was rushed down the pathway toward the crowded patio my eyes caught sight of something huge in the middle of the patio....

What was that? It was covered with white paper, and bows and balloons Oooh! It looked big enough to be a...CAR! I gasped, as I realized that hidden behind all that paper was a big gift for me and began tearing the paper off. Cameras were flashing to catch the absolute shock and amazement on my face as I unveiled a brand new, silver 2005 Toyota Camry XLE with leather interior and a rear spoiler. I couldn't help letting out a shriek as it dawned on me, "This is my car!"

Then the stories began to come to the surface about how difficult it was to hide all this from me...how my daughter came into my kitchen asking me to help her ice some cookies, when it was really time to leave for church. She seemed desperate for me to help, so I delayed leaving and hurriedly spread icing. They were trying to hide the car from me and were frantic that I might go up to the library where they temporarily parked it. They surely maneuvered around me and successfully maintained their secrecy!! I was indeed absolutely surprised and thrilled!

I learned later that the alumni planned this over almost a year, raising the money from F.G.B.I. friends and alumni. I once sneaked and saw the list of donors and was humbled and amazed. My heart is very thankful and appreciative for the love and efforts of so many.

One Extraordinary Summer

When summer of 2006 rolled around and it was time for that journey to camps and churches, I surely was travelling high class—in my new Toyota! For part of that journey, it was again my privilege to go to Bristow campmeeting. Many people were arriving and I was able to get a seat between two great ladies, Sister Kazie and Sister Doreen Cox. We were waiting for the night service to begin when two men came down the aisle and stopped at our row. One brother leaned into the row and looked in my direction.

"Sister Beam, may I have a word with you?"

I agreed and quickly stepped out into the aisle. The second brother was James Martin and seeing the uncertainty on my face, he said: "You don't know who this is, do you?"

He certainly looked familiar, but I could not recall who he was. It was embarrassing, as I momentarily stumbled with words until Brother Martin rescued me.

"This is Brother Bob Goodwin!"

I immediately knew him and flew into a flurry of words. "Of course, I know you, Brother Goodwin. Brother Beam and I came to OBI at your invitation and preached for the graduation convention while you were president. I was in your house and met your wife and family. She prepared such a great meal, and I especially loved her angel biscuits. She sent the recipe to me. I remember that she was having terrible problems with arthritis. How is she doing?"

And then the unexpected came like a thunderbolt—"Oh...she passed away. She's with the Lord now." He had been married to his wife Joyce for fifty-five years.

It stunned me. Something about that announcement affected me. I can't explain the unanticipated feeling that I suddenly sensed deep inside.

"I am so sorry, Brother Goodwin. I didn't know," was all that I could say.

The conversation faded to an end as the service began. At the close of the service I saw him briefly, and then he was gone, but something unexplainable had been planted in my soul.

The next day as I gathered and loaded catalogs, CDs, and display board in my car Brother James Martin was also leaving. In passing, he simply said, "Let the Lord have his way." What did he mean? It was always my commitment to let the Lord have his way in my life!

I still had hundreds of miles to travel and several camps and churches to go to before I would arrive back home in Export; yet that journey was one like I had never experienced before. This was not like me. I have never been a lonely person, yet these unfamiliar feelings of loneliness began to come in waves. "God," I said, "what are you doing to me?" Did five minutes in the aisle do this to me?

I couldn't understand it. Thoughts of Bob Goodwin wouldn't stay out of my mind. For the eight years of my widowhood I sought to conduct myself in a godly way, keeping my thoughts on the Lord and his will. Now, with great effort I struggled to put my mind on the ministry ahead, crying out to God for his anointing and power. More than anything my desire was to be used of God, to be his handmaiden wherever He wanted me. Yet every mile I travelled, there was one thing I was strangely sure of—there would be a letter from Bob Goodwin waiting for me when I arrived home.

I was thoroughly enjoying this time of my life. It was thrilling. The Lord had caused me to step through a great door of opportunity, and my heart was filled with joy for the privilege of involvement in this kind of ministry. I loved it and did not entertain thoughts of marrying again. I was satisfied. However, when I arrived home after that journey, the first place I went was to my mailbox. I unlocked the office door, walked through the main office, stepped into the area for mail and looked at my box. Something was there. Could it be? Could it really be what I had been thinking? The thought was loaded with a million flashes of wonder.

There it was—a small envelope addressed to Claire Beam—but it had no return address. What was this Missouri postal stamp? Of course, it had to be from him. I slowly opened it and read each word, and reread it—a greeting: "It was good to see you…I pray that the Lord will bless your trip to the Philippines." It was short and thoughtful. What a gentleman! Now what? What did this mean? We had only talked for five minutes in the aisle. I hadn't even remembered his name.

Testing the Waters

Was this esteemed man of God now testing the waters? I knew he was. I could hardly believe that this was happening. Now it was my turn. What would I do? This was the first time in eight years of widowhood that a man may have been showing personal interest in me.

My hiding place, my refuge, my place of peace and assurance called to me loudly. "He that dwelleth in the secret place of the most high, shall abide under the shadow of the Almighty" (Psalm 91:1). Where his shadow is, the Almighty is also. That is where I want to be. I have learned to flee to the place of prayer, to take all to my God who knows all and doeth all things well. God saw that little letter lying on the floor before my outstretched hands. In fact He already had it all figured out, because He who is sovereign initiated it, He who promised to direct the paths of those who trust in Him planned it and, in his own way and time He would bring to pass his divine will for his child's life.

This was a new experience for me at my age and while still uncertain as to God's plan, I guarded my thoughts and moved cautiously. "Oh, Lord," I would pray, "what are you doing? Is this of you? You know that I don't want anything that is not part of your plan for my life." Yet, deep down inside I had a growing inclination toward believing that our meeting at Bristow was not a coincidence, but a divinely providential moment. I felt free to respond to his letter, telling him about my plans for the mission trip to the Philippines.

Early in the mornings I walked the campus praying before the sun came up...seeking...wondering...asking for only God's will. With each little step of progress I found my heart filling with greater joy. A few more letters and numbers of phone calls would follow, pulling each of us more seriously to the place of prayer for God's direction.

I was sixty five years old. I had been a widow for eight years. It was different to begin thinking about the possibility of a new relationship. One night in the dark, I took a slow walk across our campus, past the little white church, across the wet grass, and to the little cemetery where David was buried. I just stood there in the dark, with light sprinkles of rain coming down, my hand resting on David's grave headstone.

I knew he wasn't there but, spontaneously, I began to talk to him, knowing he was not really hearing me. It just came from deep inside. "David, we had thirty blessed years. Now Bob Goodwin seems to be coming into my life. What would you think about that? I know you thought highly of Bob. I think you would approve..." and, like a fountain my tears suddenly poured out, my body trembling, as I stood there in the night. I cried hard for several minutes. I didn't expect that but believe it was an emotional response to "letting go" of the past and a release to "step into the future." I walked back to my apartment in wonder and peace, knowing God had everything in control.

Things were moving forward with Bob and I. It soon became evident that the hand of God was guiding our thoughts. Our lengthy phone calls always wound up with praying in the Holy Ghost. What a great joy it was to hear Bob talking to me one minute and then hear him suddenly begin to pray in tongues. I would get down on my knees with my phone in my hand as both of us prayed across the miles in the Spirit, for some time.

Philippine Missions Trip

Several weeks after meeting Bob at Bristow, I was scheduled to leave for a missionary trip to the Philippines. Along with Brother Charles Pahlman, founder and director of the SENT (Student Evangelism to the Nations Teams) missions program, I was to accompany a team of students from Free Gospel Bible Institute. This was a dream coming true and actually my second trip to the Philippines! My heart beat with great anticipation of the opportunity to minister in what would be like another world to me. Mike and Luann Petit, diligent and dedicated directors of the Free Gospel Church missions work in the Philippines, gave me a room in their house. There I sought the Lord and met Him as I lay flat on the floor praying. I felt his mighty power and presence. I knew I could do nothing without his touch. I needed the Lord now and longed to see Him work powerfully on this mission trip. Nothing compares with that sense of his anointing when you stand up to minister to the people.

What happened during those days was nothing less than a mighty rushing wind blowing through that church and igniting people everywhere with Pentecostal fire. The anointing and power of God was manifested in such an amazing way, bringing another upper room experience. God poured out his Spirit like a river flowing until all over the place students were falling, kneeling, standing, and weeping as they were filled with the Holy Ghost. The Third Person of the Trinity came in fullness, and the sounds of people speaking in tongues was heard from one side of the church to the other. I believe there were sixteen baptized with the Holy Ghost during that revival.

The ten-day ministry was packed with continual opportunity for each of the team members to minister. There were Bible school classes and chapels to teach and preach in the day and revival meetings at night. I preached eleven times in ten days.

Brother and Sister Petit found a multitude of ways for us to reach out to the people. They took us to minister in the prison. They took us to churches in the mountains and out of the way *barangays* (small villages). They arranged and took us to an outdoor crusade that was another highlight of my life. They organized a caravan of vehicles, filled with students, musical instruments, lighting, electrical and sound equipment and took off through these narrow roads until they pulled into a very dark area where I could see nothing.

I thought, "This is where they are having this crusade? Where are all the people? It is pitch-dark here."

And then my eyes were opened. I began to see shadows of movement that became people scattered all over what I thought was an empty field. They were already there—some with little chairs, some sitting on a wall, some standing. The word had gone out that we would be here, and the people came from all over. So quickly the men set up a generator, put up lights and prepared the huge concert-like platform for the amazing things that God would do. Talented pastors played and sang so beautifully drawing the crowd closer. It was glorious to hear and see. I was to be the speaker, and was so deeply moved by the opportunity that I walked around in the shadows, brokenly, yet excitedly observing this gathering of needy people. I felt such awe at the privilege to reach out for their souls. It is an indescribable joy to plead for the souls of men, to pull them in, to passionately persuade them to come to Jesus. At the altar call thirteen people came for salvation. I will never forget it.

Such experience causes the Lord's Great Commission to burn so much more intensely in my soul: "...Go ye into all the world and preach the gospel to every creature" (Mark 16:15).

Our F.G.B.I. mission team was moving with God, touching many with his message. God used each member powerfully. They were great. They worked in so well that they became like brothers and sisters to the students there at Faith Bible Institute.

Another exceptional blessing was the ability to bring great joy to some of the pastors and their families. Before leaving for the trip, our team had raised enough money to give brand new motorcycles to four needy pastors. We also paid up front for the school-related financial responsibilities of the entire school of students for one year.

During those days in the Philippines I received several emails from Tom Peretic, president of Free Gospel Bible Institute. I was stunned and unprepared for one particular message. When I read the words, "CONFIDENTIAL: I have asked Bob Goodwin to become part of the faculty at F.G.B.I.," I couldn't believe my eyes. I read it again and again. I thought it must be a joke...but it was true.

There was nothing official going on between Bob Goodwin and me yet. Things appeared to be moving in a predictable direction, but now this! My mind went in a whirl. Now what? Sudden apprehension over all the possible implications gripped me, but it wasn't long until that uncertainty seemed to slip down beneath rising waves of expectation. The hand of God was surely shaping things up. I had reason to believe that his promise was becoming reality—

"Commit thy way unto the LORD; trust also in him; and he shall bring it to pass" (Psalm 37:5).

Violent Illness Interupts Witness

Our wonderful ten-day mission soon came to an end and we began our flight back to America. It has always been my prayer that the Lord would seat me by someone that I could witness to. This time it was two Chinese young people, probably in their mid-twenties—a man and a lady whom I assumed were either married or in a relationship of some kind. They were busily looking at laptops and books so I waited for an opportunity to start a conversation. Eventually I asked the lady seated next to me where she was from and learned they were returning to the USA from China to finish their degree programs. I prayed for the Lord to direct me and felt impressed to show her a picture of my daughter Becky and her husband, Jim, with their four children (at that time)—Jessica, Briana, Andrew, and David.

"These are my four grandchildren!" I exclaimed.

She stared at it for a long moment. "Four children? They are all your daughter's children?" You could almost feel her amazement. She quietly spoke to me with a sad look on her face, "In China we can only have one child."

I knew the Lord had directed me right. This opened the door wide. I began to tell her more about my grandchildren.

"They sing together and sound so wonderful. They sing songs about God and how He loves all people and wants them to come close to Him. They sing songs about Jesus and how he can bring salvation, peace and joy into lives."

She was listening with interest as I wondered what direction to go in next. Then the Lord put the thought in my mind to give her the Chick tract that I had in my purse, "This Is Your Life." She received it readily and began intensely reading it, page by page. After a few pages she tapped on her "husband's" arm, interrupting his studies, and seemed to tell him (in Chinese) to look at the booklet with her. They both began reading it, and I was earnestly praying that they would grasp the message. Just think of it! What an opportunity it was to give the gospel to two people from atheistic China whom I may never see again.

I was anxious and ready to get to say more to them, but something began to happen to me that was very distressful. I was suddenly becoming terribly sick. I had to quickly jump up and race to the bathroom, all the way down the long aisle, and there became violently sick. I could hardly stand up and had to lean against the wall. When it was possible, I opened the door a little and signaled for help, asking for one of the mission team to come to me. I needed almost a full change of clothing. The young lady put her arm around me and held me, assisting me back to my seat.

Just as I thought I was feeling a little better, a second wave of sickness hit me. I had to find a different restroom to race to since the other one was unusable (so violent had been my vomiting). Such weakness overtook me that I was not able to stand. My condition deteriorated until a call was made for any doctor who might be on board the plane. How special it was to have a young doctor respond who was actually returning from his honeymoon. He stayed with me the whole time. My blood pressure had dropped and he was administering oxygen to me. I lay back with no strength. The Captain even came into the room and expressed to me the option to turn back and land somewhere sooner than planned.

I told him, "No, I'll be all right. Please don't turn back."

It was a very long flight that finally landed in Minneapolis. No one moved. In through the front entrance came paramedics with a stretcher who gently moved me down the aisle and out to a waiting ambulance. Can you imagine this great trip ending like this?? All that I can conclude is that it was some bad tasting food that we ate in flight or the devil trying to stop me from giving further witness to that Chinese couple. I survived it all and was sorry for all the stress I probably caused everyone. I stayed in the emergency room for a couple of hours and seemed over the episode so was released to try to catch our connecting flight to Pittsburgh.

It was such a blessing to have Joanna Brady stay with me and accompany me the rest of the journey. We pooled our remaining money together and paid for a taxi to catch our connecting flight back to Pittsburgh. We almost didn't have enough, since most of us gave all our extra cash to needy people in the Philippines. The devil was mad and I'm glad. Great were the victories won and lives changed by the gospel message and the outpouring of the Holy Ghost. To God be the glory!

Bob and Claire Goodwin, married December 15, 2006.

Bob Goodwin, preaching. It became revival time across the country.

Lolo, Montana- Some of the wonderful people at Sun Valley Church where God brought a mighty revival. Pastor Mike Metzger is standing in the center back, behind his wife with the yellow top.

Mighty revival praying at Lolo, Montana.

Choir at the Holy Church of God in Savannah, Georgia where Ryan Ralston is Pastor. God's power was manifested nightly in the revival.

Claire ministering in the Philippines.

*Ministering at the national convention of El Faro de Santidad,
in Ahuatlan, Jalisco, Mexico, near Guadalajara.*

*Bob praying for people at the Fountain of Life conference
of many tribal people at Juja, Kenya, East Africa.*

*Claire praying with many receptive women
at woman's conference in Kenya.*

*Massai Security Guards at our tent city during a
safari in the Maasai Mara National Reserve.*

Eastleigh, Nairobi, Kenya- "Little Somalia"-
where we were surrounded by Muslim people.

19

A SUCCESSFUL PURSUIT

B ack at Export, we were immediately in full swing with preparations
for the opening of the new school term. Communication between
Bob and I continued, and plans were solidified for him to come to
Export to teach an intensive course on the Book of Acts to senior
students 9:00 a.m. until 4:00 p.m., Monday through Friday, one week
per month; September, October, and November. The spirit of Bob
Goodwin was about to invade the F.G.B.I. campus.

It was an exciting night when the Peretics acted as "chaperones,"
driving me to the Pittsburgh International Airport to pick up the
arriving Rev. Bob Goodwin. It would be the first time we would see
each other since our meeting at Bristow, three months earlier. We had
been sending some pretty nice e-cards back and forth, and the Lord
was confirming his will in each of our hearts. I guess we both agreed
that "older" people can't waste any time, because before that week was
over, I had said a happy "yes" to his proposal in the middle of a very
busy airport terminal. It was hard to believe, but true: I, Claire Helen
Beam, age 65, was now officially engaged to be married!

This man, Bob Goodwin—my husband-to-be—was no ordinary
man. God saved him at seventeen, baptized him with the Holy Ghost,
and soon after called him to preach the gospel. For over sixty-five years,
he faithfully fulfilled that call in evangelistic work, pastoring churches,
serving years in district youth work; as a sectional and general presbyter,
district secretary/treasurer, as president of a Bible college, administrator
of A.C.E. (Accelerated Christian Education) schools, in radio ministry,

Bible institute and college teaching. He is an anointed Pentecostal preacher, a true revivalist, and a prayer warrior. Surely Bob Goodwin became my gift from Heaven for these latter days of my life, and he loves me and I love him.

God's Unique Planning

How unique it is that we met at Bristow, Oklahoma, campmeeting on June 15, 2006, and that Bob would propose to me on September 15, and that we would marry on December 15 of the same year! F.G.B.I. was the place, and all the students, plus hundreds of other guests, were present. My daughter Becky was maid of honor. My son David walked me down the aisle. My granddaughters, Jessica and Briana, were flower girls. My grandson Andrew was the Bible bearer. Bob's son Tom was his best man; his grandchildren, Benjamin and Jenna, lit the candles. Almost all of our family members participated in the ceremony. It was an unforgettable event that not only united Bob and I in holy matrimony, but also brought together two families as one.

One highlight of the wedding was when Bob sang to me so beautifully *Ever Faithful to You* by Jeff and Sherri Easter. The presence of God was powerfully felt as we knelt together in prayer and communion. His Spirit swept over us with sweeping surges of heavenly language. Tears of joy and worship flowed freely. We were committed to do his will together! All of this culminated in the greatest announcement of all: "I now present to you Mr. and Mrs. Bob Goodwin," and down the aisle we jubilantly marched!

We will always remember how Brother and Sister Peretic rescued us when the expected caterer for our wedding reception unexplainably dropped out of sight just days before the wedding, sending a message that she could not take care of the reception. What a catastrophe! What would we do now? Bob tried to reassure his distressed bride-to-be that the Lord would work everything out and sure enough, within a few hours the Peretics had begun to organize the entire school to carry out the work. It was one of the most beautiful sights one could see... all those students lined up at the food-filled buffet tables, wearing their white aprons and big white chefs' hats. We will never forget their great labor of love.

Off we went on our honeymoon to Virginia. Our hearts swelled with great joy and excitement. Bob was almost seventy-six and I was sixty-five. Imagine two old folks like us getting married! All dressed up and walking together hand in hand, we often draw smiles from people, especially if we are wearing matching colors and Bob has his Stetson on his head. After all, it is not possible to hide our happiness. We are so blessed. God has been so good to us. Our lives remain committed to Him and his will.

Returning to Export, we settled into our residence on the campus of Free Gospel Bible Institute and continued the next several years teaching, preaching, praying, and laboring for the Lord. It was a time of great opportunity to influence the lives of students preparing for ministry.

We rejoice to know that the directions of many students' lives were clearly changed by the Lord. How often Bob would be kneeling beside young men with his arm over their shoulders, earnestly praying for them, dealing with them, urging them to make the surrender to what God wanted in their lives. Tears would flow. You could see their body shake as they broke in submission, saying that vital "Yes!" to the Lord.

Late at night the prayer rooms would echo the voices of prayer. Battles were fought and won on bended knees and often flat on the floor. God was preparing a mighty army to go forth into all the world with his gospel. Jesus said, "...I will build my church; and the gates of hell shall not prevail against it" (Matthew 16:18). I believe He was doing that very thing in those prayer rooms—building his church, person by person. These are the ones whose lives will make a great impact in turning their world upside down for Christ.

A New Dimension to my Life

Marriage to Bob added an enriching, new dimension to my life that included traveling to do the work of an evangelist. At the close of the 2007 spring semester we headed out for summer revival meetings and much more. I was so excited as I anticipated all the new places we would go and what great things the Lord would do. It was a long journey to Dimmit, Texas but exciting to see Bob and Doris McCutchen and begin preaching in their church. I had never before met Brother McCutchen, but as we all met for a morning prayer meeting and I listened to him pray, I already knew what kind of a man he was. Oh, what prayer I heard, coming from deep within—a heartfelt crying out to God with a passionate earnestness! I had no doubt that he was a man in touch with God.

Our travels continued Northward into Colorado and to the unforgettable Royal Gorge. It took some effort, but Bob persuaded me to ride the aerial cable tram that glides along at 1,178 feet above the Arkansas River. At a time like that, it is reassuring to be ready to meet God. After you have been on that cable ride, and then walked across that Royal Gorge Bridge (one of the world's highest suspension bridges), and then dared to ride one of the world's steepest incline railways all the way down to the river, what else is there to fear in life? The worst part of walking across the bridge is that the walkway planks have space between them enabling you to see all the way down and, to top that off, the bridge sways!

My sense of awe increased even more as we came to Colorado Springs and drove the nineteen-mile mountain highway up to the summit of 14,000-foot Pikes Peak. There you can see for 130 miles and look down to view the tops of mountains. It was a breathtaking sight that became the inspiration for the writing of *America The Beautiful*. It is also the backdrop for the amazing rock formations that we saw at the Garden of the Gods.

Back at our car, we headed toward our more serious purpose, ministry in Denver. Chad Hardin had pioneered the Bible Way Tabernacle, a greatly needed ministry. He was reaching the homeless, drug addicts, people of the street, and others. With great desire we also longed to see these souls pray through and find hope in Jesus. Some came without shoes, poorly dressed, and hungry. Some slept in little tents in the woods. Yet the altars were filled after the preaching of God's Word. Heaven has recorded the eternal results of that work.

During this summer, we took our special companion with us— Truffle, our little chocolate poodle. He was so obedient and gentle and a joy to have with us, but one night we almost lost him. Pastor Hardin took us to a restaurant after the meeting and as the food arrived, our phone rang. "You had better come for your dog right now. He has been barking and we have called the police." It was incredible! This was the motel manager calling us! Truffle was never any trouble but evidently reacted to noises. Whenever security came into the room he would be as calm and quiet as ever. Not knowing what this manager might do with Truffle, we hurriedly left our food and raced back to the motel to rescue our beloved poodle. It was a lesson learned. We couldn't ever leave him alone in a motel. That eventually led to a sad departure when we had to give him away to friends.

Wonderland was yet before us. How breathtaking it was to visit Rocky Mountain National Park! I had never before seen mountains like these and, at every turn of the road, it seemed I'd say, "Ooh, look at that!" The beauty never ended. What an awesome Creator is our God! This was to be the journey of journeys for me. I had never traveled to these parts of the country and Bob was giving me a trip I would never forget. We had only been married six months at this time and were treasuring this time together.

It was almost like a second honeymoon to stop at the unique Victorian village of Ouray, Colorado, called the Switzerland of America. Departing, we entered the scenic and harrowing Million Dollar Highway from Ouray to Silverton, Colorado, called a dangerous ride. The two-lane blacktop forms a swirling ribbon through the San Juan Mountains—the wildest and most rugged peaks in the Colorado Rockies, with high cliffs and thousand-foot drop-offs, and no guardrails in places where you wanted them. My heart beat faster and I held my breath at some turns. Bob couldn't help but drive carefully with all of my little shrieks. It surely was an incredible experience for someone raised in New York City!

Passing Durango we were anxious to see the Cliff Dwellings of Mesa Verde National Park. We hiked down the hilly path and stood right there where Pueblo Indians once lived in these dwellings carved out of the cliff rock. I wondered, did anyone ever take the gospel to them?

What Hit Our Car?

Our journey took us next into New Mexico where we were heading for a campmeeting. When we traveled through Albuquerque, a most unusual thing occurred. Traffic wasn't bad on I-25 and we were moving along, enjoying the beautiful scenery. That's when we were suddenly startled by a very loud noise that sounded like a large rock crashing into our car. Bob pulled over to the side of the road and we both got out and examined the car on all sides but could find no sign of damage.

We soon headed back down the road, wondering what that noise was. It was only a matter of minutes until we came upon a terrible accident scene. Cars were stopped and people were peering over the side of a restraining wall, down into what must have been quite a drop-off. A child's bicycle, a small puppy, and other debris were scattered on the road. How horrifying and how sad! Evidently a family's RV camper had gone over the side of the mountain. Instantly, we understood why we were delayed down the road. God's mercy had prevented our involvement in this dreadful crash. It must have been an angel of the Lord who banged on our car!

Miles piled up on the odometer. I adjusted my position in the passenger seat. Gospel music filled the air from Enlighten XM radio and my eyes glanced over at my husband. "How blessed I am!" I thought, married to this wonderful man who treated me like his queen. Surely he is a special gift from Heaven for me for this time of my life."

Now as we headed southwest of Alamogordo, he promised to take me to a place advertised as being "Like No Place On Earth." What I saw convinced me in a hurry. As far as my eyes could see, everything looked like hills and fields and dunes of white sand. We were standing in one of the world's great natural wonders, the glistening White Sands of New Mexico—275 square miles of the world's largest gypsum, dune field. Bob parked the car at the edge of what looked like a massive river of snow. It was all sand, pure white sand. It wouldn't be right to leave without the most unusual experience of climbing these snowdrift-like hills. We laughed, and sunk in, and climbed some more. At the top, we stretched our necks to drink in the magnificent panoramic view, then sat to slide down, tumbled and laughed some more.

Seeing all of these amazing things on this journey filled my heart with wonder and praise to my God. How great and mighty He is! There is no God like our God. I kept praising Him over and over for his great and beautiful creation. Surely God is the God of wonders; yet He is more wonderful than all the wonders He has created! The Psalmist declared it: "Thou art the God that doest wonders..." (Psalm 77:14a).

We were about to see more of his mighty works as we made our way to beautiful Cloudcroft, New Mexico, where we would stay during the holiness campmeeting in the Sacramento Mountains. Devin Birdsong was the director and Aaron Brock was one of the preachers. Bob also preached. It was a great time in God's presence. He poured out his Spirit and touched many lives.

It was a dark contrast to leave the place where the Spirit of God was alive and working and drive through a place where the spirit of evil was alive and working—Roswell, New Mexico, New Age and UFO Capital. "Aliens Welcome" read posters at restaurants. A large UFO museum seeks to draw in visitors. The common view at Roswell is that there is no God; aliens are our creators, and they are coming back to invite us into a larger cosmic community and a new age of enlightenment. However, it is to these the Lord of the harvest sends us: "...Go ye into all the world and preach the gospel to every creature" (Mark 16:15).

A Disastrous Yard Sale

Following this summer of travel and evangelism, we returned to Export to prepare for the opening of the 2007 fall semester. Much needed to be done, but we didn't anticipate how challenging a task it would become to finally clear out my remaining possessions from my former apartment and storage cabin at the school. I had so much accumulated and really did not know what to do with all of it. Bob and I had moved much of it to our present dwelling on campus, but much remained. Many of these possessions represented forty years of my life. Some stored items were accumulated "junk" but much was of personal value to me. I gave quite a bit away and sold some larger furnishings to antique dealers. Brother Jeff Hough came and purchased my treasured, small baby grand piano. Due to space limitations, Bob and I had chosen to keep only his beautiful Yamaha keyboard in our home.

The final conclusion of the matter was that we needed to have a yard sale. Our time was limited. We had to get things moved out for incoming staff. For days we worked feverishly to organize and box what we were able. By the time we lugged about ten long and heavy folding tables out of the little white church storage place, set them up in the upper parking lot, carried all our belongings there and set them up, we were very tired. We tried to stay hopeful that people would see our advertisement signs in several locations and come ready to buy.

It was a disaster. A small number came and purchased items but, by the end of the day, we could see the trouble we were in. We tried to stay late, hoping others would come. We couldn't put it all back and couldn't find anyone who would take it. Finally we concluded that we had to dispose of it. I can still hear the cracking and breaking glass as we dropped box by box of my things into the dumpster. For all kinds of things that night, it was "goodbye!" I must admit that was difficult: yet my life has been built upon eternal values, and the things of this life are not as important as my relationship with the Lord and his wonderful peace. I count it all joy to walk in the center of his will at any cost.

As students began to arrive for the fall semester, excitement built and everyone was in high gear. Students found their rooms, unpacked and met roommates. Faculty busily divided their time between greeting incoming students and parents, and helping all kinds of things go smoothly. I, for one was anxiously waiting the first day of teaching. To me, it was ministry poured out of my heart.

When you love what you are doing, time flies, and that is exactly what happened from that August 2007 opening registration day through the first and second semesters. Another graduation sent twenty-seven more into the waiting harvest field.

Honking horns and revving engines signaled the dramatic departure of students, heading for summer destinations. Final goodbyes echoed across the campus and soon everything came to a dead stop. The week had spun like a whirlwind, with activities and end-of-year administrative responsibilities, and now the place was almost emptied out. In the next few days, faculty and staff would roam about completing maintenance and cleaning tasks to enable the semester school closing.

Heart Surgery: Is this Really Happening to Us?

Bob and I looked forward to the summer of revival meetings

scheduled on our calendar. We were filled with anticipation of what the Lord would do. In spite of the very busy recent days, we had even managed to organize what clothes we would take on the journey. However, at the moment, we had some assigned tasks to complete.

We headed for the library to complete work there when suddenly everything changed. Very casually, Bob looked at me as we entered the library doors and said that he was having chest pain. He hadn't told me that he had actually been experiencing them for a while. Now those pains were intensifying. All other plans came to a halt as I quickly drove Bob to the hospital where he was given immediate care, including an EKG.

"There are some abnormalities on this EKG that we shouldn't ignore. I would like for you to have a stress test today," the doctor told us as he proceeded to make the necessary arrangements.

This was so unexpected! Bob was unable to pass the stress test. The cardiologist immediately scheduled him for a heart catheterization for the next day. This was unbelievable! So quickly every plan changed for us. He was kept in the hospital overnight and went for the catheterization in the morning. I waited and waited for a report. It seemed to take so long. I had called our family members to let them know what was happening.

Then I saw him. I rushed into the hall to meet with the doctor and heard these words: "Well it looks like he has five blockages to his heart that will require heart bypass surgery."

I was stunned. It was an absolute shock. "Are you sure? This is hard to believe," I objected.

"Come with me and I'll show you," he beckoned, as he headed through secure surgery department doors. Illuminated and enlarged computer images revealed the truth. He pointed out the undeniable blockages and took me to my husband. There it was agreed that a quintuple coronary bypass surgery would take place on Monday.

It was Memorial Day Weekend 2008, when Bob was admitted as a patient at the Westmoreland Regional Hospital in Greensburg, Pennsylvania, a short distance from our home. He spent the long weekend there, waiting for surgery on Monday. Together we prayed earnestly for the Lord to take control of the whole situation. Sometimes the unexpected happens, but not unknown to our God. It was a disappointment for Bob to take his phone in his hand and call all the pastors who had scheduled revivals, and cancel each one. Doctors had confirmed that he would need the summer to recuperate and receive therapy.

How grateful I was for the presence of our families at this time. Some came from Pennsylvania and from as far away as Alabama and Texas. Understanding the seriousness of this surgery and recovery kept me praying. I remember a moment in the waiting area when the gravity of it all weighed down on me and brought tears. We were all facing this together. It was our son-in-law Jess who, at that particular moment, put his arm around me and comforted me. I found it necessary to make a trip to the hospital chapel to pray and then called some preachers to pray.

What a wonderful sight it was to finally enter the recovery room and see Bob's eyes open! It was all over. He would be all right. The Lord would see us through…and He did. All of that summer Bob progressed through therapy and exercise and when school reopened in the fall, he was able to begin teaching again.

First Corinthians 15:57 expresses my praise so well: "…thanks be to God, which giveth us the victory through our Lord Jesus Christ." He is the source of our continuous strength and joy. Things happen in life that make us wonder, but He keeps us from going under. All of my life I have felt the assurance of the Lord's leading and direction. It is in the place of prayer where I have met with Him and struggles have melted away. His Word brings assurance of his continuous working in our lives. "Being confident of this very thing, that he which hath begun a good work in you will perform it until the day of Jesus Christ" (Philippians 1:6).

20

A Dramatic Next Step

Following God's Leading

God had blessed Bob and I in bringing us together for these latter days of our lives. We were both very happy and fully committed to the will of God. As the days turned into weeks and months became years, our thoughts in prayer began to turn toward a new step. The Holy Ghost was speaking to our hearts. Separately, Bob and I waited on the Lord and sought his will, trying to stay sensitive to the voice of the Spirit. After lengthy time the Lord gave us the assurance of his direction. His time had come. It would be a dramatic move for me to depart from F.G.B.I. after forty years of ministry there. Much prayer produced an excitement in our hearts about stepping out into full-time evangelism. In God's time we submitted our resignations and began extensive plans for our departure. The Lord began to open the doors for revival meetings in several places and our ministry calendar began to come to life!

I had many responsibilities and desired to provide the best help I could for whoever would step into those roles when we were gone. While I continued teaching and taking care of the library and Academic Dean responsibilities, I also stayed up late compiling an Academic Dean policy and procedure manual. At the same time, we were packing, disposing of many things we could not take, and planning for a final auction of most of our belongings. Bob and I had thousands of books accumulated. Some were given to the library, some were sold, and many were given away to students. We knew we couldn't take everything with us and needed to put some things into storage. The questions were "Where?" and "How?" but God so faithfully made the way where there seemed to be no way. Two Oklahoma pastors, Bruce Ganze from Bartlesville and Doug Peper from Chelsea, along with Bob's son, Tom Goodwin from Plano, Texas, willingly drove all the way to Export to load and transport our belongings and take them to storage in Oklahoma. How thankful we are for their friendship and help!

It was May 30, 2009 when we drove off the F.G.B.I. campus onto Italy Road, heading out into a brand new life. As we drove away, I couldn't help looking back toward the last view of the property with mixed emotions, memories of forty years of my life, and great joy for all the Lord had accomplished. It was with awe that I anticipated the life of an evangelist's wife. I could not have imagined how thrilling it would be. I had taught Personal Evangelism for forty years. Now I would be even more actively involved in personally reaching the hearts of sinners, ministering the saving, delivering, Gospel of the Lord Jesus Christ across the United States and in other countries, along with my wonderful "preacher-husband," Bob.

As we made our initial plans, we incorporated our ministry under Calvary Pentecostal Revivals and also established our web page (www.calvarypentecostalrevivals.org) to publish our schedule of meetings and revival reports.

Living the Life of an Evangelist

Our first preaching service near the close of our time at Export was at Midway Pentecostal Church, Carlisle, Pennsylvania, pastored by my son-in-law, Jim Hawk, and my daughter Becky. It was a very special time that included the privilege of dedicating our grandbaby, Wesley Philip Hawk, to the Lord. As our journey continued family visits would become less frequent. It would be a price to pay to be away from my children, Becky with her five children, husband Jim, and David with his son River.

After meetings in Lewisberry, Pennsylvania, with Pastor John Andrews, we headed out on the first long trip of our new life together on the road.

Preaching Revivals

Bartlesville, Oklahoma, here we come! Bob was mightily anointed by the Holy Ghost as he preached night after night. What a blessing it was to see how God was using him! We saw the Lord put his seal on these beginnings, as he saved souls and baptized hungry hearts with the Holy Ghost at Pastor Bruce Ganze's church.

During one service, I noticed a lady standing near the altar with hands raised and lips moving in prayer. The Lord drew me to this lady named Barbara, and together we prayed that she would receive the baptism of the Holy Ghost. She was coming closer. The Spirit of the Lord was all over her, soon evidenced by stammering lips. Then like an explosion, she was filled and out of her mouth came a language she had never learned. It was such a thrill to her to finally receive that, at one point, she stopped speaking in tongues and, with a big smile on her face, just sighed loudly in amazement, "Oh, my!" and went back to speaking in tongues. What human words can appropriately express the wonder of the Third Person of the Trinity coming to dwell within a human vessel! Barbara's "Oh, my!" expressed it for her!

Before we left Export, Bob had said to me, "You know, we are going to sing together!" This was a new and challenging venture for me. I had to learn songs. I had to learn to harmonize. I prayed earnestly for the Lord's help. Most of all, if I sang, I wanted to be anointed. There was much to learn and prepare for in these evangelistic days ahead, and I was thoroughly enjoying it!

It wasn't far from Bartlesville to Bristow and we had reason to head that way. Bristow holiness campmeeting is the largest USA open-air meeting of the independent holiness movement. In a way it was a celebration for us to come back once more to the place where God initially began to bring us together. It was exciting to greet many as we came into the service. It happened to be a very special service consisting of the funeral for our beloved Sister Gail Myers. This one little lady was used of God for over fifty years to establish over 150 churches in Mexico, Panama, and Columbia. What a challenging 2 hours it was, hearing from many speakers, including preachers and converts all the way from Mexico!

The tires on our 2006, red Chevrolet Equinox continued to roll down many thousands of miles of road. We had it packed to the ceiling because we expected to just keep going. It was our "red salsa" and a place where Bob and I were always together and always conscious of God's hand upon us, and his angels watching out for us. During those first seven months of evangelizing, the Lord opened ministry doors in many places including: Oklahoma, Illinois, Ohio, Indiana, Virginia, West Virginia, Alabama, Kentucky, Arkansas, Kansas, Tennessee, Texas, and North Carolina. We stayed in many kinds of places as we held revivals, including church evangelist quarters, pastors' homes, motels, bed and breakfast housing, homes of church people, trailers, and even a beautiful lakeside home in Florida.

We were sure we were about to see the Lord move in the scheduled revival meetings at Chelsea, Oklahoma, when the devil tried to stop us only a few miles from our destination and our car came to a swerving halt. All the way from Texas the roads were fine. Then suddenly we came on a low area where snow had melted and turned into a slushy freeze. We immediately saw several cars in the ditches on both sides of the road. A truck was heading toward us and, at the same time, a pickup slammed on its brakes right in front of us. There was a lot of sliding that night, but the angel of the Lord certainly encamped around us and protected us in that moment. Bob kept tight hold of the steering wheel and got us through. Fenders were lying in the snow near one car; others were thrown to the side. In just a few minutes, we saw several ambulances, police cars, and fire trucks. So many times we have thanked the Lord for the prayers of God's people and his continuous protection as we have traveled over thousands of miles.

We were happy to arrive at Calvary Lighthouse Church and to be greeted by Pastor and Sister Doug Peper. It was thrilling to walk into a church, full of people who were excited for revival to begin. Each night was an adventure of climbing higher spiritually. Many sought the Lord earnestly at the altars.

One night a pastor brought a homeless man who was an alcoholic. It was evident that the Word of God and the move of the Spirit were affecting him. Conviction kept him restless, getting up and down, going in and out, and then to the altar where several prayed for him. Toward the close of the service he had not "gotten through" but spoke out during some final testimonies, declaring, "I'm not going to leave this place without getting saved." Back to the altar he headed to earnestly pray again. Thank God, no case is too hard for the Lord.

Testimonies verified that numbers came through to fresh fire in their souls, including many young people who were praying. Some broke free from the oppression of the enemy as the power of God moved within them. The sound of heavenly language rang through the building. Some were refilled and claimed renewed victory. "I feel like the Lord came and saved me all over again," declared one young lady.

It was a joy to see the Spirit of God moving upon one praying young lady and to hear her say, "He refilled me with the Holy Ghost and called me to the ministry. I believe he wants me to go to the mission field." Gifts of the Spirit were present in almost every service.

On what was supposed to be the final night of the revival we saw the greatest move of God of the whole week. Bob preached a powerful message on "A Challenge to Pentecostal Revival," anointed by the Holy Ghost, and God brought the breakthrough. Almost the entire church headed to the altar in response to the altar call, but one young man stayed seated in the back. As I prayed with others I kept watching him and sensing that the Lord was dealing with him. "Yes, Lord, I'll go to him." I knew it was God and turned around and walked down the aisle to that last row and slipped in beside him.

"Young man, are you saved? Are you sure you'd go to Heaven if you die tonight? Is everything right between you and the Lord?"

In just a few minutes he responded to the tug of the Holy Ghost on his soul and made his way to the front with me at his side. A miracle was about to take place. He knelt in front of Brother Goodwin, who laid hands on him and prayed with him as he surrendered his life to the Lord. After a while he returned to his seat. However, this was just the beginning. A newfound experience had begun to stir his life. He was hungry for more and headed back to the altar again, where many gathered around him praying. It turned into a glorious time of old-fashioned seeking the Lord, hands raised, tears flowing, the Holy Ghost changing the heart and life of an earnest seeker. What a joy it was to see the work of God in progress and the evidence of brand new salvation reflected in the glow and broad smile on this young man's

225

face. Before the revival was over he was also gloriously baptized with the Holy Ghost.

During all of this, others broke loose in holy dance and a Jericho march. The pastor leaped for joy at all God was doing and asked Brother Goodwin if he could come back on Sunday and continue for that week. Amazingly, our next scheduled revival had just been canceled due to severe ice conditions, so God made it possible to continue at Chelsea. The pastor declared that they "have had many good revivals, but never one like this." That's what happens when the Lord takes control! How thrilling it was to see the Lord save more souls the second week and fill more with the Holy Ghost! One young lady, who got saved the first week, was filled with the Spirit the second week. She brought her mother the next night, and she also got saved.

The amazing final night of revival became another mighty demonstration of the Spirit of God working, as conviction drew people to the altar even before preaching began. Some were getting saved, some were seeking the Holy Ghost, and only God knows all that was accomplished. There was shouting, dancing, weeping, rejoicing, praying in the Holy Ghost.

This all culminated in a grand public display of true revival and changed lives during an outdoor burning of worldly things that several people brought in bags. Everyone rejoiced, praised God and sang as many bags went up in flames. One newly saved and baptized young man stepped forward to testify, "There goes all my worldliness. I give myself completely to the Lord." To God be the glory! Great things He hath done.

This life of an evangelist brought great unexpected blessings like what happened at Florence, Montana. We will never forget our revival at Sun Valley Church, where Mike Metzger is pastor. Even before the revival began, there was fasting and prayer for a move of God. It is evident that the Lord heard those prayers and a joy to see the response to the preaching that filled the altars with earnest prayer.

The power of God stirred one young man to step forward and pour out his heart to the congregation. It seemed he just could not stop telling what God had done for him and how he now wanted his life to be different.

In the midst of it all, the father of this young man came to the platform and joyfully put his arm around his son as he declared to all, "This is the greatest thing that has ever happened." That son later confessed that God took him "out of his shell." Truly changed, he urged people to press on and acknowledged his own spiritual need.

God had amazing plans for this revival. Soon people headed for the altar and the rest of the service was a powerful outpouring from Heaven. Groups of people prayed for each other. Even young converts were crying out to God and getting filled with the Spirit. Four were baptized with the Holy Ghost and several came through to needed re-fillings. Struggling lives won great victory.

While there in Montana, we witnessed a snowball fight in June and had the privilege of enjoying meats we had never eaten before: bear, elk, moose, and mountain lion. All of it was delicious!

Witnessing Along the Way

While in Branson, Missouri, for a three-day minister's conference, we took time to do some shopping. We were about to make a purchase when we discovered that a good discount was available if we obtained a free coupon book. So while my husband waited, I headed down past several stores in this outlet mall to find the tiny specialty nut shop that provided them. Mouth watering aromas filled the place, featuring still warm praline pecans, chocolate covered hazelnuts, and giant cashews. However, my objective was to get a coupon book. My entrance drew the immediate attention of a decent looking young man behind the counter, who was working on a computer. In just a minute, I had what I came for, but I had a hope for something more. Could I somehow get an opportunity to witness to this college-student-appearing young man who seemed to be about twenty-five years old with neat brown hair and a slight beard?

Attempting to engage him in conversation I casually asked, "Have you worked here long?"

"Just a few months" was his reply.

"It seems like a nice place to work. Do you enjoy it?" I continued.

"Yes, it's quiet and I have time to do my work."

"Are you doing school work?" I asked.

He looked up with a serious half grin and answered, "No. Actually I'm writing a book."

I was immediately intrigued and inquired, "What kind of a book?"

His quick and excited response showed me he was more than ready to talk about it.

"It's about culture and how it has affected various people groups historically."

He began to briefly describe the cultures of the Greeks and Romans, and others. He spoke of their religious cultures, their gods, and their society.

Meanwhile, my mind was spinning and my heart was praying, "Lord show me how to break through to him with your message."

"That is so interesting. I've written a book too."

His eyes lit up. "Really! What is it about?"

"It's about culture too and how it has woven itself into the most intricate parts of people's lives. It's easy to see how the conditions of a culture can strongly influence people's thinking, their marriage, their future and so much more," I asserted.

He was alive with comments and agreement.

Still praying for the Lord's direction, I continued. "I have written about people whose lives have been negatively affected by their culture and my experiences in pointing them to help for their lives." (I was referring to my book, Reach Them One By One, filled with witnessing and soul-winning experiences.)

"That's incredible." He was listening and interested.

"The Romans had their gods. The Greeks had theirs. India lists 330 million gods. Yet none of them could lift their devotees out of the mire of despair and hopelessness. I point people to Jesus as the Savior, who can give them new lives."

He was very receptive and immediately let me know that he is also going to include Jesus in his book as one who had a great influence on the culture and people of his day.

"How much do you know about Him?" I asked.

To his weak reply I responded with conviction, "How can you

write about Jesus unless you first come to know who He really is? Before you go very far, you should at least read the Gospel of Saint John in the Bible. It is a true picture of who Jesus is. Do you know that He claimed to be God?"

He was nodding his head and hearing me, at least acknowledging Christ's existence.

"If he knew he wasn't God and deliberately tried to deceive the people, then He was a deceiver and a liar. If He wasn't God but simply had delusions of grandeur, then he was a lunatic, not to be believed. But if what he claimed is true and He really is God, then we all need to hear what He has to say."

I wanted so much to continue our conversation, but knew I had to leave. He had enjoyed the talk and thanked me for the insight as I left.

May God move this young man to inquire further and discover true salvation through faith in the Lord Jesus Christ. It was time for me to return to my patiently waiting husband.

21

BEYOND OUR BORDERS

Mexico Ministry—March 2010

"Habla usted espanol?" I have asked that question many times when encountering people who appeared to be Hispanic. Texas is home to more than 9.5 million Spanish-speaking people. When I speak those Spanish words to them, they light up thinking I know their language. However, I know only a series of phrases—just enough Spanish vocabulary to sometimes get me in trouble—like the time I meant to say "Dios le bendiga, hermano," which means "God bless you, brother." Instead, I said, "Dios le bendiga, hermoso" and wondered why that old man's eyes got so big as he stepped away from me. To my embarrassment, I had said, "God bless you, handsome." So much for my Spanish!

My interest is to catch their attention and gain an audience so I can leave them with the gospel message in their language. I love witnessing to them, sometimes even in very limited broken phrases—just enough to turn their thoughts to Jesus. Once when Bob and I were witnessing in a trailer park we came to a couple who knew hardly any English. Our feeble attempt to communicate with them brought smiles from all of us. Finally I just began to sing to them a Spanish chorus that I knew:

"Soy feliz Cristo me salvó, Soy feliz Cristo me salvó,

Soy feliz Cristo me salvó, Canta gloria aleluya,

Cristo me salvo."

Their faces brightened with broad smiles as they grasped the message that Jesus can save. I love the Spanish language and Spanish people. Once in a very early Oral Roberts crusade in New York, I was a personal worker and led a Spanish lady to the Lord simply by reading the "soul-winning scriptures" to her from a Spanish Bible and praying with her. Maybe someday before we go to Heaven we can become more fluent in the Spanish language. It certainly is a need for these days.

Bob and I rejoiced when plans finalized for us to go to Mexico in response to Missionaries Marvin and Isabella French's invitation. We were requested to preach at the National Convention of El Faro de Santidad, a fellowship of churches headed by Brother French.

It was March of 2010 when we said farewell to our son and daughter-in-law, Tom and Jeanna Goodwin and departed Dallas-Fort Worth International Airport on a two and a half hour flight to Guadalajara, Mexico. This journey would take us about fifteen hours below the border. We were excited as we anticipated this wonderful opportunity to minister where we have never been. The French's met us and transported us about an hour to their home in Ahuatlan, Jalisco, a small town filled with people needing the hope of the gospel.

Suddenly we were in a new world and our hearts were stirred with a desire to touch some of these lives for the Lord. As the meetings began, people came from long distances, filling every seat in the church, in the aisles, and outside the church, where many more were seated and standing. Well over 300 people came.

It was an overwhelming experience to see how God moved in these services. From Friday through Sunday night, we were in church nineteen hours. On Saturday, the morning service went from 10:00 a.m. until 2:00 p.m. We had lunch and then continued from 4:00 p.m. through 8:30 p.m. No one was in a hurry. They sang and worshipped, and prayed with great devotion and love for God. The altar services went on hour after hour, seemingly with no desire to stop.

Bob preached the night services and I preached on Sunday morning, with the help of an anointed interpreter—one of the best, Missionary Jeremy Brooks, who pastored another church about an hour away. Missionary Craig Benner preached a tremendous message one morning on "The Second Mile," and the Mexican brethren from the fellowship blessed us with their testimonies. Missionary Marty French interpreted powerfully for Evangelist Doug Cornet, as he shared his miraculous testimony of God raising him from the dead after a head-on, fatal crash.

Pronounced dead and with his body covered with a sheet in the hospital, the doctor suddenly felt like lifting the sheet and checking him again. To his amazement, there were signs of life. For the next period of time, although alive, Brother Doug suffered extensively but experienced miracle after miracle as his body was gradually healed. His lower jaw bone was crushed, broken in 100 places. It was painfully wired together and his mouth wired shut. His excruciating pain came to an end suddenly when God miraculously healed him in a church service. The next day, the doctor compared x-rays and told him, "I don't know how it happened, but someone has given you a brand new jaw bone that has no evidence of ever having been broken."

No wonder Brother Doug shouted his message theme: "GOD IS GREAT! DIOS ES GRANDE!" The people lined up from the front of the church all the way to the back and out the door waiting to be prayed for. There were testimonies of victory and healing ringing out. God surely moved!

The power of God was manifested mightily during these meetings, as people came to the altar for salvation. One backslidden man ran to the front and earnestly cried out to the Lord; a young man bound by drugs and terribly oppressed by the devil dropped to his knees seeking God's help and deliverance. God brought victory to a very depressed and suicidal young man.

An entire Catholic family came to give their lives completely to the Lord on Sunday morning. What a joy it was to see numbers baptized with the Holy Ghost! Others testified to being healed. Numbers of young people testified to being "set free" by the Lord. Hallelujah! The Lord was present to save, heal, baptize, deliver, and sanctify. It was great!

Missionaries Marvin and Isabella French are two amazing people who came into Mexico many years ago, when they were in their mid-twenties. They came to nothing but a land of idolatry, with a burden and vision to reach these people with the Gospel of Christ. They won souls, built churches and houses, making their own bricks.

In those early days as opposition to the gospel mounted, they experienced much persecution and danger, but God watched over them. Opponents sought to drive them out, even sending a truck load of soldiers to do the job, but the Lord was with them and caused the truth to triumph! Due to the prevalent "law of vengeance," people shot and killed their enemies. Brother French had a body guard that carried two guns because some opponents infiltrated the church services wearing their guns, wanting to kill this missionary. Through much sacrifice, prayer and hard work, they paved the way for the gospel and established many churches that believe in and practice old-time Pentecost and holiness.

During the convention, I heard what sounded like a group of people singing in the street, as they marched past the church property. Sister French informed me that it was the Catholics, who would like to close down the work. They sing and chant prayers for it to happen. What a great joy and liberty comes to these dear Catholics when their eyes are opened to the wonderful love of God, to the forgiveness and Salvation that Jesus gives!

In between services we enjoyed eating a true Mexican meal with a lovely Mexican family and also sampling cactus, green gravy made with many crushed peppers, and so much more, with all the people seated at tables on the church property.

The dusty narrow roads of Ahuatlan are filled with people selling tacos, burritos, fruit, rice and beans. Modest, open store fronts line the streets that are crowded with traffic from many bicycles, people walking or riding on horses, in cars, trucks, and motorcycles. Dwellings built close together created a tight neighborhood, where countless noises filled the air. Donkeys brayed, roosters crowed, and birds chirped through the background sounds of laughter, people and their families talking, children playing, and even a loud band practicing almost nightly in the village.

We will never forget this wonderful experience and privilege of involvement in this great work of God. As we flew back to America our hearts burned within to see a continuing move of God in our meetings.

"I Have to Get this Holy Ghost"

Every revival rekindles strong desire to see lives redeemed, recharged, and changed. Once while preaching in Jacksonville, Florida, an elderly man approached Brother Goodwin. His wife had prayed for his salvation all their married life and both were now so happy that he was saved. With great emotion and excitement he pleaded, "I have to get this Holy Ghost. I want it; I can't go without it." Well, that surely lights a preacher's fire! That night the man was at the altar with others praying but in his earnest desire, he would hardly stop talking. He talked so fast, almost non-stop, telling the Lord what he wanted, until Brother Goodwin gently advised him that he wasn't giving God a chance to do anything. He had to stop so much talking and let God do his work.

Perhaps he didn't like that. At any rate, he soon got up and went back to his seat. Yet there, he continued on with hands raised and his mouth moving rapidly, pouring fourth his continued plea to the Lord. I felt the Lord send me back to him where I said, "Brother, the Spirit of the Lord is all over you." It truly was! "He wants to fill you and do the talking, but you have to let Him. Just stop talking so fast, and open your mouth, and worshipfully express your love and praise to the Lord. "Jesus, I love you. Hallelujah!" "Give Him your voice." As he relaxed his talking and began to worship, the Spirit of God took over and quickly filled him. No one has to persuade the Lord to give him the gift He has already promised! It surely was a shouting time for everyone who witnessed it.

A brand new family had all recently been saved except the youngest son. Much to the family's joy he finally did surrender to the Lord the next night. What also happened then to his mother is a strong reminder that God can choose when He wants to work in a service. This service was ending and people were beginning to leave when something happened that would have a lasting effect on this entire family. The mother had been praying for quite some time in the service, at her seat near the back, when she was suddenly moved on by the Holy Ghost. It didn't matter to her that people were leaving. Her voice rose above all others and soon began to echo heavenly words of the Spirit, as the Lord baptized her with the Holy Ghost.

This newly converted family looked on in utter amazement. They had never seen their mother behave like that! What we call the end of a service may only be the beginning of new things God wants to do. Suddenly people came back into the church, returning to their seats and to the altar, as a Pentecostal wave swept across the congregation, filling more hungry seekers in the same wonderful way.

Kenya, East Africa 2010

Vibrant memories of our earlier ministry opportunity in Mexico were still fresh in our hearts as we prepared to venture out in this same year on an even more challenging missions journey. What a thrill it was when we received the offer of an all-expense-paid trip to Kenya, East Africa! Students, whose lives had been affected by the ministry of Free Gospel Bible Institute twenty-five years before, now wanted us to come and see what God had done through those seeds planted in their hearts so many years ago. These three men have been best friends and co-laborers in Kenya for many years. Their testimony is that what they learned and experienced at Export grounded and motivated them to do what they have done for the Lord.

Bishop Armstrong Cheggeh has planted and built many churches and serves the Fountain of Life fellowship of 150 churches in Kenya, Uganda, Tanzania, and Burundi as its Presiding Bishop and General Overseer. He has over seventy ministers serving with him. His wife Rhoda, was our student at Export.

Bishop Steven Kabachia and his wife Jennifer pastor the Agape Fellowship Center in the heart of Nairobi. I asked him how he built such a large church. His reply was, "Just like you taught us in Personal Evangelism. We went house to house and reached the people where they lived." Their ministry is mainly evangelistic and church planting, targeting the unreached and the un-churched in East Africa. They have 120 Agape churches now, scattered all over Kenya, and they have started to enter other African countries. When Steven and Jennifer sat in our classes at Export we did not know how God would use their lives.

I still remember teaching Rev. Geoffrey Njuguna during his three years at F.G.B.I.. He and his wife Elizabeth pastor the Deliverance Church at Langata, Kenya, a ministry that began in a small tent and grew to this very large facility. The Deliverance Church is very active in evangelism, reaching out to the unreached in many areas. They have planted six churches around the Nairobi area and far away in Garissa where they have established a day-care center near the border with Somalia. They have reached out and even built a church in the Kibera slums, the largest slum in Nairobi, and the largest urban slum in Africa, where over 170,000 highly impoverished people live.

Reality sunk in when our airline tickets arrived and we saw the itinerary. We were really going to Africa! Our lengthy journey took us from airports in Dallas, Texas, to Frankfurt, Germany; to Addis Adabba, Ethiopia; and finally to Nairobi, Kenya, East Africa. That in itself was an unforgettable experience! Although we had not seen Bishop Steven Kabachia in many years, we were excited to recognize him approaching as we filled out visa papers in the large Nairobi Kenyatta airport. We were amazed at the very developed city of Nairobi and very blessed to have the first week of accommodations at the lovely Grace Guest House. It was a new experience to see mosquito netting hanging from a frame above our bed ready to be drawn around us. The on-site restaurant provided wonderful meals.

A Muslim from Senegal

The Lord planned in advance that right here we would have our first opportunity to minister the gospel. Several times a day we got our exercise walking up and down four flights of stairs. One afternoon as we descended, a tall African man was coming up. He was the same man we had seen and greeted before and it became obvious that he was watching us carefully. He always had a friendly smile, but this time he stopped us. He stood there and stared at us with what seemed to be a look of admiration, as he said he was so glad to see such a nice couple.

Something caused this dignified stranger to be attracted to us. Slowly his hand slipped down into his pocket where he seemed to feel around for something. We didn't know anything about this stranger. Was this to be a moment that eternity would enlighten? It was hard to know how to react as his hand came out of his pocket holding a silvery multi-stranded necklace. It must have been valuable to him. With fingers gently grasping the clasp, he displayed the necklace in his outstretched hand. "I want you to have it. You make me think of my grandparents."

It was a touching moment, an unexpected, noble gesture of respect. Clearly, this was a heartfelt gift that could not be refused.

"Thank you! I feel honored. Your kindness is greatly appreciated." As I spoke my heart was stirred. I knew the Lord was right there in the middle of this unusual scene on a third floor staircase.

"May I ask your name, Sir?" I ventured.

"My name is Abdoul. I am from Senegal."

"It is very nice to meet you, Abdoul."

He began to tell us a little about himself, about his education, and continued, "You are from the United States? I lived in Stroudsburg, Pennsylvania for a while. My wife is a teacher at the University of Stroudsburg and is presently here in Kenya advocating education for women of Senegal."

As I stared intently at him, listening, my mind wandered to scenes of multitudes without the Lord, reaching out from a valley of decision. My spirit prayed. My heart could hold it back no longer. I had to ask.

"Abdoul, you are an educated man. Do you know who Jesus is?" I waited and tried to analyze his facial expression. It was blank as he stared back.

"Abdoul, I am talking about Jesus Christ. Have you heard of Him? He came to earth from Heaven to die for our sins so we can go to Heaven some day. Do you know Him?"

It was a heartrending moment as I beheld the slightly bewildered look on his face and heard him quietly respond, "No, I do not."

It felt like my insides trembled! There I, from eight thousand miles away, stood in Kenya, face to face with a man from the Republic of Senegal, West Africa, who has never heard of Jesus. It is hard to imagine that such a setting could have occurred by accident.

Immediately and with great joy, I continued, "Oh Abdoul, I would love to have the opportunity to tell you about Jesus. He is so wonderful. You must hear about Him!"

He showed no reluctance and very politely suggested that "a little later, maybe we can talk."

With joyous expectation Bob and I returned to our room that

afternoon. We knew Abdoul was leaving the next day and we prayed for a fruitful opportunity to share the gospel with him. We didn't have to wait very long for as we were taking a little rest a knock came on our door. It was Abdoul! He stood there very politely, as he bowed slightly and humbly stated, "Just wanting to say 'Good Afternoon." We asked him to meet us in the adjoining guest area, and quickly gathered some materials and joined him. We learned he is a Muslim, but he listened intently as we gave him the beginnings of the gospel story, the Old Testament sacrificial lambs and how Jesus became that final Lamb, lived, died, rose again, providing the only way of forgiveness of sins and Salvation. We told Abdul that the God of Heaven knew him and saw him, and cared about him, and caused our paths to meet. We gave him helpful literature to take with him.

There was no resistance and he said he would like to speak to us again about it tomorrow. He is in need of a job for the year; he will be here in Nairobi, so we joined hands and prayed that God would help him get that job and reveal his love and care for him. What an amazing opportunity God gave us! We continued to pray for Abdoul, but we never saw him again. Perhaps he got a job, but the gospel seed is planted and the Holy Ghost will water it. I can't fully describe the joy of telling someone about Jesus for the first time! In Arabic, Abdoul means "servant." May he become a servant of the Lord Jesus Christ.

God gave us multiple opportunities to minister and to experience his mighty power at work. The work of the gospel is reaching and changing many lives in Kenya. Once we ministered in the five-story Great Physician Church in the city of Nairobi, where Christ was working in hearts on each of the levels. Many responded to the preaching, yielding their lives to the Lord at the altar call. We were welcomed exuberantly in conferences where we were also able to minister along with many others.

There are forty-two tribes in Kenya and twenty-five of them are considered unreached with the gospel. Pray for the efforts of these ministries and others who are diligently endeavoring to obey the Great Commission of Jesus. We found Kenya to be a country of great contrasts—from the beautiful buildings and homes of Nairobi, to the extreme poverty of close-by slums.

At the conference in Juja we witnessed people from many Kenyan tribes hearing the gospel, praying, weeping, rejoicing, worshiping, speaking in tongues, and committing their lives to the Lord Jesus Christ. The enthusiastic, heartfelt worship of Kenyan believers was evident every place we went. We learned that each tribe not only has its own language, but also its own style of worship and dress. The Maasai were especially unique and memorable.

During a special time of ordination of ministers we could sense the vision and determination of these men to take the gospel throughout their land. It was a great joy to be present for the formal appointment of Joseph Gitau Kamau, an F.G.B.I. alumnus, as the Director of Christian Education for the Fountain of Life churches.

In Kenya, our eyes most certainly beheld massive amounts of fruit that indeed grew from those small seeds planted with faith in classrooms at Free Gospel Bible Institute. To God be the glory for the great things He has done!

A Real Safari

I never thought I would ever see lions, giraffes, wildebeests and zebras, elephants, ostriches, antelopes, gazelles, baboons and cheetahs right outside my window, plus hippos and crocodiles in the Mara River. But there they were, some by the hundreds, as we hung on for dear life inside a safari vehicle traveling over very rough, hilly grasslands. It was almost literally a breathtaking experience! The definition of safari is "an expedition to observe or hunt animals in their natural habitat." Our hosts planned this exciting safari adventure for us at the Masai Mara National Reserve in southwest Kenya, on the border of Tanzania's Serengeti, not to hunt, but to observe things we had never seen before. This massive home for innumerable wild animals encompasses about 583 square miles, and is situated in the Great Rift Valley. In one spot, we closely viewed a family of lions, resting after their pursuit of food. Their successful hunt was evident by a large wildebeest, stretched out on its back, mortally torn, lying beside one of the lions.

Our home during the safari was a large tent joined to a concrete extension that included a bathroom. When we first arrived, I stared out our tent window in amazement and said to Bob, "Look at who our neighbors are!" Climbing out of the tent next door were three Massai tribal warriors, wrapped in their traditional, ornately decorated, bright orange sheeting, with colorful shoulder draping, neck and ear ornaments, and holding raised spears at their sides. We were stunned and intrigued. I suppose they were just as shocked when I climbed out of the tent with a camera and called to them, asking if I could take their picture. Such boldness these Americans have! They looked at me, then at each other, mumbled some words unintelligible to me, and then nodded and stood there posing. Later we learned that these men were the camp security guards!

The captivating allure of this unforgettable safari was at least partly matched by the daily comical antics of colonies of monkeys that inhabited our tent city. It was hilarious to watch them race and leap from tree to tree, slide wildly down tent roofs, and aggressively wrestle with each other. Someone surely should have taught them to draw a privacy curtain when they decided to give group bug-picking therapy to sunbathing relatives. Looking behind us we could see the open-sided dining area where some brave monkeys would venture to steal food and quickly flee the instant swats of attending staff. While eating our meals, we could hear unfamiliar languages all around us. We were no doubt very privileged to have had this most unusual safari experience that was desired and chosen by people from countries around the world.

Surrounded by Muslims

So many things from our three weeks in Kenya will never be forgotten. The drive through Eastleigh shook us to the core. Suddenly we were surrounded by moving, shifting crowds of Muslim men in long robes and turbans, women covered from head to toe with only eyes showing. They filled every available space. They were next to our car. They were walking in front of us. Our tinted windows made it possible for me to take pictures, and as I snapped so many, I wondered if we were safe. This was a little "Somalia" on the outskirts of Nairobi that had become home to a whole generation of Muslim Somali immigrants who had left their own violent, war-torn country.

Clothing and other products for sale hung from windows of dark deteriorating buildings that poked their way into the dusty sky. Overflowing merchant tables and boxes cluttered the narrow disintegrating roadway, leaving little room for maneuvering vehicles, donkey carts, and bicycles. Rivers of pedestrians wove their way through litter, generated by the diverse commodities on display. At one point, a bus in front of us got stuck in a huge rut, and we were trapped there for a while very anxious to be able to move forward again. This was sort of a "shock and awe" trip into a different world, a world for which God sent his only begotten Son. The sight of this huge mass of humanity without Christ put an ache in my heart. Does anyone have the right to hear the gospel twice when there are multitudes that have never heard it once?

22

"OUT OF BREATH PURSUING SOULS"

You Don't Need a Pulpit to Be a Soul Winner

Flying back to America, we had many hours to allow that burden to grow. The longing to win the lost burned in my heart. One of John Wesley's biographers said, "He was out of breath pursuing souls." I would like my life to have that kind of a testimony. Ahead for us were revivals in Florida, Virginia, West Virginia, Pennsylvania, Illinois, Oklahoma, and Texas, and many miles of travel where we would have contact with lost people. I yearned to urge them to come to Christ.

Have you felt that kind of stirring in your soul that made you want to go out and find the unsaved? Many Christians have no such desire. Something is wrong! Is God still looking and searching for someone to stand in the gap for the lost and sadly saying, "I found none"? What would He find if He looked your way? Have the cares of life and other interests distracted you from the vital call of the Lord's Great Commission?" What would happen if you and every Christian you know would pray through, catch a vision for the lost, and begin to do all you could to reach them? You don't need a pulpit to be a soul winner. Jesus showed us how to do it. His passion for the lost compelled him to go and find them.

"And he said unto them; Let us go into the next towns that I may preach there also: for therefore came I forth" (Mark 1:38).

Have you let his words capture your heart?

"...as my Father hath sent me, even so send I you" (John 20:21).

We were in a restaurant in Dallas when I saw a young man walk past,

243

wearing a tee shirt with that same scripture on the back. It immediately made me want to go to him and at an opportune moment, I walked up to his booth where he sat eating his salad. I pointed at him and said, "Do you know that you are a 'sent-one'?" He looked at me a bit puzzled until I said, "Your shirt says so." A sudden smile of recognition hit him as he explained he had gone on a missions trip back a few years ago, and that's where he got that shirt. I wouldn't let him off the hook. "Don't forget it! You ARE a 'sent-one'! Go and preach the gospel!" He looked thunderstruck as I walked away and out the exit door. God, send him!

Dear reader, you are also a "sent-one"! Listen carefully and you will hear God's voice calling you as Isaiah did, "Also I heard the voice of the Lord, saying, whom shall I send, and who will go for us?" Will you answer as Isaiah did, "Then said I, Here am I; send me" (Isaiah 6:8)?

Beyond the walls of the church, beyond the confines of a pulpit and a platform, the souls of the lost call out for you to come minister to them where they are in your neighborhood, in your town, at the park, at laundromats, shopping malls, restaurants, gas stations, the post office, on the job; by letter, phone call, text message, e-mail, by distributing tracts, praying for the sick where you meet them. The Lord is calling to you, "Go ye..." (Mark 16:15a). How will you answer Him?

Three Rough Suspiscious Guys

As we headed down the revival road, we found many who needed the gospel. One time we stopped to get gas at a truck stop and I noticed a rough- looking group standing outside the store. One big, dark guy was decked with jewelry and flashy clothes. The three acted suspicious, with their eyes darting in all directions as if watching their surroundings and keeping alert to who was nearby. Could it be a drug deal in the making?

As I watched the scene from inside our car, it appeared that something shady was going on. There was no doubt in my mind that here were people who needed the Lord. It was daylight, and there were plenty of people going in and out of the store, so I grabbed my purse and searched my tract supply, chose several, and headed straight toward them. They quickly noticed me heading for them and watched my every move. With my eyes focused on them and my heart focused on the power of Spirit of God, I approached them with a smile and a greeting that interrupted their activities.

"Hi! Are you having a good day?" I didn't wait for an answer and really didn't expect one. "Here's something that will give you an even greater day!" I quickly handed gospel tracts to each of them and kept moving into the store. Their empty stares revealed the misery that is in the path of those who journey the dark road of sin. I was full of joy that I had just invaded the devil's territory with the written message of Jesus Christ who will deliver all who come to Him.

The Omelet Maker Without Christ

God had already prepared the heart of a lady in a town up the road. We had no idea that Merridian, Mississippi, would be the place where we would find her. This hotel had a great free breakfast, including omelets made to order, and she surely could make them! She was a sweet little lady, friendly, and carefully observing us. She seemed to like what she saw and that made my approach to her so much easier. "Something" about us attracted her to us. Isn't that the way it is supposed to be for Christians? There should be "something" about us that doesn't drive people away from us but draws them to us so we can present Christ to them. That "something" is Jesus inside us!

When things were slower and I felt she had time to talk, I went over to her as she was cleaning up her table and pans. I asked her if she went to church and she replied, "Not enough!" That opened the way to tell her that the Lord cared about her and has sent us to invite her to give her life to Jesus. She allowed me to come back into the kitchen area with her and there I was able to pray for her and with her to settle her relationship with God.

We later found a Pentecostal pastor's wife working in one of the local restaurants and told her about this lady so she could follow up and hopefully get her in church. The harvest is great and it is exciting to have opportunity to reap it for the Lord!

Go Ye into all the Malls

It is not unusual for Bob and I to go into malls in search of people to witness to. We see a mass of humanity, hurrying on their way to eternity with no hope of salvation. We arm ourselves with tracts and other witnessing supplies and start walking. Recently during one such mall trip we were able to witness to people from Costa Rica, the Philippines, India, and Mexico. The harvest field is at our doors. The world has come to America. We can almost hear Jesus tell us today, "Go ye into all the malls and preach the gospel." All the gods of this world are there, and we have the saving, delivering message that they need.

It was 105 degrees on this Texas day as we left our car. Off to the side of the mall's main entrance we saw a man whose appearance caught our attention. There he stood with a defiant pose. It was those long dreadlocks and his facial expression that made me wonder if I should approach him. This was no time to wonder. I reached into my purse's tract supply, found what I wanted and headed towards him praying.

"Hi! How are you doing today?" I said with a smile.

He didn't smile but stared at me and just said. "Okay."

"Has anyone ever lied to you?" I asked?

His interest seemed to perk up. Maybe he felt like a wrongfully oppressed person.

"Yeah!" he said with eyebrows raised.

"Well, then you really need to read this," I said as I handed him Mark Cahill's latest soul-winning booklet, The Second Greatest Lie Ever Told.

He grabbed it, read the title, and his face lit up with a big smile. "Yeah, thanks a lot!" he said, already glancing through the pages.

I don't know what he was expecting, but God has a way to reach every desperate soul, if only we claim his promise of boldness and go.

That was just a simple act that got the gospel into the hands of "who knows what kind of a person," with "who knows what kind of a life"—a soul for whom Jesus died.

That booklet asks if the reader has ever been lied to. The most dangerous lie of all is the one that says there are many ways to Heaven. The beliefs of the top nine religions in the world are summarized, revealing how they contradict each other. It then shows proofs that the Bible is true and offers the only way to be saved—through the Lord Jesus Christ.

A Hindu Sellling Body Jewelry

As we walked inside past multiple stores we came upon an Indian man selling body jewelry at a kiosk. He was furiously attacking the keypad of his cell phone when I approached him and remarked, "It looks like you are an expert at texting. Your fingers are moving as fast as lightning." That brought some laughter and broke the ice. I asked if he was from India and after his positive response, I told him about some friends that we had in India. He was quick to show interest and begin describing the particular parts of India where these friends lived. The door was opening and I was anxious to step through it.

"Do you speak another language besides English?" I asked him and learned that he spoke several, including Hindi. I knew that this was one of the languages on the gospel material I had and showed it to him. "Here, is this your language?" His positive response paved the way for me to offer it to him as a gift. As he turned it over, He saw the word JESUS in big bold letters. I must admit I was not expecting his reaction.

"I am happy to see this about Jesus, for I have been researching about Him. I am a Hindu, but I believe He is real. His name keeps coming to me. I can't get it out of my mind."

Standing in front of me was a young man totally unaware of what was causing the name of Jesus to keep coming to his mind. With awe at how God was already working in his life, I inquired, "Do you know why the name of Jesus keeps coming to your mind? That is the work of God's Holy Spirit. He is drawing you to Jesus." What a great joy it was to continue this conversation with this young man! He was so sincere and interested in learning more. Our invitation to come to church was received without objection. I pray that the Lord will reveal Himself to this young man as Savior and Lord!

A Goth Who Needed Jesus

As we were concluding our conversation, I saw an amazing sight out of the corner of my eye and just had to turn to see if what I thought I saw was really what was standing there. The moment I fully saw these two young men, my heart was stirred to reach them for the Lord. One stood tall, with long black hair, dark black makeup around his eyes and one eye superimposed with a strange gothic-type, eye contact lens. His face was filled with many piercings also on his tongue. He wore gothic-type pants with chains and straps. The other young man seemed to be a follower.

I turned away from my Indian friend and reached out and touched the young gothic on the arm. He looked at me, as I walked up to him with a smile and said:

"Wow! How did you get this way?" "How long did all of this take you?"

"What do you mean?" he cautiously asked.

"I mean all your tattoos and piercings. They caught my attention."

"About two years. I am a piercer and a tattoo artist."

"Well," I said, "I couldn't help but notice you, and I'd like to give you a gift of the greatest story ever told."

He took it in his hand, looked down and saw the title "JESUS" printed in large letters, and said, "Oh, I know all about Jesus. Give it to him (nodding to his friend). He's an atheist."

He handed it to his friend, the little guy, and I said, "Oh, no! You need it too and I have enough for both of you, so here, you take this one. You see it's not enough to 'know all about Jesus,' That won't save you! The devil even knows all about Jesus, and what he knows makes him tremble, but he's not saved and isn't going to Heaven. But you can know Jesus in a greater way than just in your head—you can know Him in your heart when you surrender your life to Him. There's no way to escape it—Jesus is the one we will all have to bow and submit to someday. The Bible says, ...every knee shall bow..." (Romans 14:11). He loves you and will save you if you, will come to Him."

They both took the gospel presentation and even posed for me to take their picture so I would not forget them and would pray for them. I do pray that they will truly come to know this Jesus and be born again by the Spirit of God.

It was Bob Pierce who long ago wrote a book entitled, "Let My Heart Be Broken with the Things That Break the Heart of God." God is "not willing that any should perish, but that all should come to repentance" and salvation (Second Peter 3:9). The same blood of Jesus that was shed for you, was shed for these two young men, and can save them too.

Meeting Micah the Levite

Time is about to stand still. Walking through another mall, we suddenly become aware that the Dead Sea is in Texas. As we almost pass by one of many kiosks, we are enticed to stretch out our hands to receive precious mineral ointment, squeezed from a turquoise tube by a hopeful salesman. He is interested in restoring harmony and balance to our skin but with delicate caution, we hope to engage him in conversation.

"These products are from Israel and contain amazing beneficial minerals from the Dead Sea. One of the natural wonders of the world is the Dead Sea in Israel, which is 1200 feet below sea level."

Politely, I edge my way into the sales pitch: "Israel! I love Israel! I have been there!"

Slight amazement creeps to the surface of the man's facial features. "You have? When?"

"Many years ago," I reply," probably around 1985."

"Did you see the wall? I am from Israel and I live by the wall. I am here only two weeks now."

In such a location, he no doubt lived in the proximity of constant danger. I conjecture, "You must have seen some terrible things."

A weather-worn, creased brow seemed intrinsically connected to the squint of his eyes as his solemn words poured forth—"I thanked God every morning that I woke up."

His mid-fiftyish appearance seemed strained, yet determined. A Jewish kippa (cap) crowned his browned, tired-looking face setting him apart from the passing crowd.

"Yes, I saw the wall of the city and the Western wall, where many Jews were praying."

Immediately Micah is pulling out his cell phone to show us pictures of his home.

He seems a bit anxious as he slides one picture after another and then smiles as if he has just found a treasure. "This is my home. These are my streets." It seemed evident that he was already missing that familiar place. We were strangers; yet he risked sharing personal facts. "I have children. Slowing down with a noticeable pause, he continued, "My two sons are in the military." As if a dark cloud passed over him, his appearance suddenly changed, revealing obvious concern.

I sense the unsettling moment and attempt to seize it. "We keep up with the news and are alarmed at the attacks and violence against Israel. We believe God has given the land to his chosen people, the Jews. The Torah declares it. Do you read the scriptures?"

Not a second was wasted. With a quick twist of his body, his hand reached only inches away to his counter where he grasped his own very worn, coverless copy of the Torah. Its edges were curled upward from use. He seemed almost offended that anyone would even question his use and familiarity with the scriptures. He made us aware of his knowledge of Hebrew and his studies of the mystical Kabbalah. With strong Hebrew dialect and fingers pouring through the pages of that sacred book, he began to reveal his educational background, his deep studies of the Jewish Bible, and his love for it.

After sharing our own love for the Bible, in a leap of faith I asked him, "Micah, are you looking for the Messiah to come?"

"Of course," he shot back "and the time is near!" Intensity drove his words as he began to describe chaotic world conditions, devastating weather patterns. "These all are signs that his coming is near."

He paged through his Torah and pointed to portions describing how wickedness brought God's judgment of the flood in Noah's day. "It is like today. Something is going to happen." Micah is from the tribe of Levi.

I cautiously interrupted him. "Micah, your Messiah has already come. He came for you. His name is Jesus and He is about to come again."

Like a streak of lightning, he stretched his arm out toward me with an upturned palm, as if to say, "Stop! Say no more!"

Somewhat yielding, I still continued with a question. "Then tell me, Micah, how would you identify the Messiah if He came tomorrow? How would you know for sure that He is the Messiah?"

I hoped he would describe some of the messianic characteristics prophesied in the Old Testament but avoiding such an answer, he simply stated, "I will know. In my heart I will know." His face was set.

As gently as possible I protested his conclusion, suggesting that many have come in the past, saying they were the messiah. "How would you know for sure if they were really the Messiah? Surely there are attributes, qualities, unique features you should look for...prophetic details..."

Again, he waved me off, apparently understanding where I was headed. "Some things we don't need to know. Some things we are not to know."

I wondered why he turned to Exodus 19 and detailed the account when Moses went up into Mount Sinai to meet with God. The people were not to come near or touch the mount lest they die. He inferred that the people were not to know what Moses was to know. Some things are too sacred. He seemed to associate that with having knowledge of the Messiah. "We don't need to know everything."

He conveyed such a depth of knowledge of the Old Testament that I wondered who he really was. Could it be that this man was a rabbi? Regardless, he knew enough to be aware that his Torah revealed many prophecies concerning the Messiah to come. If all these Old Testament messianic prophecies were pulled together they would paint a picture of the One who has fulfilled them all—Jesus Christ, the Promised One. Micah chose to ignore those unique prophecies. Was he afraid of Who they pointed to?

Our conversation was intense. At one time I tried to excuse myself, saying that we were interfering with his business, as customers were coming by. Another shopkeeper was standing nearby at the door of his business, listening to our entire conversation with no attempt to hide it. Micah was not about to stop. "This is more important," he insisted.

Many minutes passed by. I had to move forward with this discussion. "Micah, we love Jerusalem and pray for its peace. We love our Jewish friends."

It was his turn again. "I know that Christians love Israel and Jewish people. They do many things to show that."

"Yes, and I want to thank you for the part Jewish people had in preserving the Holy Scriptures. I also want to thank you for giving to us our Jewish Messiah, Jesus."

This brought him to another full stop with his hand outstretched, palm upraised as if to say, "Enough!" Yet I could not help but sense that something was going on inside Micah's heart that he fought to hide. He did not want to stop this conversation. I knew I could not push him further but felt the Holy Spirit directing my words.

"Micah, we are not going to keep you any longer." As he stood by that two week old, Dead Sea product Kiosk, he made me think of one of the Old Testament prophets, before they knew anything about the Babe who would be born of a virgin. He could quote the scripture. He was waiting for the Messiah but was unwilling to acknowledge the Truth. Gently, I put my hand on his shoulder, looked into his Jewish face, and pleaded, "Micah, please look one more time at Isaiah 53, and read it with an open heart. His face said that he knew what was in that Messianic chapter of the Torah.

We stepped away from that sacred spot, where Heaven was yearning to reach one of God's chosen ones, with a prayer that has continued to ring out from our heart: "Lord Jesus, reveal yourself to Micah." In a moment we were again mingling with more of the very ones Jesus died for, continuing to desire to reach them for Him. Worthy is the Lamb to receive the reward of his sufferings. Every day we are planting seeds and God is watering them.

23

A FINAL CHALLENGE

Lord, Give Me Souls

Please come with me as I step into one more scene. I am standing in the middle of a multi-level shopping mall, with emotion building inside me. My hands grasp the cold railing and I lean forward to scan the scene before me. Time seems to stand still as my mind absorbs the sight of multitudes walking, laughing, chattering, and rushing about. Smells from the nearby food court and drifting sounds of music endeavor to break into my space, but it is this passing mass of humanity that grips my moment. Lost! That's what they are. Lost! My heart is bursting with passion to give them the gospel. Have you felt that kind of stirring inside you? The longing intensifies as my yearning spirit cries to the Lord, "God, let me reach them."

I could not have anticipated what happens next. A sudden grinding noise behind me draws my full attention. I turn and am overwhelmed to see a back wall shifting inch by inch, in slow motion, across the floor like a huge sliding door. Shadowy forms become visible behind a previously hidden space and are transformed into a huge crowd of people seated at round tables. They are all looking at me. Instantly, the indescribable burden that had been building in my spirit burst forth with powerful words as I stretch my arms out to these people and call out passionately, "Come to Jesus. He will save you now."

Then I woke up! I was in my bed. The half-conscious, mumbling cry of my dreaming words echoed into our bedroom, waking my startled husband. As I poured out the story of my dream, my spirit continued to swell with that same passion and thrill of reaching out and urging those lost souls to come to Jesus.

Although it was a dream, it is a picture of what motivates me. It is a piece of my inner being. On my knees before my Lord, I continuously cry, "Lord, give me souls." I still have some years left, and I never want to stop trying to bring to Jesus the reward of his sufferings. Did He not pay an excruciating price so that all may be saved who come to Him? Lost souls who come to Him are his due reward.

This Joy is No Dream

I am overwhelmed with joy at the blessing God gave me today. We stopped in a little thrift store just to browse and, as I was paying for a purchase, I noticed a man walk in the door. He was dressed shabbily and had the appearance of a homeless person. It didn't take much to realize the man had little. I felt like I wanted to help him in some way so, as I put my change away, I grabbed a couple of dollars and then pulled out of my purse a very good, colorful and clearly presented gospel tract, as well as a million dollar tract. I asked my husband if he would watch my cart as I headed through the store in search of that man. I went all the way through and headed back, unable to see him anywhere.

A worker at the store, probably in his sixties, was seated on the side and, as I passed him, he asked if I found everything I was looking for. "No," I said. "Did you see that man who came in the store who appeared to be homeless?" He said, "Oh, yes. He asked if he could use the restroom."

So that's where he disappeared to! Walking over to this gentleman, I said, "When I saw him, I just felt I wanted to help him. When he comes out, would you tell him a lady wanted to give him these couple of dollars, and would you also give him these gospel tracts? They tell all about how we can be saved and ready to meet the Lord."

"I sure will," he replied, as he looked more closely at me. "You're a holiness woman, aren't you?"

"Yes, sir. I am, all because of Jesus."

"Yes...because of Jesus. You're Pentecostal, aren't you?"

"Yes, I am...." I hardly got the words out of my mouth until I noticed his eyes begin to squint and tears begin to slip out....

"I could tell," he said, as his body began to tremble with emotion. His quivering lips spoke with a voice broken by tears: "It's all over you. I can see it." His big eyes just stared up at me.

This was amazing! I had never seen this man before and I couldn't help being awed at what God seemed to be doing right before my eyes. I had an immediate awareness of the presence of God and of a divine moment in process. It all happened so quickly. I could feel the Spirit of God moving me as I stepped closer and put my hand on the man's shoulder.

"What you see and feel is the presence of God! Are you ready to meet Him? Is your heart right with God?"

A cloud of sadness hung over him as he shook his head from side to side and told me, "No. I drifted away."

I knew I was facing an event prepared by Heaven. God was in control! It was powerful!

"Then what are you waiting for?" I urged him, "You need to pray now and get back to God," and I started to pray for him. "Lord, help this man to repent of his wandering and return to you right now."

He was crying and praying with me: "Yes, Lord. Yes, Lord."

I kept praying. "Ask the Lord to forgive you and cleanse you from all sin." I felt his power and knew that He was at work in this man's life. "God brought me here, just for you. What is your name?"

"James," he replied.

"Now, James, are you ready to meet the Lord? You prayed with me. Did you repent? If Jesus came tonight, would you be ready to go with Him?"

He hung his head and said, "No."

"Then we need to pray again, James. Whatever stands in the way— whatever whatever you are holding on to that will keep you out of heaven, whatever is still sin in your heart...has to go. Are you willing to turn away from all sin and let Jesus come in and give you a new beginning right now?"

As he positively responded, we prayed some more until he acknowledged that he had surrendered it all and was ready to live for God again.

His background was in good churches, and I urged him to come to the church where we were presently holding a month-long seminar called "Commissioned to Discipleship, Commissioned to Ministry, and Commissioned to Evangelism."

What great thrill filled my heart as I left that store and realized what God had done! And the story isn't over yet. What about that homeless man? Wouldn't it be an ironic twist if James gave those tracts to that homeless man, and then gave him his newfound testimony, and won him to the Lord?

How many more are out there just like James, away from God and ready to come to the Lord at the urging of someone who cares—someone who has a burden to see the lost get saved. Will you let the Lord lead you and use you today?

A Little White-Haired Man from Australia

Allow me to introduce you to a little white haired man named Frank Jenner. He lived on Max Street, Sydney, Australia. When God saved and delivered him from sin, he was so thankful that he vowed to witness to ten people every day. For twenty-eight years, Jenner stepped out of his doorway and addressed passersby, "Excuse me, sir, but if you died today, do you know for sure whether you would be going to Heaven or Hell?" After all those years of faithful, simple witness he never knew of one person who genuinely got saved. No wonder he wept, as a preacher found him and reported what he had discovered. Through the years, this preacher had heard the testimonies of growing numbers of people serving God who said it was the same simple witness of a little white-haired man on Max Street that brought them to salvation. Who was this man? He determined to find him.

Tears flowed down Jenner's face as the preacher told him of Peter, Noel, Corporal Murray Wilkes, a sailor from Perth; about the pastors in Britain, about the former Hindu who was now a missionary in India, about several missionaries in Jamaica and a naval chaplain in the United States who all were saved as a result of this man's humble, faithful witness. No one knows the total number of persons who will make it to Heaven some day because of Frank Jenner or how many people were reached through the missionaries and pastors that were saved after talking to Jenner. But the promise of God is final: "He that goeth forth and weepeth, bearing precious seed shall doubtless come again with rejoicing, bringing his sheaves with him" (Psalm 126:6).

Maybe someday when I get to Heaven, I'll see the tallest man in the world come running down those golden streets shouting, "You gave me that tract and I got saved! I'm here! Hallelujah!"

Maybe I'll see some of those thirteen who made their way down to the altar in that outdoor Philippine crusade, rejoicing before the throne of God.

Maybe I'll see the man who was dead five minutes before, whose breath God restored and who repented on that hospital gurney as I prayed with him.

Maybe many who received the hundreds of tracts that we distributed will be there. What rejoicing there will be!

This book reaches back to that dead-end street in Corona, New York, to that teenage girl sitting on her front stoop, with no idea of how the hand of God would direct her life. It is a testimony of how Almighty God will take any yielded, willing vessel and mold it for his use. It is evidence that whom He calls, He will enable to do anything He wants done. It is confirmation of the continuing presence and power of God directing the path of his servant into the greatest and most wonderful life, for now and all of eternity.

ENDNOTES

1. Hudson, Ralph E. I'll Live for Him. New York: A. C. Armstrong & Son, 1880

2. Brown, Mary. I'll Go Where You Want Me to Go. Philadelphia: Heidelberg Press, 1922.

3. Lowry, Robert. Nothing But the Blood. Chicago: Glad Tidings Pub. Co, 1921.

4. Taylor, J. Hudson. "J. Hudson Taylor Quotes." GoodReads. Jan 2007.. http://www.goodreads.com/author/quotes/594568.J_Hudson_Taylor (retrieved Apr 2013).

5. Howard, Mary L. I've Placed My Life Within the Hands of God. Used by permission.

6. The Math Forum @ Drexel (a research and educational enterprise of the Drexel University School of Education). Counting to One Billion. <http://mathforum.org> (Retrieved Mar 2013) Used by permission.

7. Jenner, Frank. "Living Testimonies of People in Christ." The Story of Frank Jenner. Video produced by <http://www.personaltract.com> (Retrieved Feb 2013)

8. McPherson, Aimee Semple. This Is That: Personal Experiences, Sermons and Writings of Aimee Semple McPherson, Evangelist. Los Angeles: Bridal Call Publishing House, 1919. Used by permission from the International Church of the Foursquare Gospel.

9. Spurgeon, Charles. Earnestness, Speeches at Home and Abroad. (London: 1878) G.H. Pike, ed. <http://books.google.com/> (Retrieved Jan 2013)

CPSIA information can be obtained at www.ICGtesting.com
Printed in the USA
LVOW08s1035270913

354317LV00003B/4/P